日本語５つの

とびら

TOBIRA

－初級編１－

FOUNDATION JAPANESE1

JAPANESE TEXTBOOK FOR STUDENTS FROM OVERSEAS

立命館アジア太平洋大学

RITSUMEIKAN ASIA PACIFIC UNIVERSITY

Preface

"日本語（にほんご）５つのとびら The Five Doors to Japanese" is for students who study Japanese in a Japanese university. This series has 5 textbooks from the survival to the advanced levels. They are written for the purpose of learning academic Japanese. "日本語（にほんご）５つのとびら　初級 1-Tobira Foundation Japanese 1" is designed for complete beginners as well as those who have already studied a little Japanese. It consists of 10 lessons which cover frequently encountered topics for foreign students in a Japanese university. Using the video and audio materials through the internet, you understand situations better and communicate in Japanese faster. We hope this textbook will help you start your college life in Japan.

Video and audio materials are available in the home page:

URL　http://www.apu.ac.jp/tobira

目次 Contents

もくじ

How to Use This Textbook

Each topic in the textbook is divided into 9 sections. The purpose of each section is as follows:

1. **Introduction**

   Before starting the lesson, you will listen to new vocabulary using the vocabulary list and watch the video on the APU website to grasp an idea about what you will learn in the lesson.

2. **Model conversation**

   Listen to the conversation and understand the communication procedure at the beginning of the lesson. Practice the conversation and memorize formulaic expressions through the lesson.

3. **Vocabulary exercises**

   Building vocabulary and expressions is crucial in order to develop Japanese proficiency at the introductory level. Practice the vocabulary with many illustrations prior to learn new sentence structures and skills.

4. **Grammar exercises**

   Grammatical points based on the model conversation are explained in detail to develop fundamental sentence structures and functions. Use the pictures to practice the correct grammar to form your own sentences.

5. **Speaking and listening exercises**

   Practice the model conversation by yourself using the audio tool on the APU'S website. In class, practice the conversation interacting with classmates using vocabulary, expressions and the sentence structures you have learned. In this section there is a self evaluation section. You can use it to check the level of your conversation ability on your own, which is useful in helping you keep track of your progress.

6. **Reading exercises**

   Practice key words and comprehend a variety of texts using vocabulary, Kanji and grammar learned. Strategies are introduced to help students understand the texts.

7. Writing exercises

Practice writing simple passages on your own or about your own life by using the vocabulary, grammar and Kanji you have learned. In this section there is a self evaluation sheet. You can use it to check the level of your writing ability on your own, which is useful in helping you keep track of your progress.

8. Cultural challenge

Learn about Japanese culture by examining, understanding and comparing Japanese culture to your own. While observing the customs of Japanese culture you may feel uncomfortable at times, but it is all part of the experience of living in another country. Please try to observe Japanese customs as an opportunity to improve yourself and gain new perspectives about your home country by learning about another culture.

9. Additional information

Useful vocabulary, expressions, and other cultural information are introduced.

10. Kanji and Vocabulary

Practice Kanji relating to each topic. Exercises include stroke orders, meanings, formations and signs used in real life.

Japanese Writing System, Pronunciation and Accent

1. Hiragana

(1) Syllables

There are 46 basic Hiragana syllables. See the Hiragana chart.

(2) Hiragana with diacritical marks

With short diagonal strokes (゛), *k*, *s*, *t*, and *h* become g, z, d, and b, respectively. The consonant *h* changes to *p* with a small circle (°).

Examples:

か (ka) → が (ga)　　さ (sa) → ざ (za)　　た (ta) → だ (da)

は (ha) → ば (ba)　　ぱ (pa)

(3) Contracted sounds

Small や (ya), ゆ (yu), and よ (yo) follow after letters containing the vowel (i). The contracted sound presents a single syllable.

Examples:

Horizontal Writing	Vertical Writing
きゃ (kya)　きゅ (kyu)　きょ (kyo)	きゃ きゅ きょ

(4) Double Consonants

① Small letter っ (tsu) between two sounds indicates a pause. It is transcribed as tt or pp.

Examples:

Horizontal Writing	Vertical Writing
きって (kitte=stamp)　きっぷ (kippu=ticket)	きって

② Letter ん with Hiragana（な、に、ぬ、ね or の）is written as follows:

Examples:　しんねん（shinnen=new year）　おんな（onna=female）

（5）Long vowels

When the same vowels appear one right after the other, pronunciation of the vowel becomes about twice as long as the single vowel. It becomes a continuous sound rather than as two separate vowels.

Examples:

aa　おかあさん（okaasan=mother）　おばあさん（obaasan=grandmother）

ii　おにいさん（oniisan=elder brother）　おじいさん（ojiisan=grandfather）

uu　くうき（kuuki=air）　すうじ（suuji=numbers）

ee　The long vowel ee is usually written by adding Hiragana い（i）. There are few words with Hiragana え（e）：とけい（tokee=clock, watch）おねえさん（oneesan=elder sister）

oo　The long vowel oo is written by adding う（u）. There are words with Hiragana（お）：おとうさん（otoosan=father）　とおり（toori=street）

（6）The pronunciation ん（n）changes depending on the sound preceded.

Examples: Become *m* before *m*, *n*, *b* and *p*：こんばん（komban=tonight）

Become *ng* before *k* and *g*：まんが（manga=comics）

（7）Vowels to be dropped

The vowels い（i）and う（u）are sometimes dropped between consonants（*k*, *s*, *t*, *p*, and *h*）or at the end of an utterance preceded by（*k*, *s*, *t*, *p*, and *h*）.

Examples:

すし（s[u]shi)=type of Japanese food）　ひと（h[i]to=people）

2. Katakana

（1）The long vowels are written with "ー".

Examples:

Horizontal writing	Vertical writing
チーズ（chiizu=cheese）　コーヒー（koohii=coffee） メール（meeru=mail）	チ ｜ ズ

（2）Additional combinations with small vowel letters

Examples: ウィ（ui）、ウェ（ue）、ウォ（uo）、シェ（she）、ジェ（je）、チェ（che）、ファ（fa）、フィ（fi）、フェ（fe）、フォ（fo）、ティ（tii）、ディ（di）、デュ（dyu）

（3）The sound v is sometimes written with ヴ.

Examples: ビーナス or ヴィーナス（venus）

3. Accent

Whereas English uses stress for accent, Japanese uses two pitches: high and low. Japanese each syllable is pronounced approximately in equal length and stress.

Examples:

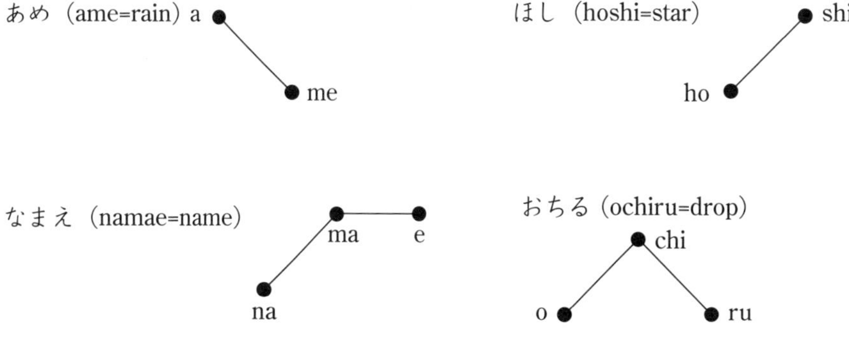

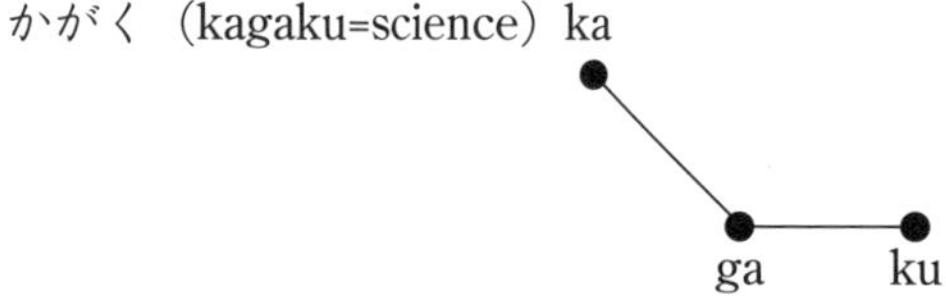

Classroom Expressions

おはようございます。	Good morning.
こんにちは。	Good afternoon.
すみません。	Excuse me. / I'm sorry.
ちょっとまってください。	Wait a moment.
もういちどおねがいします。	Please say it again.
ゆっくりおねがいします。	Please say it slowly.
かいてください。	Please write it.
おねがいします。	Please.
しつもんがあります。	I have a question.
××はなんですか。	What is ××?
どういういみですか。	What does it mean?
わかりました。	I understand.
わかりません。	I don't understand.
ありがとうございます。	Thank you.
さようなら。	Good-bye.
またあした。	See you tomorrow.

Teacher's Instructions

みてください。	Look here.
よんでください。	Read it.
かいてください。	Write it.
きいてください。	Listen.
いってください。	Say it.
しずかにしてください。	Be quiet.

Hiragana and Katakana

ひらがな (Hiragana)

	a	i	u	e	o
	あ	い	う	え	お
K	か	き	く	け	こ
S	さ	し	す	せ	そ
T	た	ち	つ	て	と
N	な	に	ぬ	ね	の
H	は	ひ	ふ	へ	ほ
M	ま	み	む	め	も
Y	や		ゆ		よ
R	ら	り	る	れ	ろ
W	わ				を
	ん*				
G	が	ぎ	ぐ	げ	ご
Z	ざ	じ	ず	ぜ	ぞ
D	だ	ぢ (zi)	づ (zu)	で	ど
B	ば	び	ぶ	べ	ぼ
P	ぱ	ぴ	ぷ	ぺ	ぽ

	ya	yu	yo
K	きゃ	きゅ	きょ
S	しゃ	しゅ	しょ
T	ちゃ	ちゅ	ちょ
N	にゃ	にゅ	にょ
H	ひゃ	ひゅ	ひょ
G	ぎゃ	ぎゅ	ぎょ
Z	じゃ	じゅ	じょ
Z	ぢゃ	ぢゅ	ぢょ
B	びゃ	びゅ	びょ
P	ぴゃ	ぴゅ	ぴょ

ん /N/

カタカナ（Katakana）

	a	i	u	e	o
	ア	イ	ウ	エ	オ
K	カ	キ	ク	ケ	コ
S	サ	シ	ス	セ	ソ
T	タ	チ	ツ	テ	ト
N	ナ	ニ	ヌ	ネ	ノ
H	ハ	ヒ	フ	ヘ	ホ
M	マ	ミ	ム	メ	モ
Y	ヤ		ユ		ヨ
R	ラ	リ	ル	レ	ロ
W	ワ				ヲ
	ン*				
G	ガ	ギ	グ	ゲ	ゴ
Z	ザ	ジ	ズ	ゼ	ゾ
D	ダ	ヂ (zi)	ヅ (zu)	デ	ド
B	バ	ビ	ブ	ベ	ボ
P	パ	ピ	プ	ペ	ポ

ン /N/

	ya	yu	yo
K	キャ	キュ	キョ
S	シャ	シュ	ショ
T	チャ	チュ	チョ
N	ニャ	ニュ	ニョ
H	ヒャ	ヒュ	ヒョ
G	ギャ	ギュ	ギョ
Z	ジャ	ジュ	ジョ
Z	ヂャ	ヂュ	ヂョ
B	ビャ	ビュ	ビョ
P	ピャ	ピュ	ピョ

目次(もくじ) Grammar and Skills Contents

Topic 1　はじめまして

Objectives:

In this lesson, you will learn how to:

1. Introduce yourself to others.
2. Gather information about others whom you meet for the first time.
3. Read self-introductions.
4. Write a self-introduction.

リー

よしだかずお

Introduction:

1. Listen to the vocabulary and check the meaning on pages 3-5.
2. Watch two videos then answer the following questions.

1st video：The following questions are about Lee-san.

① くにはどこですか。

② なん年生(ねんせい)ですか。

③ しゅみはなんですか。

2nd video：The following questions are about Yoshida-san.

① 専門(せんもん)はなんですか。

② なん年生(ねんせい)ですか。

Ⅰ. Let's introduce ourselves

Lee is a first-year student from Australia. She introduces herself at the welcome party.

はじめまして。ナンシー・リーです。
くにはオーストラリアです。けいえい学科(がっか)の
1年生(ねんせい)です。しゅみはすいえいです。
どうぞよろしくおねがいします。

Ⅱ. Introducing oneself to others

Lee introduces herself to Yoshida at the welcome party.

リー：はじめまして。リーです。
吉田(よしだ)：吉田(よしだ)です。はじめまして。
　　　リーさんのおくには、どちらですか。
リー：オーストラリアです。
吉田(よしだ)：専門(せんもん)はなんですか。
リー：ビジネスです。
吉田(よしだ)：ぼくの専門(せんもん)はこくさいかんけいです。
リー：1年生(ねんせい)ですか。
吉田(よしだ)：いいえ、2年生(ねんせい)です。
リー：よろしくおねがいします。
吉田(よしだ)：こちらこそ。

New vocabulary

Nouns

Countries：

くに	country
インド	India
インドネシア	Indonesia
オーストラリア	Australia
かんこく	Korea
タイ	Thailand
ちゅうごく	China
にほん	Japan

People：

私（わたし）	I
ぼく	I (used by men)
学生（がくせい）	student
先生（せんせい）	teacher, professor
友達（ともだち）	friend
留学生（りゅうがくせい）	international student

Nationality：

〜人（じん）	〜 people (suffix attached to a country)
にほん人（じん）	Japanese (people)

School：

大学（だいがく）	university
〜年生（ねんせい）	〜 year student
専門（せんもん）	major
けいえい	management
けいざい	economics
こくさいかんけい	international relations
ビジネス	business
学部（がくぶ）	college
学科（がっか）	department
社会学部（しゃかいがくぶ）	college of sociology

Nouns

Language：

～ご	～ language
えいご	English (language)
にほんご	Japanese (language)

Hobbies：

しゅみ	hobby
えいが	movie
おんがく	music
カラオケ	karaoke
どくしょ	reading
ピアノ	piano
りょうり	cooking
スポーツ	sport
サッカー	soccer
すいえい	swimming
テニス	tennis
バスケットボール	basketball
バドミントン	badminton
たっきゅう	table tennis

Others：

でんわばんごう	telephone number
なまえ	name
～さん	term used when addressing people
ほん	book

Question words

だれ／どなた	who
どこ／どちら	where
なに／なん	what

Numbers

れい／ゼロ	0	zero
いち	1	one
に	2	two
さん	3	three
し／よん	4	four
ご	5	five
ろく	6	six
しち／なな	7	seven
はち	8	eight
きゅう／く	9	nine
じゅう	10	ten

Vocabulary exercises

1. Self-introduction

Exercise A **Profile**

Look at the table below and fill in the blanks with the appropriate word from the New vocabulary list on pages 3-5.

A	Your profile	B
リー	Your face ______	吉田（よしだ）
オーストラリア	National flag ______	______
______ご	______ご	______ご
1年生（ねんせい）	______	2年生（ねんせい）
けいえい学部（がくぶ）	______学部（がくぶ）	こくさいかんけい学部（がくぶ）
0977-78-10 ××	______	080-5287-49 ××

APS…アジア太平洋学部（たいへいようがくぶ）　APM…こくさいけいえい学部（がくぶ）

Exercise B **Hobbies**

What are your hobbies? Check the box next to the pictures below.

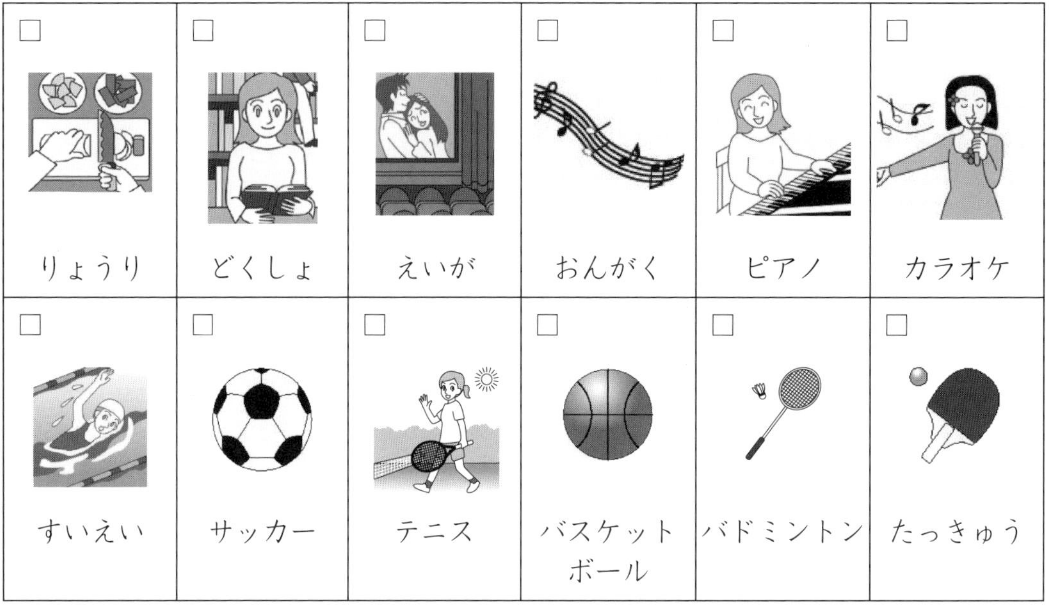

2. 先生（せんせい）／友達（ともだち）

Write your teacher's name and friend's name in Japanese.

先生（せんせい）のなまえ：　　　　友達（ともだち）のなまえ：

Grammar explanations and exercises

1. Identifying someone or something. A は B です

① This sentence structure means 'A is B'. は is a topic marker and comes after the sentence's topic (noun 1). Thus, は is attached to noun 1 in order to indicate the topic of the sentence. It is pronounced "wa".

② です is a copula verb meaning "to be" and is attached to nouns and adjectives at the end of a sentence. It implies that a speaker shows politeness towards a listener.

Topic		Comment	
Noun 1	Particle (topic marker)	Noun 2	Copula Verb
(私（わたし）)	は	なかむら	です。
I am Nakamura.			
くに	は	インド	です。
My country is India.			

れんしゅう Write about yourself then introduce yourself to your classmates.

① なまえ　　② くに　　③ 学部(がくぶ)　　④ しゅみ

2. Particle の（Connecting two nouns）

の is a particle that connects two nouns. The following example shows how の connects two nouns. The second noun（N2）provides the main idea and the first noun（N1）makes the second noun（N2）more specific.

	N1	Particle	N2	
Possession	私(わたし)	の	ほん	my book
Personal relationship	私(わたし)	の	友達(ともだち)	my friend
Descriptive relationship	にほんご	の	先生(せんせい)	a Japanese teacher
The organization to which N2 belongs	大学(だいがく)	の	先生(せんせい)	a university teacher
The place of origin	かんこく	の	学生(がくせい)	a student from Korea

れんしゅう Write the appropriate particle in the（　　）and complete the following sentences.

① 私(わたし)（　　）くに（　　）＿＿＿＿＿＿＿＿＿＿＿＿＿＿＿＿です。

② ＿＿＿＿＿＿さん（　　）くに（　　）＿＿＿＿＿＿＿＿＿＿＿＿＿＿です。

③ 私(わたし)（　　）にほんご（　　）先生(せんせい)（　　）＿＿＿＿＿＿＿＿＿＿先生(せんせい)です。

④ 私(わたし)（　　）友達(ともだち)（　　）＿＿＿＿＿＿＿＿＿＿＿＿＿＿＿＿さんです。

3. Question sentences

① Yes-no questions

When asking whether a statement is correct or not, か is added to the end of a sentence to make it a question.

Positive answer：If you agree with the statement, your answer begins with はい followed by the statement. You can also use そうです "That's right" instead of repeating the statement. (You can use そうです only when you answer with a yes-no question).

A：1年生(ねんせい)ですか。　　Are you a first-year student?

B：はい、1年生(ねんせい)です。　　Yes, I am a first-year student.

　　はい、そうです。　　Yes, that's right.

Negative answer：If you disagree with the statement, your answer begins with いいえ and uses the negative form of です；じゃありません. ではありません is more formal than じゃありません.

A：2年生(ねんせい)ですか。　　Are you a second-year student?

B：いいえ、2年生(ねんせい)じゃありません。　　No, I'm not a second-year student.

Question

Noun	Copula verbs	Question marker
1年生(ねんせい)	です	か。
Are you a first-year student?		

Positive Answer

Yes	Noun	Copula verbs
はい	1年生(ねんせい)	です。
Yes, I'm a first-year student.		

or はい、そうです。 Yes, that's right.

Negative Answer

No	Noun	Copula verbs (negative)
いいえ	1年生(ねんせい)	じゃありません。
No, I'm not a first-year student.		

② Question words

Asking about names and things using なん. なん means "what" and can be used when it is connected to most counters such as ねんせい (～year student), and ばん (number). なん can also be used as a word by itself.

1) A：しゅみはなんですか。　　What is your hobby?

　B：すいえいです。　　(My hobby is) swimming.

2) A：なん年生(ねんせい)ですか。　　Which year are you?

　B：1年生(ねんせい)です。　　I'm a first-year student.

3) A：でんわばんごうはなんばんですか。　　What is your telephone number?

　B：78-1111（ななはち［の］いちいちいちいち）です。　　It's 78-1111.

れんしゅう1　What is your hobby? Ask your classmates about their hobbies.

When asking about places, どこ or どちら is used. どちら is more polite than どこ.

A：おくにはどちらですか。　　Which country are you from?

B：タイです。　　I am from Thailand.

* お is added to a word concerning the listener or a third person to show the speaker's respect towards the listener.

When asking which department one is in, どちら is also used.

A：学部（がくぶ）はどちらですか。　　Which department are you in?

B：けいざい学部（がくぶ）です。　　I am in the department of economics.

When asking who the person is, だれ or どなた is used. どなた is more polite than だれ .

A：先生（せんせい）はどなた／だれですか。　　Who is your teacher?

B：山田先生（やまだせんせい）です。　　My teacher is Mr. Yamada.

Topic	Question word	Copula verbs	Question Marker
しゅみは	なん	です	か。
What is your hobby?			
おくには	どちら	です	か。
Which country are you from?			

れんしゅう２　Ask your classmate's name, country, college, year, telephone number and hobby. Fill in the blanks after you ask all questions.

なまえ	くに	学部（がくぶ）	なん年生（ねんせい）	でんわばんごう	しゅみ

れんしゅう３　Make a sentence by putting the words in the proper order.

① なん・です・専門（せんもん）・か・は

② は・どなた・先生（せんせい）・か・です

③ どちら・は・おくに・か・です

④ です・どちら・は・学部（がくぶ）・か

⑤ 私（わたし）・あゆみ・です・の・なまえ・は

4. Particle も（Describing similarities）

も means "also" or "too". When the statement about a topic is the same as a previous topic, も is used instead of は.

1）田中(たなか)さん**は**学生(がくせい)です。	Tanaka-san is a student.
2）ユンさん**も**学生(がくせい)です。	Yun-san is a student, too.
3）山中(やまなか)さん**は**学生(がくせい)じゃありません。	Yamanaka-san is not a student.
4）太田(おおた)さん**も**学生(がくせい)じゃありません。	Oota-san is not a student, either.

れんしゅう　Complete each sentence as in the example.

e.g. ハンさんはタイ人(じん)です。ピムさん（も）タイ人(じん)です。

① ジムさんの学部(がくぶ)はけいざい学部(がくぶ)です。チンさんの学部(がくぶ)（　　）社会学部(しゃかいがくぶ)です。

② ジャルさんのくにはインドです。オンさんのくに（　　）インドネシアです。

③ メイさんはちゅうごく人(じん)です。キムさん（　　）かんこく人(じん)です。

④ トムさんは２年生(ねんせい)です。ピンさん（　　）２年生(ねんせい)です。

はなします　Speaking

Check the following points:

1. Starting the conversation: はじめまして。How do you do?
2. Closing the conversation: どうぞよろしくおねがいします。Nice to see you.
3. Replying to "どうぞよろしくおねがいします"：こちらこそ。Nice to see you, too.
4. Self-addressing term "ぼく" is used by males while "わたし" is used for both.
5. わたし is not used repeatedly.

＊ Note that to say "あなた(you)" when addressing someone is not polite and sometimes quite rude.

れんしゅう１　Practice the conversation using the listening material.

れんしゅう２　Practice to introduce yourself.

【はなしたあとで】After speaking 〈Self-check〉 Evaluate your speaking.

I was able to introduce myself in Japanese.	☺	😐	☹

よみます　Reading

Ⅰ. 【よむまえに】Before reading

The Japanese writing system is composed of Hiragana, Katakana, and thousands of Chinese characters called Kanji. The three scripts generally have different functions. Hiragana is used to write grammatical elements. Katakana is used to write foreign loan words. Kanji are used to write the core of the Japanese vocabulary, particularly nouns.

【よみましょう】Let's read

Below are two self-introduction passages which are the same. However, one uses only Hiragana and Katakana whereas the other uses Kanji as well. Check how Hiragana, Katakana and Kanji are used. Answer the following questions.

しつもん　Questions

Read the questions before reading the passages.

① What kind of words are written in Kanji?

② は、の and です are not changed to Kanji. What are they?

③ What is バスケットボール？　Is this word Japanese?

ほんぶん　Paragraph

はじめまして。うえだかずお[1]です。りつめいかんアジアたいへいようだいがく[2]のいちねんせい[3]です。しゅみ[4]はバスケットボール[5]です。どうぞよろしくおねがいします。

↓

はじめまして。上田一男[1]です。立命館アジア太平洋大学[2]の一年生[3]です。趣味[4]はバスケットボール[5]です。どうぞよろしくおねがいします。

Ⅱ.【よむまえに】Before reading

New words

きょういく education　　じゅうどう judo

【よみましょう】Let's read

The following passages are the profiles of volunteer tutors who will help you study Japanese. Answer the following questions.

しつもん　Questions

1. Answer the following questions based on the text below.

① 山田(やまだ)さんはなん年生(ねんせい)ですか。

② ふじもとさんのしゅみは、なんですか。

③ 山下(やました)さんの大学(だいがく)は、どこですか。

④ 山下(やました)さんの専門(せんもん)は、なんですか。

⑤ 上田(うえだ)さんは、立命館(りつめいかん)アジア太平洋大学(たいへいようだいがく)の学生(がくせい)ですか。

2. Which person would you like to be your friend?

e.g. ___④___　reason：上田(うえだ)さんのしゅみはじゅうどうです。

ほんぶん　Paragraph

① はじめまして。山田(やまだ)はなです。かわい大学(だいがく)の四年生(よねんせい)です。しゅみはりょうりです。どうぞよろしく。

② ふじもとあいです。ぶんか大学(だいがく)の二年生(にねんせい)です。専門(せんもん)はにほんごきょういくです。しゅみはどくしょです。どうぞよろしく。

③ 山下(やました)はなこです。まつば大学(だいがく)の三年生(さんねんせい)です。専門(せんもん)はけいざいです。しゅみはカラオケです。よろしくおねがいします。

④ はじめまして。上田(うえだ)けんです。立命館(りつめいかん)アジア太平洋大学(たいへいようだいがく)の一年生(いちねんせい)です。しゅみはじゅうどうです。どうぞよろしくおねがいします。

かきます　Writing － My profile －

【かくまえに】Before writing

1. Punctuation　わたしのくには、インドです。

The Japanese period and comma are a different shape from their English equivalents. The Japanese period is a small circle（。), and the Japanese comma is a short line written from the upper left to lower right（、).

2. Particles　わたしのくには、インドです。

A particle (*joshi*) is a word that shows the relationship of a word, a phrase, or a clause to the rest of the sentence. Some particles have English equivalents (e.g. prepositions). Others are post-positions such as は and の.

れんしゅう 1　Read the following text, then put a period at the end of each sentence and circle all the particles.

わたしはやまもとよしおですおおやまだいがくのにねんせいですせんもんはけいざいですしゅみはすいえいですどうぞよろしくおねがいします

【かきましょう】Let's write

1. List the items you want to include in your writing.
2. Put sentences together using punctuation marks to form a paragraph correctly. A paragraph is a group of sentences about one topic. The first sentence is indented; there is a space before it. The second sentence follows the first sentence on the same line. It doesn't go on a new line.

【かいたあとで】After writing

〈For your patner's writing〉 Read your partner's writing out loud. Tell your partner if something is not clear.

〈For your writing〉 Improve your writing by including your partner's questions and comments.

〈Self-check〉Evaluate your writing.

I was able to write my profile.	☺	😐	☹

Cultural Challenge

The way Japanese people greet each other is different from it in my country.

1. How do you greet people in your country? Do you bow? Demonstrate your greeting to your classmates.
2. Personal culture notes: Write about what surprises you in Japan. Share your experiences with your classmates.
3. Your challenge: How many friends have you made? List their names.

Additional information

How to address people in Japanese

- ～さん is a commonly used suffix. It is used in every situation, even when just meeting or greeting someone.
- ～さま（様）is more honorable than ～さん. This is the common way to address clients/customers (for example, at stores). It is also used after the name of the addressee when writing an address on an envelope.
- ～ちゃん is typically used after a girl's name, but is also used for small children of either sex. Among adults, it may be used between close friends.
- ～くん（君）is typically used after a boy's name. It is also sometimes used when referring to males of equal or lower status than oneself (for example, when a boss speaks to a subordinate, or a professor speaks to a student).
- ～せんせい（先生）refers to teachers, doctors, or politicians.

How to greet other people in Japanese.

If you meet the same person again later that day, rather than use a verbal greeting, it is common to only smile or slightly bow your head. This is called "えしゃく".

Topic 2　きょうしつはどこですか

Objectives:

In this lesson, you will learn how to:

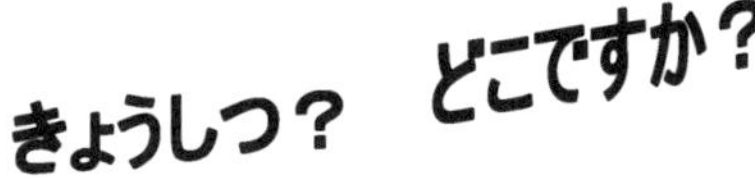

1. Ask for directions.
2. Understand the directions given to you.
3. Read a short paragraph explaining some directions.
4. Write a self-introduction.

Introduction:

1. Listen to the vocabulary and match it to the pictures on pages 20-21.
2. Watch two videos. If the statement is correct, write a ○. If the statement is wrong, write an ×.

1st video：

① オリエンテーションのきょうしつは204きょうしつです。　(　　)

② 1ごうかんはとしょかんのとなりです。　(　　)

2nd video：

① 1ごうかんは大学院棟（だいがくいんとう）のとなりです。　(　　)

3. Circle all places you have been to.

ゆうびんきょく	はなや	コンビニ	スーパー	ほんや
100えんショップ	ぎんこう	でんきや	くつや	
びょういん	こうえん	えいがかん	はなや	

Asking for directions

1. Lee asks a staff in the Academic Office about the location of the orientation meeting.

リー　　　　　：すみません。オリエンテーションのきょうしつはどこですか。
きょうむかの人：1ごうかんの2かいです。203きょうしつと204きょうしつです。
リー　　　　　：1ごうかんはどこですか。
きょうむかの人：としょかんのまえです。
リー　　　　　：ありがとうございました。

2. Lee asks a stranger for the location of Building 1 on campus.

リー：すみません。ここは1ごうかんですか。
学生：いいえ、ちがいます。ここは大学院棟(だいがくいんとう)です。1ごうかんはこのたてもののとなりです。
リー：そうですか。ありがとうございました。

New vocabulary

Nouns

Places:

たてもの	building
キャンパス	campus
こうどう	auditorium
しょくどう	cafeteria
生協（せいきょう）／コープ	CO-OP shop
たいいくかん／ジム	gymnasium
としょかん	library
りょう	dormitory
ATM	Automatic Teller Machine
おてあらい／トイレ	toilet
オフィス	office
けんきゅうとう	faculty building
学生課(がくせいか)／スチューデントオフィス	Student Office
きょうむか／アカデミックオフィス	Academic Office
きょうしつ	classroom
クリニック	clinic
へや	room
アパート	apartment house
えいがかん	movie theater
ぎんこう	bank
くつや	shoe shop
こうえん	park
コンビニ／コンビニエンスストア	convenience store
スーパー／スーパーマーケット	supermarket
でんきや	electrical appliance shop
ドラッグストア	drug store
はなや	flower shop
100 えんショップ	100 yen shop

Nouns

Places:

びょういん	hospital
ホテル	hotel
ほんや	bookstore
まち	town
ゆうびんきょく	post office
レストラン	restaurant

Locations：

あいだ	between
うしろ	back
そと	outside
ちかく	near
となり	next to
なか	inside
ひだり／ひだりがわ	left (to the left)
まえ	front
みぎ／みぎがわ	right (to the right)

Things：

ペン	pen
じしょ	dictionary
ちず	map

Demonstrative pronouns

これ	this one
それ	that one
あれ	that one (over there)
どれ	which one
ここ	here
そこ	there
あそこ	over there

Demonstrative pronouns

この〜	this (noun)
その〜	that (noun)
あの〜	that (noun), over there
どの〜	which (noun)

Counters

〜かい	counter for floors (of a building)
〜ごうかん	counter for buildings
〜ごうしつ	counter for rooms/room number
〜さつ	counter for books
〜とう	counter for large buildings
〜まい	counter for papers

Others

オリエンテーション	orientation
けんきゅう	research
じどうはんばいき	vending machine
大学院（だいがくいん）	graduate school
ふんすい	fountain

Vocabulary exercises

1. Places

Match the words and the pictures as in the example.

~~(a) きょうしつ~~	(b) りょう	(c) ゆうびんきょく	(d) スーパー
(e) 先生のオフィス	(f) へや	(g) たいいくかん（ジム）	(h) おてあらい
(i) としょかん	(j) ぎんこう	(k) 生協（コープ）(せいきょう)	(l) クリニック
(m) しょくどう	(n) きょうむか（アカデミックオフィス）		

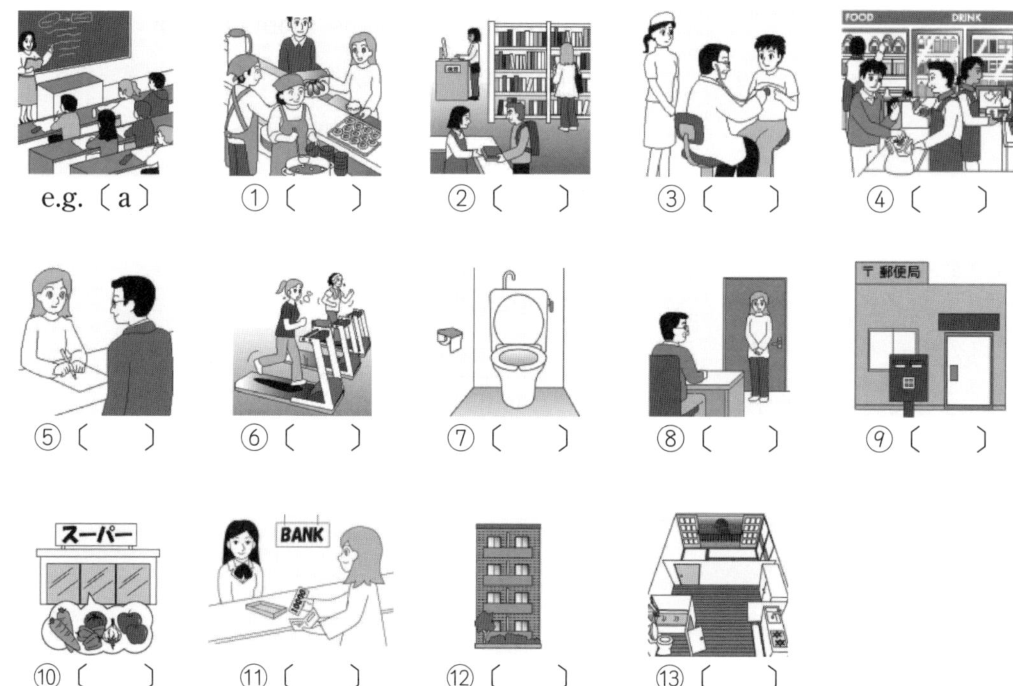

e.g.〔 a 〕 ①〔　〕 ②〔　〕 ③〔　〕 ④〔　〕
⑤〔　〕 ⑥〔　〕 ⑦〔　〕 ⑧〔　〕 ⑨〔　〕
⑩〔　〕 ⑪〔　〕 ⑫〔　〕 ⑬〔　〕

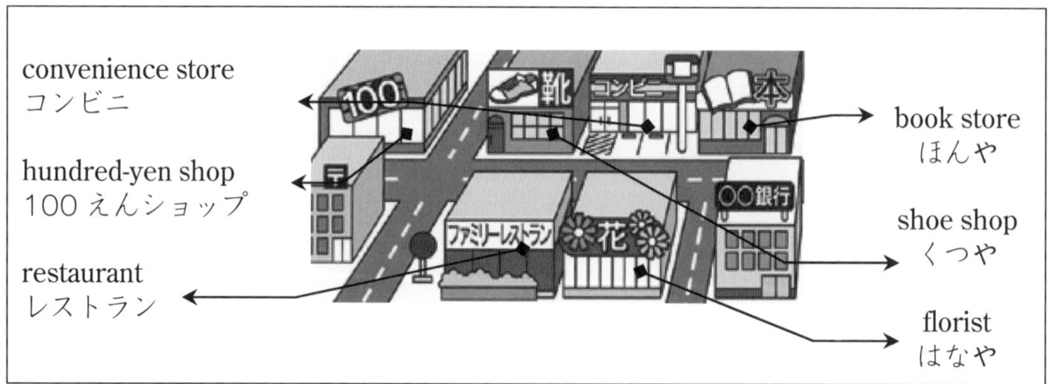

2. Locations

Exercise A

Look at the pictures below and complete the blanks with an appropriate word from the Locations of New vocabulary listed on page 18.

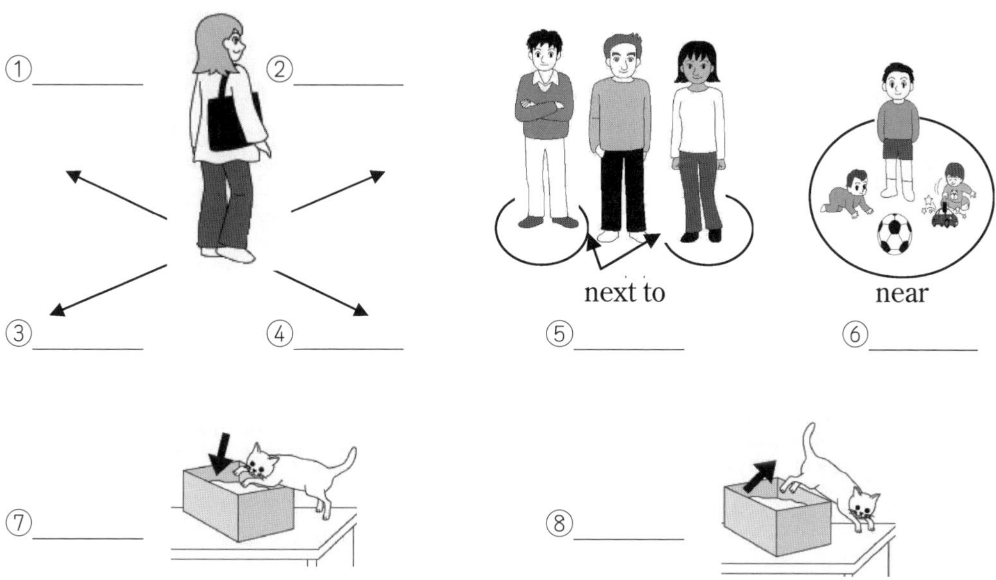

Exercise B

Lee goes down the street. Find the building and fill in each blank as shown in the example.

e.g. レストランのまえ　〔　i　〕

(1) レストランのとなり　〔　　　〕　(2) コンビニのひだり　〔　　　〕

(3) ゆうびんきょくのみぎ　〔　　　〕　(4) りょうのうしろ　〔　　　〕

(5) コンビニのまえ　〔　　　〕　(6) りょうのとなり　〔　　／　　〕

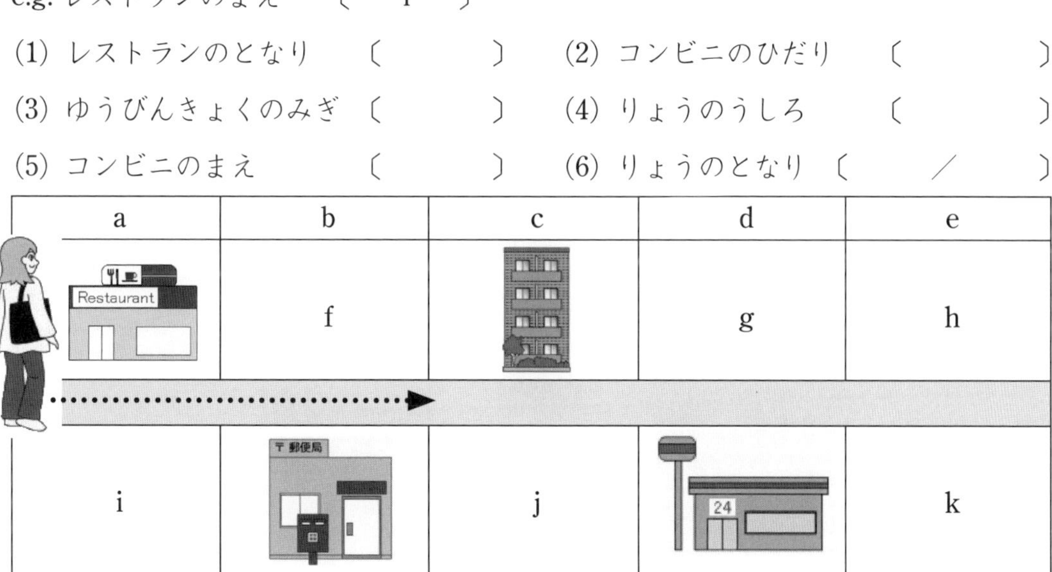

Grammar explanations and exercises

1. Counters

There are a variety of counters in Japanese. The counters are attached directly to the number.

Number ＋かい：counter for floors
いっかい、にかい、さんかい、よんかい、ごかい、ろっかい……
Number ＋まい：counter for papers
いちまい、にまい、さんまい、よんまい、ごまい、ろくまい……
Number ＋さつ：counter for books
いっさつ、にさつ、さんさつ、よんさつ、ごさつ、ろくさつ……

2. Numbers

① Notice how the pronunciation of *hyaku* changes in the following numbers.
300 *sanbyaku*　600 *roppyaku*　800 *happyaku*
1,000 *sen*　3,000 *sanzen*　8,000 *hassen*

② Japanese uses the marker *man* for ten thousand as follows:
10,000 *ichi-man*　1,000,000 *hyaku-man*　10,000,000 *issen-man*
In Japanese 100,000 is juu-man. The next unit marker 1,000,000 is one million in English whereas in Japanese it is hyaku-man.

れんしゅう

① Read the following numbers.

24　125　489　703　1970　2009

8153　6094　36294　53712　167319

② 〈Pair work〉 Write down the numbers you hear from your partner.

3. こ・そ・あ・ど words

こ・そ・あ・ど are used when identifying things, people, or places.

① これ・それ・あれ・どれ

これ(this one here), それ(that one there), あれ(that one over there), どれ(which one) are used to refer to things.

これ：used when referring to things near both the speaker and the listener.

それ：used when referring to things that are a short distance from both the speaker and the listener or things near the listener but far from the speaker.

あれ：used when referring things far away from both the speaker and the listener.

どれ：used when asking "which".

Yes／No Question

Topic	Noun Phrase	Copula	Question Marker
これは	先生(せんせい)のペン	です	か。
Is this your pen ? (asking to the teacher)			
それは	りーさんのほん	です	か。
Is that Lee's book ?			
あれは	としょかん	です	か。
Is that a library ?			

Answer: はい、そうです。／いいえ、ちがいます。

Question with a question word and Answer

	Topic	Noun/Question Word	Copula	Question Marker
Q1	あれは	なん	です	か。
	What is that ?			
A1	あれは	としょかん	です。	
	That is a library.			
Q2	りーさんのほんは	どれ	です	か。
	Which one is Lee's book ?			
A2	りーさんのほんは	それ	です。	
	Lee's book is that one.			

② この・その・あの

この・その and あの are used as indicators with a noun to refer to things and people.

Topic	Noun/Question Word	Copula	Question Marker
このたてものは	としょかん	です。	
This building is a library.			
そのたてものは	ぎんこう	です。	
That building is a bank.			
あのたてものは	ゆうびんきょく	です。	
That building is a post office.			
このたてものは	なん	です	か。
What is this building?			

③ ここ・そこ・あそこ

ここ・そこ and あそこ are used as indicators to refer to places.

ここ means "here" or "this place" and refers to a place close to both the speaker and the listener.

そこ means "there" or "that place" and refers to a place a short distance away from both the speaker and the listener or a place near the listener.

あそこ means "over there" or "that place over there" and refers to a place far away from both the speaker and the listener.

Topic	Noun	Copula
ここは	しょくどう	です。
The cafeteria is here.		
そこは	きょうむか	です。
The Academic Office is there.		
あそこは	学生課(がくせいか)	です。
The Student Office is over there.		

れんしゅう１　Choose the right answer.

①

（これ・それ・あれ）はなんですか。

②

ヤン　リー

リー：じしょはどこですか。

ヤン：（ここ・そこ・あそこ）です。

③

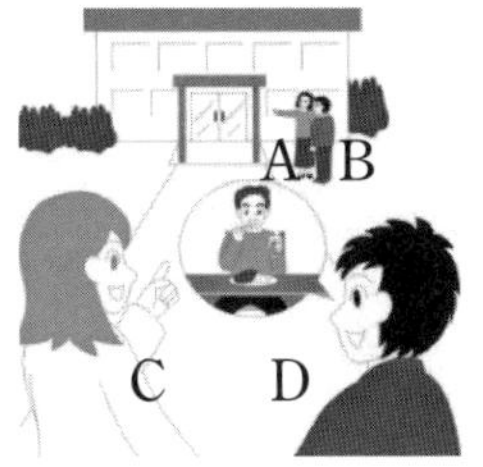

A：（この・あの）たてものはなんですか。

B：しょくどうです。

C：（この・あの）たてものはなんですか。

D：しょくどうです。

④

B　A

A：これはだれのペンですか。

B：（これ・それ）はハナさんのペンです。

れんしゅう２　Bring in an interesting thing from your country or Japan. You may also bring in a picture instead. Show it to your classmates and tell them about it.

e.g. A：それはなんですか。　　B：これは＿＿＿＿＿です。

4. Describing locations

Giving the location of a building
Topic は＋ Landmark ＋の＋ Location word ＋です。

Topic	Place	Particle	Location word	Copula
びょういんは	ぎんこう	の	となり	です。
The hospital is next to the bank.				
ぎんこうは	スーパー	の	まえ	です。
The bank is in front of the supermarket.				

Question with a question word

Topic	Place	Copula	Question Marker
としょかんは	どこ	です	か。
Where is the library?			
たいいくかんは	どこ	です	か。
Where is the gymnasium?			

Answer

Topic	Place	Particle	Location-word	Copula
としょかんは	しょくどう	の	うしろ	です。
The library is in back of the cafeteria.				
たいいくかんは	コープ	の	ちかく	です。
The gymnasium is near the CO-OP shop.				

れんしゅう　Complete each sentence using the following picture and map. Write the name of a building in the (　　) and a location word in the [　　] as in the example.

<キャンパスちず>　e.g. としょかんは（大学院棟（だいがくいんとう））の [まえ] です。

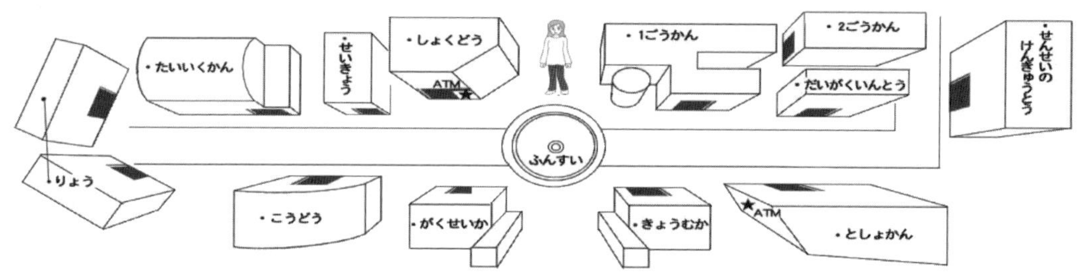

①ATMは（　　　　　）の [なか] です。

②2ごうかんは（　　　　　　）の [うしろ] です。

③生協（せいきょう）は（　　　　　）と（　　　　　）の [あいだ] です。

④学生課（がくせいか）は（　　　　　　）の [ひだり] です。

⑤きょうむかは（　　　　　　）の [まえ] です。

＜私(わたし)のまちのちず＞　e.g. 本屋(ほんや)は（アパート）の ［となり］ です。

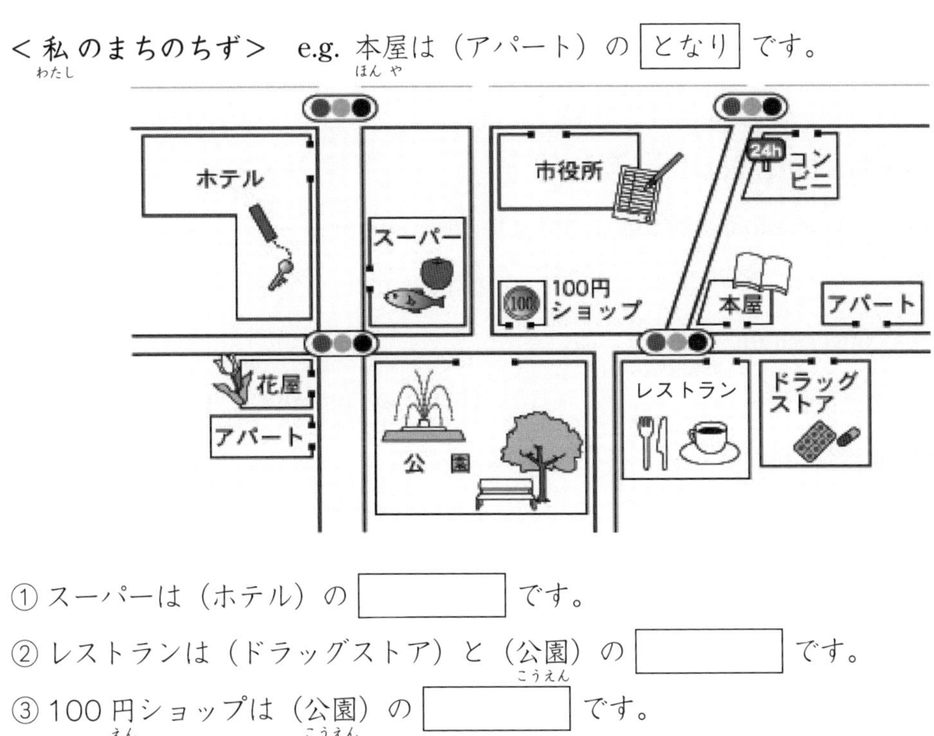

① スーパーは（ホテル）の ［　　　　］ です。

② レストランは（ドラッグストア）と（公園(こうえん)）の ［　　　　］ です。

③ 100円(えん)ショップは（公園(こうえん)）の ［　　　　］ です。

④ 私(わたし)のアパートは（花屋(はなや)）の ［　　　　］ です。

⑤ 本屋(ほんや)は（レストラン）の ［　　　　］ です。

はなします　Speaking

Check the following points:

1. Starting a conversation: (Say this in order to get attention.)

すみません。	Excuse me.

2. Closing a conversation:

ありがとうございました。	Thank you for your help.

3. Correcting a statement:

ちがいます。	It's not correct.

4. Asking for directions using the following underlined expressions:

・としょかんは<u>どこですか</u>。	Where is the library?
・としょかんは<u>どのたてものですか</u>。	Which building is the library?
・としょかんは<u>ここですか</u>。	Is the library here?

れんしゅう１　Practice the conversation using the listening material.

れんしゅう２　〈Role play〉 Practice the conversation. You take role A and your partner takes role B using the illustration on pages 26–27.

A	B
・Start the conversation. ・Ask the location of a building. ・End the conversation.	・Explain the location.

れんしゅう３

1. Bring a map of a town, a shopping center, a campus, etc. Practice asking and describing locations with it.
2. Where is your favorite place downtown? Why do you like it there?

【はなしたあとで】After speaking 〈Self-check〉 Evaluate your speaking.

I was able to ask and explain locations.	☺	😐	☹

よみます　Reading

【よむまえに】Before reading

カタカナ

Katakana is most often used for transcription of words from foreign languages. As you found in this lesson, these words are written using the Japanese sound system. For example, "clinic" is written *kurinikku*（クリニック）. Other examples of Katakana include:

1. *Konbini*（コンビニ）which is "convenience store"; note that the Katakana shortens the English word.
2. *Basutee raunji*（バスてい）which is "bus stop"; note the combination of Katakana with a Japanese word:
3. *Amerika*（アメリカ）which is "America"; foreign places and personal names.
4. *Tonton*（トントン）which is "knock-knock"; note that it is an onomatopoeia when letters are used to represent sounds.
5. スズキ、トヨタ ; company names.
6. Others: to emphasize keywords on signs and advertisements throughout Japan.

Guess the meanings of the following words.

① ちゅうしゃじょう　② ゲームセンター　③ えいがかん　④ じどうはんばいき
⑤ めがねや　⑥ かばんや　⑦ ようふくや　⑧ クリーニング
⑨ くつや　⑩ ファストフード

【よみましょう】Let's read

しつもん

Read the passage and find the stores. Fill in all blanks, 1-6 on the following picture.

Reading tip

When you read the paragraph, scan all places and locations in the paragraph first and mark them.

ほんぶん

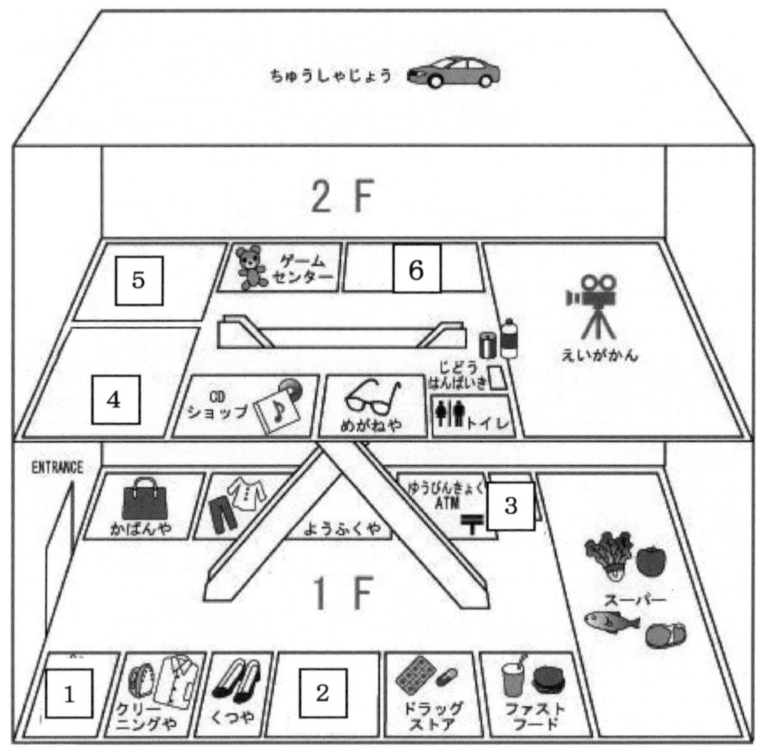

はなやと 100 えんショップは 1 かいです。はなやはかばんやのまえです。100 えんショップはくつやのとなりです。1 かいのトイレはゆうびんきょくのみぎがわです。ほんやとでんきやとレストランは 2 かいです。ほんやはゲームセンターのとなりです。レストランはゲームセンターのひだりがわです。でんきやはレストランのとなりです。

かきます　Writing － Describe a location －

【かくまえに】Before writing

Write the following words in Katakana as in the example.

	English	Japanese pronunciation	
e.g.	America	*amerika*	アメリカ
①	Asia	*ajia*	______
②	toilet	*toire*	______
③	calendar	*karendaa*	______
④	schedule	*sukejuuru*	______
⑤	coffee	*koohii*	______
⑥	elevator	*erebeetaa*	______
⑦	shop	*shoppu*	______
⑧	convenience store	*konbini*	______

【かきましょう】Let's write

Answer the following questions based on the picture on the previous page.

1. Find the following shops from the picture and write them in Japanese.

book store______　100 yen shop ______　laundry______

drug store______　supermarket______　optician______

restaurant______　shoe shop ______　fast food______

2. See the picture on the previous page and describe the locations of the following shops:

ドラッグストア、めがねや、クリーニングや、えいがかん、ファストフード

【かいたあとで】After writing

〈For your patner's writing〉 Read your partner's writing out loud. Tell your partner if something is not clear.

〈For your writing〉 Improve your writing by including your partner's questions and comments.

〈Self-check〉 Evaluate your writing.

I was able to:			
use Katakana properly.	☺	😐	☹
describe locations properly.	☺	😐	☹

Cultural Challenge

> The way Japanese people count numbers with their fingers is different from the way we do it in my country.

1. How do you count numbers and money in your country? Explain your way of counting to your classmates.
2. Your challenge: Find interesting places to go on campus. Explain the location of the places to your classmates.

Additional information

Learning strategies

1. Make notes and find meanings of Katakana words in your daily life like food, signs, magazines etc. When you eat or drink something, don't just throw away the bottle, can or box. Read what is written on it. You can learn a lot of Katakana words. Bring them to class and share them with your classmates.
2. It's a good idea to keep a small notepad and pen with you. If you don't know how to get to a place, ask someone to draw a map for you. Most streets in Japan don't have names, so it is very common for Japanese to do this as well!
3. Pictures help you understand or guess a word that you don't know.

Topic 3　今何時(いまなんじ)ですか

Objectives:

In this lesson, you will learn how to:

1. Ask and understand the date and time.
2. Read schedules and business hours.
3. Write schedules.

Introduction:

1. Listen to the vocabulary and match it with the calendar on the page 37.
2. Watch the video. If the statement is correct, write a ○. If the statement is wrong, write an ×.

　① オリエンテーションは今日(きょう)じゃないです。　(　　)
　② オリエンテーションは明日(あした)です。　(　　)
　③ オリエンテーションはごごです。　(　　)

3. Write your birthday and ask the birthdays of your classmates.

　① わたしの誕生日(たんじょうび)：＿＿＿＿＿＿年(ねん)＿＿＿月(がつ)＿＿＿日(にち)
　② XX さんの誕生日(たんじょうび)はいつですか。

At the Academic Office

Lee asks a staff in the Academic Office about the schedule for orientation.

リー　　：あのう、すみません。今日(きょう)、オリエンテーションがありますか。

じむいん：いいえ、今日(きょう)はありません。

リー　　：いつですか。

じむいん：明日(あした)とあさってです。

リー　　：何時(なんじ)からですか。

じむいん：12時半(じはん)からです。

リー　　：何時(なんじ)までですか。

じむいん：2時(じ)までです。

リー　　：どうもありがとうございました。

New vocabulary

Verbs

あります	to have
わかります	to understand

Nouns

Years, months, days and time :

あさ	morning
今（いま）	now
～時（じ）	o'clock
～分（ふん／ぷん）	minute
半（はん）	half past
ごぜん	a.m.
ごご	p.m.
明日（あした）	tomorrow
あさって	the day after tomorrow
今日（きょう）	today
昨日（きのう）	yesterday
おととい	the day before yesterday
毎日（まいにち）	everyday
～週（しゅう）	week
今週（こんしゅう）	this week
先週（せんしゅう）	last week
毎週（まいしゅう）	every week
来週（らいしゅう）	next week
～月（がつ）	month
今月（こんげつ）	this month
先月（せんげつ）	last month
毎月（まいつき）	every month
来月（らいげつ）	next month
～年（ねん）	year
今年（ことし）	this year

Nouns

去年（きょねん）	last year
毎年（まいとし）	every year
来年（らいねん）	next year
Others：	
カレンダー	calendar
クイズ	quiz
じゅぎょう	class
祝日（しゅくじつ）	national holiday
しゅくだい	homework
セミナー	seminar
誕生日（たんじょうび）	birthday
テスト	test
パーティー	party
平日（へいじつ）	weekday
休（やす）み	no class/off/holiday/rest
ワークショップ	workshop
Minutes：	
１分（いっぷん）	one minute
２分（にふん）	two minutes
３分（さんぷん）	three minutes
４分（よんぷん）	four minutes
５分（ごふん）	five minutes
６分（ろっぷん）	six minutes
７分（ななふん）	seven minutes
８分（はっぷん／はちふん）	eight minutes
９分（きゅうふん）	nine minutes
10分（じっぷん／じゅっぷん）	ten minutes
11分（じゅういっぷん）	eleven minutes
20分（にじっぷん／にじゅっぷん）	twenty minutes
30分（さんじっぷん／さんじゅっぷん）	thirty minutes
40分（よんじっぷん／よんじゅっぷん）	forty minutes
50分（ごじっぷん／ごじゅっぷん）	fifty minutes

Question words

いつ　when

Vocabulary exercises

1. Calendar and Time word

Month											
1月 いちがつ	2月 にがつ	3月 さんがつ	4月 しがつ	5月 ごがつ	6月 ろくがつ	7月 しちがつ	8月 はちがつ	9月 くがつ	10月 じゅうがつ	11月 じゅういちがつ	12月 じゅうにがつ

Day／Day of the week						
日曜日 にちようび	月曜日 げつようび	火曜日 かようび	水曜日 すいようび	木曜日 もくようび	金曜日 きんようび	土曜日 どようび
1 ついたち	2 ふつか	3 みっか	4 よっか	5 いつか	6 むいか	7 なのか
8 ようか	9 ここのか	10 とおか	11 じゅういちにち	12 じゅうににち	13 じゅうさんにち	14 じゅうよっか
15 じゅうごにち	16 じゅうろくにち	17 じゅうしちにち	18 じゅうはちにち（今日 きょう）	19 じゅうくにち	20 はつか	21 にじゅういちにち
22 にじゅうににち	23 にじゅうさんにち	24 にじゅうよっか	25 にじゅうごにち	26 にじゅうろくにち	27 にじゅうしちにち	28 にじゅうはちにち
29 にじゅうくにち	30 さんじゅうにち	31 さんじゅういちにち				

Exercise A

Look at the above table and write the reading of the following dates in Hiragana.

e.g. 1／15〔いちがつじゅうごにち〕	(1) 4／20〔　〕
(2) 7／7〔　〕	(3) 9／9〔　〕
(4) 11／3〔　〕	(5) 1／15〔　〕
(6) 8／10〔　〕	(7) 3／1〔　〕

Exercise B

Today is October 18th, 2017. Look at the calendar on the previous page and fill in the blanks with the appropriate word. It is not necessarily to write in kan

ji.

Day				Week	
10／16	（　　）	10／19	（　　）	10／ 8～10／14	（ 先週 ）
10／17	（　　）	10／20	（　　）	10／15～10／21	（　　）
10／18	（ 今日 ）	every day	（ 毎日 ）	10／22～10／28	（　　）
				every week	（　　）

Month		Year	
9月	（ 先月 ）	2016年	（ 去年 ）
10月	（ 今月 ）	2017年	（　　）
11月	（　　）	2018年	（　　）
every month	（　　）	every year	（　　）

Grammar explanations and exercises

1. Time expressions

① Number ＋ counter 時 indicates the hour. e.g. 5時 (5 o'clock)
Number ＋ counter 分 indicates the minutes. e.g. 5分 (5 minutes)
② 何＋ counter 時 asks the hour whereas 何＋ counter 分 asks the minutes.

れんしゅう 1 Look at the following times and answer the questions as in the example.

e.g. A：いま、何時ですか。 B：ごぜん7時です。 [7：00 am]

① [12：10 pm] ② [4：15 pm] ③ [9：30 am]

④ [8：16 am] ⑤ [6：40 pm] ⑥ [1：09 am]

れんしゅう２ Ask your classmates about the local time of their countries as in the example.

e.g. A：今(いま)、ホンさんのくには何時(なんじ)ですか。　B：ごぜん８時(じ)です。

友達(ともだち)のなまえ	友達(ともだち)のくに	時間(じかん)

2. Calendar

① 何(なん)＋ counter 曜日(ようび) asks the days of the week.
② 何(なん)＋ counter 日(にち) asks the days of the month.
＊ いつ also can be used when asking about the time.

れんしゅう 〈Pair work〉 Practice as in the example based on the following calendar.

e.g. A：カーさんの誕生日(たんじょうび)はいつですか。　B：３日(みっか)です。

カレンダー

日曜日(にちようび)	月曜日(げつようび)	火曜日(かようび)	水曜日(すいようび)	木曜日(もくようび)	金曜日(きんようび)	土曜日(どようび)
				1 ワークショップ	2	3 カーさんの誕生日(たんじょうび)
4	5 祝日(しゅくじつ)	6 セミナー	7	8	9	10
11	12	13	14 アンさんの誕生日(たんじょうび)	15	16	17
18	19	20 先生(せんせい)の誕生日(たんじょうび)	21	22	23	24 パーティー
25	26 かんじのテスト	27	28	29	30 イムさんの誕生日(たんじょうび)	31

3. Past tense of the copula verb です

でした is the past tense of です and is used in sentences to describe something that happened in the past.

	affirmative	negative
Present	です	じゃありません
Past	でした	じゃありませんでした

れんしゅう Look at the following calendar and answer the questions.

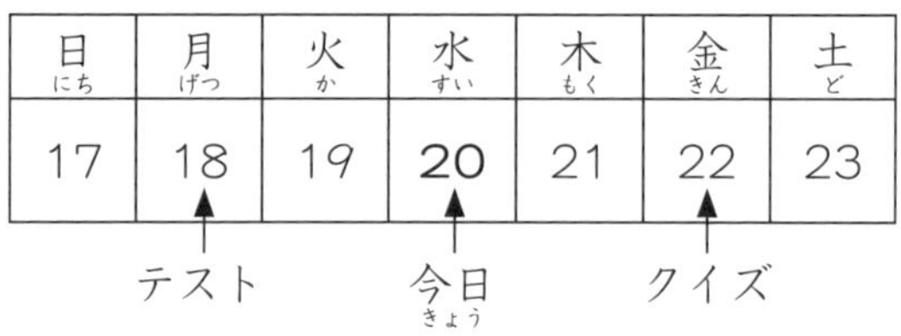

① 昨日(きのう)は、何日(なんにち)でしたか。

② おとといは、何曜日(なんようび)でしたか。

③ テストは、金曜日(きんようび)ですか。

④ クイズは、明日(あした)ですか。

4. Object + particle が + あります

あります is a verb. It means "to have".

① When the ending -ます is added to a verb, it makes it polite. The endings of verbs indicate the tense and whether they are affirmative or negative.

	affirmative	negative
Present	ーます	ーません
Past	ーました	ーませんでした

② The particle が is used with an object as in the following examples.

1) 今日(きょう)、日本語(にほんご)のじゅぎょうがあります。　I have a Japanese class today.

2) 昨日(きのう)、テストがありました。　I had a test yesterday.

3) 昨日(きのう)、じゅぎょうがありませんでした。　I had no class yesterday.

4) いつ、クイズがありますか。　When do we have the quiz?

れんしゅう Answer the following questions.

① 昨日(きのう)、日本語(にほんご)のしゅくだいがありましたか。

② 明日(あした)、日本語(にほんご)のじゅぎょうがありますか。

③ いつ、日本語(にほんご)のクイズがありますか。

④ 今週(こんしゅう)、パーティーがありますか。

5. ～から～まで

～から(from)～まで(to) is used to express start and end points. 何時＋から and 何時＋まで asks “from what time until what time”.
* どこ＋から and どこ＋まで asks “from where to where”.

1) 今日３時から５時半まで じゅぎょうがあります。	I have a class from three to five thirty today.
2) じゅぎょうは何時からですか。	From what time does your class start?

れんしゅう１ Make a sentence based on the following schedule as in the example.

e.g.	Mon	10:35-12:10	日本語	→ 月曜日は、10時35分から12時10分まで日本語のじゅぎょうがあります。
	Tue	17:55-19:30	けいざい	→
	Wed	12:25-13:50	ワークショップ	→
	Thu	8:45-09:20	テスト	→

れんしゅう２ Ask your classmates about the business hours of the following places in their country. [ゆうびんきょく、ぎんこう、スーパー、びょういん]

はなします　Speaking

Check the following points:

Variations: Asking for the day and time.

・何時からですか。何時までですか。何時から何時までですか。

・いつからですか。いつまでですか。いつからいつまでですか。

れんしゅう１ Practice the conversation using the listening material.

れんしゅう２ Tell your classmates about your weekly schedule.
Who is the busiest person?

【はなしたあとで】**After speaking** 〈Self-check〉 Evaluate your speaking.

I was able to ask and explain about a schedule.	☺	😐	☹

よみます　Reading

【よむまえに】**Before reading**

The following Japanese words, 平日（月火水木金）、土日、祝日・休日（holiday）are important to know. If you don't know these words, you won't complate your errands.

【よみましょう】**Let's read**

しつもん

Read the passage and fill in the blanks in the chart with the specific times as in the example.

ほんぶん

ばしょ	平日（月～金）	土日．祝日
としょかん	8:00 ～(e.g. 21:30)	8:00 ～（　　）
せいきょう	8:30 ～（　　）	11:00 ～ 14:00
ATM	8:45 ～ 19:00	(土)9:00 ～ 17:00(日・祝日)(　　)
スーパーマーケット	（　　）～ 24:00	年中無休（No holiday）

　としょかんは、平日ごぜん８時からごご９時30分までです。土日と祝日は８時から５時までです。せいきょうは、月曜日、ごぜん８時半からごご８時までです。土日と祝日は、あさ11時から２時までです。ATMは、日曜日と祝日は休みです。大学のちかくのスーパーは、あさ10時からです。

かきます　Writing － Today and tomorrow's event －

【かくまえに】Before writing

1. Read the sample paragraph about a schedule. Pay particular attention to underlined words.

昨日（きのう）、えいごとビジネスのじゅぎょうがありました。えいごは、10時半から12時10分までした。ビジネスは、4時5分から5時40分までした。明日（あした）、ワークショップがあります。ワークショップは、2時15分から3時50分までです。

2. Write down keywords about your schedule from yesterday and for tomorrow.

＜昨日（きのう）＞ ____________________　＜明日（あした）＞ ____________________

【かきましょう】Let's write

Write about your schedule from yesterday and for tomorrow using all the information you wrote above. Refer to the sample paragraph above.

【かいたあとで】After writing

〈For your partner's writing〉 Read your partner's writing out loud. Tell your partner if something is not clear.

〈For your writing〉 Improve your writing by including your partner's questions and comments.

〈Self-check〉 Evaluate your writing.

I was able to:			
write yesterday's events using the past tense.	☺	😐	☹
write tomorrow's events.	☺	😐	☹

Cultural Challenge

Japanese students seem very busy with part time jobs and club/circle activities.

Your challenge: Think about time management and how you organize your time.

Additional information

Japanese calendar

A new calendar starts over every time a new emperor ascends the throne. The year is preceded by the era, for example: 平成（へいせい）21年（ねん）"*heesee nijuuichi nen*". When you fill out forms, they often ask you for your birthday（生年月日（せいねんがっぴ））or the current date in the Japanese calendar.

e.g. 2017年（ねん）11月（がつ）25日（にち）or 平成（へいせい）29年（ねん）11月（がつ）25日（にち）

The Japanese native counters

1つ(ひとつ)　2つ(ふたつ)　3つ(みっつ)　4つ(よっつ)　5つ(いつつ)
6つ(むっつ)　7つ(ななつ)　8つ(やっつ)　9つ(ここのつ)　10(とお)

-tsu（つ）for counting generic objects; anything that doesn't have a counter, or anything that you don't know the counter for. The generic counter goes up to ten.

You see the following words on information about business hours.

窓口（まどぐち）service counter　営業時間（えいぎょうじかん）business hour

Topic 4　どのぐらいかかりますか

Objectives:

In this lesson, you will learn how to:

1. Use public transportation.
2. Ask someone how to get to a place and how much it costs.
3. Read a bus and a train timetable.
4. Write the way to go and get to a place.

Introduction:

1. Listen to the vocabulary and match it to the pictures on the page 49.
2. Watch two videos. If the statement is correct, write a ○. If the statement is wrong, write an ×.

1st video：

① 山田えきからしやくしょまであるきます。20分です。　(　　)

② 大学(だいがく)から山田えきまでバスで５分です。　(　　)

③ 大学(だいがく)から山田えきまでバスで360円(えん)です。　(　　)

2nd video：

① 山田えきいきのバスは12時35分です。　(　　)

② 山田えきいきのバスのりばは３ばんです。　(　　)

Asking how to get to a place

1. Lee asks Kan how to get to City Hall.

リー：カンさん、しやくしょまでどうやっていきますか。

カン：バスで山田えきまでいきます。しやくしょは山田えきからあるいて５分ぐらいです。

リー：ここから山田えきまでどのぐらいかかりますか。

カン：20分ぐらいです。

リー：いくらですか。

カン：360円(えん)です。

リー：ありがとうございました。

2. Lee asks a bus driver about a bus bound for Yamada station.

リー　　　　：あのう、すみません。このバスは、山田えきにいきますか。

うんてんしゅ：いいえ、いきません。

リー　　　　：山田えきいきのバスは何時にきますか。

うんてんしゅ：12時35分です。

リー　　　　：のりばはここですか。

うんてんしゅ：いいえ、ちがいます。２ばんのりばです。

リー　　　　：ありがとうございました。

New vocabulary

Verbs

いきます	to go
かえります	to go home/to return
きます	to come
あるきます	to walk
おきます	to get up
かかります	to take (time duration)
しょくじします	to have a meal
ねます	to sleep
べんきょうします	to study

Nouns

Time duration：

～か月（げつ）	month
～時間（じかん）	hour
～週間（しゅうかん）	week
～年間（ねんかん）	year

Time：

今朝（けさ）	this morning
今晩（こんばん）	tonight
毎朝（まいあさ）	every morning
毎晩（まいばん）	every evening/night
ゆうべ	last night

Places：

いえ	house
うち	home
えき	station
学校（がっこう）	school
くうこう	airport
しやくしょ	City Hall
のりば	bus stop/platform

Nouns

ばしょ	place
バスてい	bus stop
プラットホーム	platform
みなと	harbor
Transportations：	
のりもの	transportation
車（くるま）	car
自転車（じてんしゃ）	bicycle
しんかんせん	Shinkansen
タクシー	taxi
電車（でんしゃ）	train
バイク	motorbike
バス	bus
ひこうき	airplane
フェリー	ferry
Time table：	
うんちん	fare
時刻表（じこくひょう）	timetable
ほうめん	direction
Things relating to the transportations：	
～いき	bound for
～ばんせん	platform

Question words

いくら	how much
どうやって	how to (do something)
どのくらい	how long/many/much

Vocabulary exercises

1. Transportations

Exercise A

Match the Japanese words with the pictures.

のりもの (Transportations)	(a) バス	(b) タクシー	(c) 自転車(じてんしゃ)	(d) フェリー
	(e) バイク	(f) 車(くるま)	(g) 電車(でんしゃ)	(h) ひこうき
	(i) しんかんせん		(j) あるきます	
ばしょ (Place)	(k) えき	(l) くうこう	(m) バスてい	(n) みなと

のりもの (Transportations)

ばしょ (Place)

2. Verb words

Exercise A

Match the verbs with the pictures.

(a) おきます	(b) あるきます	(c) いきます	(d) ねます
(e) しょくじします	(f) べんきょうします	(g) かえります	(h) きます

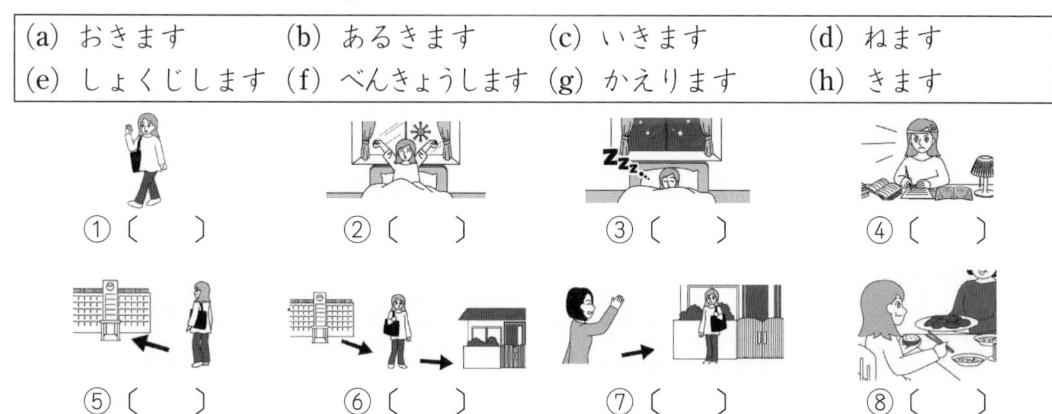

Exercise B

What time do you do the following activities? Write the time in each blank.

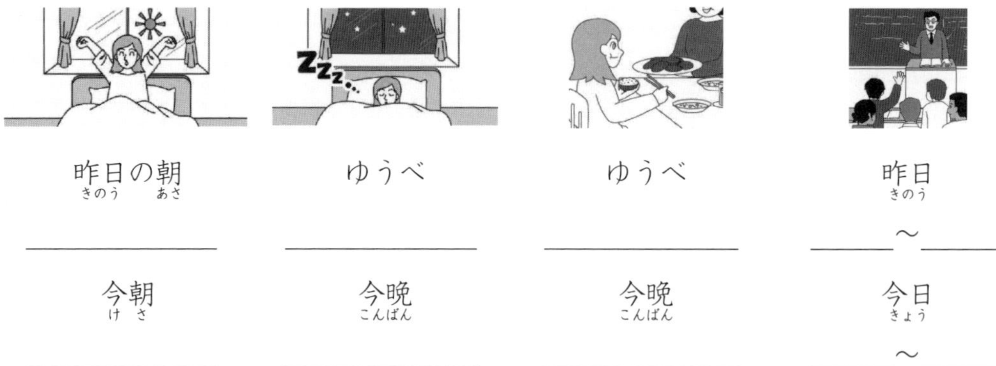

昨日(きのう)の朝(あさ)	ゆうべ	ゆうべ	昨日(きのう)
______	______	______	____～____
今朝(けさ)	今晩(こんばん)	今晩(こんばん)	今日(きょう)
______	______	______	____～____

Grammar explanations and exercises

1. Particle に／へ and moving verbs いきます／きます／かえります

① Particle に／へ

In a sentence with a verb such as いきます，きます，かえります，に or へ attached to a place noun indicates movement in some direction, or toward some destination. へ is pronounced "e".

1) 明日(あした)レオさんはくにへかえります。 Leo will go back to his country tomorrow.

2) (私(わたし)は) 今日(きょう)東京(とうきょう)にいきます。 I am going to Tokyo today.

② いきます・きます・かえります

When the ending -ます is added to a verb, it makes it polite. The endings of verbs indicate the tense and whether they are affirmative or negative.

Present affirmative	Present negative	Past affirmative	Past negative
いきます	いきません	いきました	いきませんでした
きます	きません	きました	きませんでした
かえります	かえりません	かえりました	かえりませんでした

When you move towards a place where the listener is, in English you say, "I am coming…" whereas in Japanese, you say "いきます". If you are already at the destination you are talking about, use "きます". You are on campus now and say:

1) (私(わたし)は)明日(あした)学校(がっこう)へきません。 I will not come to school tomorrow.

2) (私(わたし)は)昨日(きのう)学校(がっこう)にきませんでした。 I didn't come to school yesterday.

If you are talking about the destination you are going to, use "いきます". For example: You are now at the cafeteria and say that you are coming to cafeteria tomorrow, you say in Japanese, "明日（あした）、しょくどうに／へきます。", if you say that you are going to the library at the cafeteria, then you say, "としょかんに／へいきます。".

3) （私（わたし）は）明日（あした）１時（じ）ごろしょくどうへきます。　I will come to the cafeteria around 1:00 tomorrow.

4) 日曜日（にちようび）にとしょかんにいきます。　I will go to the library on Sunday.

③ Question

Question	Particle	Verb	Question Marker
どこ	に／へ	いきます	か。
Where are you going?			

Answer

Place Noun（Destination ／ Goal）	Particle	Verb
学校（がっこう）	に／へ	いきます。
I'm going to school.		

れんしゅう１ Fill in each blank using either いきます，きます or かえります．

① 学校（がっこう）へ＿＿＿＿＿＿＿＿＿＿＿＿

② うちへ＿＿＿＿＿＿＿＿＿＿＿＿

③ 友達（ともだち）はうちに＿＿＿＿＿＿＿＿＿＿

れんしゅう２ Now you are talking to a friend in the cafeteria. Choose the appropriate verb to make each sentence.

① 明日（あした）びょういんへ（いきます・きます・かえります）。

② 午後（ごご）先生（せんせい）のけんきゅうしつへ（いきます・きます・かえります）。

③ あさってくにへ（いきます・きます・かえります）。

④ うちへ（いきます・きます・かえります）。

⑤ 明日（あした）もしょくどうへ（いきます・きます・かえります）。

れんしゅう３　Ask your classmates where they will go next Sunday or where they went last Saturday.

2. Transportation＋particle で and asking the method of transportation どうやって（何(なん)で）

① で attached to a transportation noun indicates a method of the transportation. It means "by".
② When asking about the method of transportation, use どうやって／なんで. "On foot" is not used with で. あるいて is the expression for it.

1）A：どうやって大阪(おおさか)へいきますか。　How will you go to Osaka?
　　B：ひこうきでいきます。　I will go by plane.
2）A：何(なん)でえきまでいきますか。　How will you go to the station?
　　B：あるいていきます。　I will go to the station on foot.

れんしゅう　Ask how to go to the following places using いきます and the transportation as in the example.

e.g.　A：どうやって学校(がっこう)へいきますか。B：あるいていきます。

①　②　③　④　⑤

3. Time duration ～間(かん) and asking time duration どのぐらい／どのくらい

① かん is the counter word used for showing the amount of time.

1）１週間(いっしゅうかん)　a week
2）３時間(じかん)　three hours
3）40分(ぷん)（間(かん)）　forty minutes
4）１か月(げつ)（間(かん)）　a month
5）２年間(ねんかん)　two years

② どのぐらい／どのくらい is a question phrase used to ask about the duration of time. ぐらい is used to express approximate duration.

1) 学校(がっこう)からうちまでどのぐらいかかりますか。	How long does it take from school to your house?

＊ When the time duration for minutes or months is expressed, 間(かん) is omitted.

2) 30分(ぷん)ぐらいかかります。	It takes about 30 minutes.

＊何(なん)＋時間(じかん)、分(ぷん) are also used to ask for the duration of time.

3) くにから日本(にほん)まで何時間(なんじかん)かかりますか。	How many hours does it take from your country to Japan?

れんしゅう Ask about the duration of time to your classmates as in the example. Write it down.

e.g. A：どうやってうちから学校(がっこう)までいきましたか。　B：バスでいきました。
A：どのぐらいかかりましたか。　B：30分(ぷん)かかりました。

	～から～まで	どうやって	どのくらい
さん			
さん			
さん			

4. Time + particle に／ごろ

① に indicates specific times and dates when an action occurs. You need to use に with the day of the week such as 月曜日(げつようび) and numerical time expressions such as 7時(じ), 1時(じ)30分(ぷん), 1月(がつ), 15日(にち).

② ごろ is used with or without the particle に to express "around".

③ に is not used with 昨日(きのう), 今日(きょう), 明日(あした), and expressions describing regular intervals, such as 毎日(まいにち), 毎週(まいしゅう), 毎月(まいつき) and etc.

Use with に	Do not Use with に
6時(じ)15分(ふん)　月曜日(げつようび)　8月(がつ)19日(にち) 2009年(ねん)　何年(なんねん)　何日(なんにち)　etc.	昨日(きのう)　今日(きょう)　明日(あした)　あさって　いつ 先週(せんしゅう)　今週(こんしゅう)　来週(らいしゅう)　毎日(まいにち)　毎晩(まいばん) 今朝(けさ)　今晩(こんばん)　午後(ごご)　午前(ごぜん)　etc.

	Time	Particle	Action
(私(わたし)は)	1時(じ)	に／ごろ（に）	ねました。
I slept at (about) 1 o'clock.			
(私(わたし)は)	今朝(けさ)	−	しょくじしませんでした。
I didn't eat this morning.			

④ 〜ます is used for habitual actions, future actions or events.

1) 明日(あした)９時(じ)から12時(じ)まで べんきょうします。　I will study from 9:00 to 12:00 tomorrow.

2) 毎日(まいにち)７時(じ)におきます。　I get up at 7 o'clock everyday.

〜ました is used for actions that have already taken place and 〜ませんでした is used for the negative of 〜ました.

昨日(きのう)６時間(じかん)ねました。　I slept for 6 hours yesterday.

れんしゅう　Make sentences and ask your classmate as in the example.

e.g.　今日(きょう)　10：00　→　今日(きょう)10時(じ)に学校(がっこう)へいきました。

Q：何時(なんじ)に学校(がっこう)へいきますか。

① 毎日(まいにち)19:00−23:00　② ゆうべ 2:00　③ 毎朝(まいあさ) 7:00　④ 今日(きょう) 12:00　⑤ 今日(きょう) 6:00

5. 〜いき

〜いき attached to places to indicate the destination. It is used with public transportation.

1) このバスは福岡(ふくおか)いきです。　This bus is bound for Fukuoka.

2) 東京(とうきょう)いきのしんかんせん　The shinkansen bound for Tokyo station.

3) しやくしょいきのバスは何時(なんじ)にきますか。　What time will the bus bound for the City Hall come?

れんしゅう Practice as in the example.

e.g.  福岡（ふくおか） <u>福岡（ふくおか）いきのバス</u>

①  福岡（ふくおか）

②  かんこく

③ 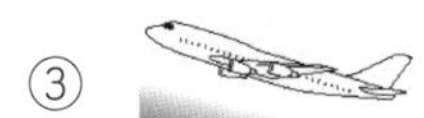 ニューヨーク

④  東京（とうきょう）

6. Number ＋ばん

The counter ばん is used for the bus stop or platform.

バスのりば：1ばんのりば・4ばんのりば・7ばんのりば・9ばんのりば

プラットホーム：1ばんせん・4ばんせん・7ばんせん・9ばんせん

A：福岡（ふくおか）いきのバスののりばは、どこですか。 Where is the bus stop for the bus bound for Fukuoka?

B：2ばんのりばです。 It's number 2.

れんしゅう Practice as in the example. Check the places on the map on page 268.

e.g.（大阪（おおさか）いき・バス・4ばんのりば）

A：大阪（おおさか）いきのバスののりばはどこですか。 B：4ばんのりばです。

①（広島（ひろしま）いき・バス・2ばんのりば） ②（大分（おおいた）いき・電車（でんしゃ）・3ばんせん）

③（東京（とうきょう）いき・しんかんせん・6ばんせん） ④（長崎（ながさき）いき・バス・5ばんのりば）

7. いくら／いくらぐらい

The question word いくら is used to ask the cost. ぐらい is used with いくら and numbers. ぐらい means about or almost. 円（えん） is used to count money.

A：福岡（ふくおか）から広島（ひろしま）まで、しんかんせんでいくらぐらいですか。 How much is the fare from Fukuoka to Hirosima by shinkansen?

B：9000円（えん）ぐらいです。 It's about nine thousand yen.

れんしゅう　How much does the transportation fee cost? Practice with your partner using the following diagram as in the example.

e.g. A：ヨンさんのくにから日本(にほん)までいくらですか。　B：86,000円(えん)です。

A：どのくらいかかりますか。　B：２時間(じかん)50分(ぷん)です。

はなします　Speaking

Check the following points：

If the statement is not right, you correct it: ちがいます It's not right.

→ Give the right information.

e.g. A：山田えきいきのバスのりばはここですか。	Is this the place to catch a bus bound for Yamada station?
B：いいえ、ちがいます。２ばんのりばです。	No, it's not here. It's number 2.

れんしゅう１　Practice the conversation using the listening material.

れんしゅう２　〈Role play〉 Practice the conversation. One student takes role A and another student takes role B using the information in the [ ]

Situation: Ask the bus driver.

A・Start the conversation.
　A・Ask：whether the bus goes to the place you want to go;
　　how long it takes;
　　how much the bus fare is; and
　　where you can catch the bus.
　・Close the conversation.

B・Give all the information.

ばしょ	時間	うんちん	のりば
鉄輪(かんなわ)	25分	420	2
石垣(いしがき)	20分	380	1
高崎山(たかさきやま)	10分	240	3

れんしゅう３　Recommend a place you would like to go with your classmates. Give the following information：ばしょのなまえ／どこですか／どうやっていきますか／どのぐらいかかりますか／いくらですか

【はなしたあとで】**After speaking** 〈Self-check〉 Evaluate your speaking.

I was able to ask:			
how to get to a place.	☺	😐	☹
how long it takes.	☺	😐	☹
how much the bus fare is.	☺	😐	☹

よみます　Reading

【よむまえに】Before reading

Look at the following timetable then answer the following questions.

しつもん

① 今４時１０分です。亀川(かめがわ)いきのバスは何時にきますか。

② 今５時です。別府(べっぷ)にいきます。電車は何時にきますか。

バス時刻表(じこくひょう)

時刻(じこく)	大学(だいがく)→亀川(かめがわ)えき
16	06　18　30　42　54
17	06　18　30　42　54
18	06　18　30　45

電車　亀川(かめがわ)えき時刻表(じこくひょう)

時刻(じこく)	くだり（大分(おおいた)ほうめん）
16	19　38
17	10　38
18	16　28

【よみましょう】Let's read

Read the passage and answer the questions using the timetable above.

しつもん

① 何時何分のバスで亀川(かめがわ)へいきますか。

② 何時何分の電車で大分(おおいた)へいきますか。

③ 大学(だいがく)から大分(おおいた)までどのぐらいかかりますか。

④ 大学(だいがく)から先生のいえまで何分ぐらいかかりますか。

ほんぶん

私は、今週の金曜日、午後７時に大分の先生のいえへいきます。午後のじゅぎょうは５時 40 分までです。大学から亀川えきまでバスで 15 分ぐらいかかります。亀川から大分まで JR で 20 分ぐらいです。大分えきから先生のいえまであるいて 10 分くらいかかります。

かきます　Writing － How did you come to Japan? －

【かくまえに】Before writing

1. Remember how you came to Japan and how long it took. Fill in the blanks.

	あなたのくにのうち→くうこう	あなたのくに→日本	日本のくうこう → 大学
どうやっていきましたか／きましたか		ひこうき	
どのぐらいかかりましたか	____時間____分	____時間____分	____時間____分

2. Make sentences using the information above to explain how you came to Japan and the university.

【かきましょう】Let's write

Write a short paragraph about how you came to Japan and the university.

【かいたあとで】After writing

〈For your patner's writing〉 Read your partner's writing out loud. Tell your partner if something is not clear.

〈For your writing〉 Improve your writing by including your partner's questions and comments.

〈Self-check〉 Evaluate your writing.

I could write how I came to Japan and the university including all necessary information.
☺ 😐 ☹

Cultural Challenge

Try to read the names of the stations written in Kanji on the board at the station.

Your challenge: What train station names in Kanji can you read?

Additional information

Riding public transportation:

Reading a timetable

You will see the following Kanji as you learned in the previous topic: 平日、土・日・祝日. If you don't pay attention to these words, you might miss your bus or train.

Riding a bus

Take a boarding ticket, 整理券 (*seeriken*). When you pay the bus fare, check the number of the ticket and find the fare corresponding to the number on the ticket. If you don't have any coins called 小銭 (*kozeni*), you can break a 1000 note into coins using the change machine located next to the bus driver. The following tickets which are cheaper than the regular fare are also available: a book of tickets, 回数券 (*kaisuuken*); a season ticket, 定期券 (*teekiken*); a bus card, バスカード (*basu kaado*).

Riding a train

1. Train categories: local, 普通 (*futsuu*); rapid, 快速 (*kaisoku*); express, 急行 (*kyuukoo*); limited express, 特急 (*tokkyuu*); super express, 新幹線 (*shinkansen*).
2. Type of tickets: a local train ticket, 普通乗車券 (*futsuujyooshaken*); a limited express ticket, 特急券 (*tokkyuuken*); a seat reservation ticket, 指定席券 (*shiteesekiken*); If you take an express train and reserve a seat, you need to pay a limited express fee and a seat reservation fee in addition to the base fare.

Topic 5　じゅぎょうはどうですか

Objectives:

In this lesson, you will learn how to:

1. Ask about how classes are going.
2. Explain daily activities.
3. Read for details about daily routines.
4. Write about daily activities.

Introduction:

1. Listen to the vocabulary and match it to the pictures on the page 65-66.
2. Watch the video. If the statement is correct, write a ○ . If the statement is wrong, write an × .

①リーさんのじゅぎょうはむずかしいです。　(　　)

②リーさんは毎日忙(いそが)しいです。　(　　)

③吉田(よしだ)さんは図書館(としょかん)でべんきょうします。　(　　)

④リーさんは生協(せいきょう)へいきます。　(　　)

Seeing a friend on campus

Lee happened to see Yoshida and made small talk on campus.

リー：こんにちは。

吉田(よしだ)：こんにちは。じゅぎょうはどうですか。
むずかしいですか。

リー：いいえ、あまりむずかしくないですけど、しゅくだいやクイズがたくさんあります。毎日、とても忙(いそが)しいです。

吉田(よしだ)：そうですか。

リー：吉田(よしだ)さんはどうですか。

吉田(よしだ)：ぼくも忙(いそが)しいです。
毎日８時45分からじゅぎょうがあります。

リー：今からじゅぎょうですか。

吉田(よしだ)：いいえ、しょくどうで昼ごはんをたべます。リーさんは。

リー：私は図書館(としょかん)でレポートを書(か)きます。

吉田(よしだ)：じゃあ、また。

リー：じゃあ。

New vocabulary

Verbs

かいます	to buy
かいものします	to go shopping
書（か）きます	to write
かります	to borrow
聞（き）きます	to listen/to hear
します	to do
たべます	to eat
使（つか）います	to use
のみます	to drink
はなします	to talk/to speak
はらいます	to pay
見（み）ます	to see/to watch/to look at
読（よ）みます	to read

Adjectives

あかるい	bright
あたらしい	new
いい	good
忙（いそが）しい	busy
うるさい	noisy
おいしい	delicious/tasty
大（おお）きい	big
おもしろい	fun/interesting
きたない	dirty
きびしい	strict/hard
くらい	dark
せまい	narrow/small (space)
たかい	expensive
楽（たの）しい	enjoyable/delightful
小（ちい）さい	small

Adjectives

つまらない	boring
広（ひろ）い	spacious/wide
ふるい	old
まずい	not delicious/tasteless
むずかしい	difficult
やさしい	easy/gentle
やすい	cheap
かんたん［な］	easy/simple
きれい［な］	clean/beautiful
しずか［な］	quiet/silent
にぎやか［な］	lively
ひま［な］	have spare time
べんり［な］	convenient
ふべん［な］	inconvenient
ゆうめい［な］	famous

Nouns

Electric goods：

コンピューター	computer
テレビ	television

Food and drinks：

たべもの	food
おちゃ	tea
コーヒー	coffee
ジュース	juice
パン	bread
朝（あさ）ごはん	breakfast
昼（ひる）ごはん	lunch
晩（ばん）ごはん	dinner/supper

Books & Stationeries：

ざっし	magazine
新聞（しんぶん）	newspaper

Nouns

ノート	notebook
Others：	
アニメ	animation
アンケート	questionnaire
お金（かね）	money
漢字（かんじ）	Kanji
きっぷ	ticket
クラス	class
クラスメート	classmate
こうぎ	lecture
コンピュータールーム	computer room
サークルかつどう	club/circle activity
CD	CD
生活（せいかつ）	life
レポート	report

Adverbs

あまり	not so much/many/often
ぜんぜん	not at all
たくさん	many/a lot
とても	very

Vocabulary exercises

1. Verb words

Exercise A

Match the word to the picture.

(a) のみます	(b) たべます	(c) 聞(き)きます	(d) 読(よ)みます
(e) 使(つか)います	(f) はらいます	(g) 見(み)ます	(h) かいます
(i) はなします	(j) 書(か)きます	(k) テニスします	

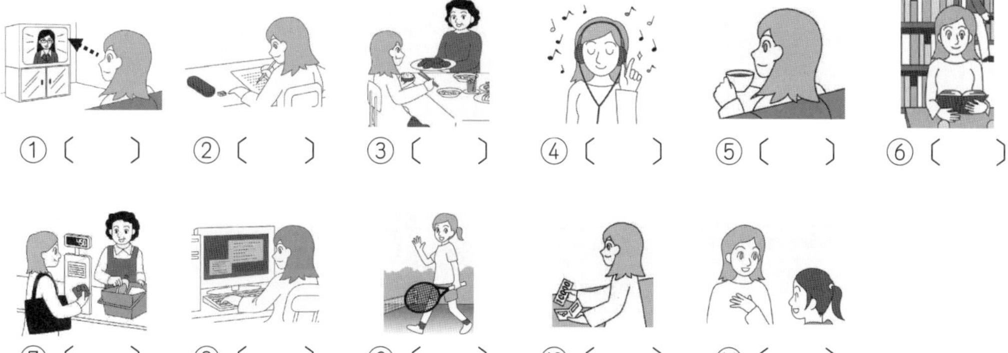

①〔　　〕 ②〔　　〕 ③〔　　〕 ④〔　　〕 ⑤〔　　〕 ⑥〔　　〕

⑦〔　　〕 ⑧〔　　〕 ⑨〔　　〕 ⑩〔　　〕 ⑪〔　　〕

Exercise B

Choose the appropriate noun which relates to each picture from ▭ as in the example.

~~テレビ~~・本(ほん)・音楽(おんがく)・晩ごはん・コーヒー・お金・コンピューター・漢字(かんじ)

e.g. テレビ

①__________

②__________

③__________

④__________

⑤__________

⑥__________

⑦__________

2. Adjective words

Exercise A

Match the word to the picture as in the example.

(a) ふるいです	(b) かんたんです[な]	(c) きたないです	(d) おいしいです
(e) あかるいです	(f) たかいです	(g) あたらしいです	(h) にぎやかです[な]
(i) まずいです	(j) べんりです[な]	(k) 広(ひろ)いです	(l) くらいです
(m) つまらないです	(n) 忙(いそが)しいです	(o) きれいです[な]	~~(p) 大(おお)きいです~~
(q) しずかです[な]	(r) おもしろいです	(s) やすいです	(t) ふべんです[な]
(u) ひまです[な]	(v) せまいです	(w) むずかしいです	(x) 小(ちい)さいです
(y) うるさいです			

Grammar explanations and exercises

1. Particle を（direct object + を）

The particle を is used to indicate the object of a verb. When you ask about an object, use the question word 何(なに). 何(なに)をしますか means to ask what someone does or will do.

Topic	Object	Particle	Verb	Question marker	
(私(わたし)は)	朝(あさ)ごはん	を	たべます。	—	I eat breakfast.
(私(わたし)は)	本(ほん)	を	読(よ)みます。	—	I read a book
(あなたは)	何(なに)	を	します	か。	What do you do?

れんしゅう Practice with your classmate as in the example.

e.g.  A：何(なに)をしますか。 B：本(ほん)を読(よ)みます。

①  ② ③  ④  ⑤ 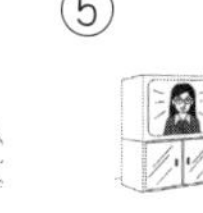 ⑥  ⑦ 

2. Particle で（place of action）

The particle で is used to indicate the place where an action takes place. When you ask about a place, use the question word どこ.

Topic	Place	Particle	Object + Particle + Verb	Question marker
(私(わたし)は)	図書館(としょかん)	で	本(ほん)を読(よ)みます。	
I read a book at the library.				
(私(わたし)は)	へや	で	テレビを見(み)ます。	
I watch TV in my room.				
(あなたは)	どこ	で	昼(ひる)ごはんをたべます	か。
Where do you eat lunch?				

れんしゅう１　Practice with your classmate as in the example.

e.g.  日本語(にほんご)のクラスで漢字(かんじ)をべんきょうします。

① うち　② 日本語(にほんご)のクラス　③ しょくどう　④ 生協(せいきょう)　⑤ えき　⑥ へや

れんしゅう２　Make 5 questions and ask your classmates as in the example.

e.g. ① どこで昼(ひる)ごはんをたべますか。　② どこでしゅくだいをしますか。

3. Particle や／とか（listing things）

や and とか are used to list nouns. や／とか suggest a list of some examples, whereas と is used to give an all-inclusive list. とか is a little more casual than や .

1) 生協(せいきょう)でペンやノートをかいます。 I buy a pen, a notebook and so on at the COOP.

2) 図書館(としょかん)で本(ほん)とかCDをかります。 I borrow a book, a CD, and other things at the library.

3) しょくどうで昼(ひる)ごはんと晩(ばん)ごはんをたべます。 I eat lunch and dinner at the cafeteria.

れんしゅう　Make 5 questions and ask your classmates as in the example.

e.g. Q：図書館(としょかん)で何(なに)をしますか。　A：ざっしや新聞(しんぶん)を読(よ)みます。

4. い adjective and な adjective

Adjectives are words that describe a person or thing such as 大(おお)きい (big) and しずか (quiet). In Japanese, adjectives are used as predicates and as noun modifiers. There are two types of adjectives, い adjectives and な adjectives. い and な are the last syllables when they modify nouns. です is placed at the end of the sentence after the adjective, the same as the sentence ending with a noun.

	Affirmative	Negative
い adjective	たかいです	たかくないです
な adjective	べんりです	べんりじゃないです

1) ロンさんの本(ほん)はあたらしいです。	Ron-san's book is new.
2) ヨンさんの本(ほん)はあたらしくないです。	Yon-san's book is not new.
3) 友達(ともだち)のへやはしずかです。	My friend's room is quiet.
4) 私(わたし)のへやはしずかじゃないです。	My room is not quiet.

*When adjectives are used as predicates, some な adjectives end with い such as きれい（な）, ゆうめい（な）. These adjectives conjugate the same as な adjectives.

1) 私(わたし)のへやはきれいです。	My room is clean.
私(わたし)のへやはきれいじゃないです。	My room is not clean.

**Exception：いいです→よくないです

2) 私(わたし)のコンピューターはいいです。	My computer is good.
私(わたし)のコンピューターはよくないです。	My computer is not good.

れんしゅう Practice as in the example.

e.g.

あたらしいです。

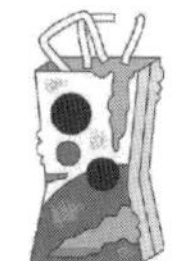

あたらしくないです。ふるいです。

①

②

③

⑤

5. Question word どう

The question word どう is used to ask one's impression or opinion about various things like: people, ideas, foods, and so on.

A：日本(にほん)の生活(せいかつ)はどうですか。	How is your life in Japan?
B：毎日(まいにち)、忙(いそが)しいです。	It's busy everyday.

れんしゅう　Ask your classmates as in the example.

e.g. 日本語(にほんご)のじゅぎょう→A：日本語(にほんご)のじゅぎょうはどうですか。
B：むずかしいです。

① 漢字(かんじ)のクイズ　② 専門(せんもん)のこうぎ　③ クラスメート　④ りょう/アパート

6. とても、あまり and ぜんぜん

とても、あまり and ぜんぜん are adverbs of degree. とても means "very". あまり means "not so much". ぜんぜん means "not at all". あまり and ぜんぜん are used with negative form.

1) A：日本(にほん)のアニメはどうですか。	How is Japanese animation?
B：とてもおもしろいです。	It's very interesting.
2) A：りょうはしずかですか。	Is the dormitory quiet?
B：いいえ、あまりしずかじゃないです。	No, it is not so quiet.
3) A：日本語(にほんご)はむずかしいですか。	Is Japanese difficult?
B：ぜんぜん、むずかしくないです。	No, not at all.

れんしゅう　Answer the following questionnaire then ask your classmates.

アンケート　大学(だいがく)のせいかつはどうですか

1. 大学(だいがく)のりょうのへや／アパートのへや

（　）せまいです　（　）とてもせまいです　（　）あまりせまくないです

2. しょくどうのたべもの

（　）おいしいです（　）とてもおいしいです（　）あまりおいしくないです

3. 大学(だいがく)のじゅぎょう

（　）むずかしいです　（　）とてもむずかしいです

（　）あまりむずかしくないです　（　）ぜんぜんむずかしくないです

4. 日本語(にほんご)の先生(せんせい)

（　）きびしいです　（　）とてもきびしいです

（　）あまりきびしくないです　（　）ぜんぜんきびしくないです

7. が／けど (contrast)

When the two sentences have contrasting ideas, they should be connected by が or けど. が is more formal than けど.

1) りょうは<u>あたらしい</u>ですけど、<u>ふべん</u>です。 The dormitory is new but inconvenient.
　　　　adjective 1　　　　adjective 2

2) 私(わたし)のへやは<u>きれい</u>ですが、<u>うるさい</u>です。 My room is clean but noisy.

れんしゅう１ Complete each sentence.

① 日本料理(にほんりょうり)はおいしいですが、＿＿＿＿＿＿＿＿＿＿＿＿＿＿＿＿。

② 日本(にほん)の生活(せいかつ)は忙(いそが)しいですが、＿＿＿＿＿＿＿＿＿＿＿＿＿＿＿＿。

③ タクシーはべんりですけど、＿＿＿＿＿＿＿＿＿＿＿＿＿＿＿＿。

④ 日本語(にほんご)はむずかしいですけど、＿＿＿＿＿＿＿＿＿＿＿＿＿＿＿＿。

れんしゅう２ Ask five questions using アンケート on the previous page to your classmates and answer with "が" or "けど" as in the example.

e.g. A：アンさんのへやはどうですか。　B：<u>せまいですけど、きれいです</u>。

はなします Speaking

Check the following points:

1. Starting the conversation: こんにちは　Hello!
2. Choosing an easy topic to start a small conversation such as:
   じゅぎょうはどうですか。　How are your classes going?
   今からじゅぎょうですか。　Are you going to class now?
3. Acknowledging new information:
   そうですか。　I see./Is that so?
4. Making the listener talk: (listener's name)＋は
   リーさんは。　How about Lee-san?
5. Taking leave: じゃあ、また。　See you again.

れんしゅう 1　Practice the conversation using the listening material.

れんしゅう 2　〈Role play〉 Practice the conversation with your partner. One student takes role A and another student takes role B using the information in the previous page.

Situation: You happen to see your friend on campus. Make small talk.

A ・Start the conversation.
・Ask how the classes are going.
・Ask what B is going to do.
・End the conversation.

B ・Answer A's questions.
・Make A talk.

れんしゅう 3　Choose a typical day and talk about what you do and how the day is for your classmates.

【はなしたあとで】After speaking 〈Self-check〉 Evaluate your speaking.

I was able to:			
ask and express how things are going.	☺	😐	☹
make others talk.	☺	😐	☹
end the conversation.	☺	😐	☹

 読みます　Reading

【読むまえに】Before reading

しつもん

Answer the following questions.

① あなたの友達(ともだち)のくにはどこですか。

② 友達(ともだち)と何をしますか。

③ 何時にうちへかえりますか。

④ うちで何をしますか。

⑤ Check the meaning of the following words.

パソコンルーム　インターネット　イギリス　アメリカ　フランス

ホームページ　ロビー　サークル　ハウスメート　ニュース

【読みましょう】Let's read

しつもん

Read the following questions then read the paragraph and find the answers.

1. If the statement is correct, write a ○ . If the statement is wrong, write an × .

①（　　　）あるいて大学へいきます。

②（　　　）うちで日本人や留学生(りゅうがくせい)の友達(ともだち)と昼ごはんをたべます。

③（　　　）図書館(としょかん)でインターネットをします。

④（　　　）りょうのロビーでタイやちゅうごくのニュースを見ます。

⑤（　　　）大学の生活(せいかつ)は楽しいですが、忙しいです。

2. Compare your daily schedule to Koi-san's below. List similarities and differences.

本文

<u>コイさんの一日</u>

私は朝、５時半におきます。日本語をべんきょうします。８時半にりょうの友達(ともだち)とあるいて学校(がっこう)へいきます。12時10分に日本人や留学生(りゅうがくせい)の友達(ともだち)としょくどうで昼ごはんをたべます。１時から２時までじゅぎょうがありません。りょうのパソコンルームでインターネットをします。イギリスやアメリカ、フランスのホームページを見ます。６時からサークルかつどうをします。９時にりょうにかえります。りょうのロビーでタイやちゅうごくのハウスメートと日本のニュースを見ます。12時ごろねます。忙しいですが、とても楽しいです。

書きます　Writing － My schedule －

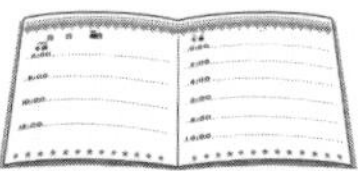

【書くまえに】Before writing

Write your schedule on a certain day and a brief comment about the day.

【書きましょう】Let's write

Write a short paragraph about your typical day. Put the information in chronological order including brief comments.

【書いたあとで】After writing

〈For your partner's writing〉 Read your partner's writing out loud. Tell your partner if something is not clear.

〈For your writing〉 Improve your writing by including your partner's questions and comments.

〈Self-check〉 Evaluate your writing.

I gave all necessary information when and what I did.	☺	😐	☹
I explained them chronologically.	☺	😐	☹
I included final comments at the end of the writing.	☺	😐	☹

Cultural challenge

I try to watch Japanese news with Japanese friends at night whenever I have spare time and ask questions.

Your challenge: Make Japanese friends and do something together.
Report what you do with your Japanese friends to your classmates.

Additional Information

1. The following expression is used to start a conversation when you happen to see your friends on campus. おつかれさま or おつかれ means "Hello, how are you?" This expresses a feeling of empathy with someone else's hard efforts but it is also used as a greeting young people.
2. Aizuchi: そうですか "I see." or "Is that so?" During a conversation in Japanese, the listener often gives short verbal reactions which are not replies but "Aizuchi" (back-channel behavior). Back-channeling is very important to have a smooth conversation with Japanese people. そうですか is said with the falling intonation.

Topic 6　どこでかいますか

Objectives:

In this lesson, you will learn how to:

1. Describe the location of things, people and shops.
2. Comment on things and shops.
3. Read about internet shopping and a description of a shop.
4. Write about a shopping experience.

Introduction:

1. Listen to the vocabulary and match it to the pictures on the page 81-82.
2. Watch two videos. If the statement is correct, write a ○. If the statement is wrong, write an ×.

1st video：

① ヨンさんの誕生日(たんじょうび)のプレゼントは電子辞書(でんしじしょ)です。　(　　)

② リーさんはあたらしいショッピングセンターへいきました。　(　　)

③ あたらしいショッピングセンターは大きくないです。　(　　)

2nd video：

① 電子辞書(でんしじしょ)はカウンターの右(みぎ)です。　(　　)

② 小さい電子辞書(でんしじしょ)がほしいです。　(　　)

Shopping

1. Lee and Hon talk about the new shopping center.

リー：ホンさん、ヨンさんの誕生日（たんじょうび）に何をあげましたか。
ホン：電子辞書（でんしじしょ）です。
リー：どこでかいましたか。
ホン：あたらしいショッピングセンターです。いきましたか。
リー：いいえ。どんなところですか。
ホン：大きいショッピングセンターです。みせもたくさんあります。
リー：どのみせでかいましたか。
ホン：1かいの電気屋（でんきや）さんです。今、セールですよ。
リー：そうですか。

2. Lee is looking for an electronic dictionary and asks the store clerk to show her other models.

リー　　：すみません。電子辞書（でんしじしょ）は、どこにありますか。
てんいん：あのカウンターの前（まえ）にあります。
. . . .
リー　　：あのう、もうすこし小さくてかるい辞書（じしょ）がほしいんですけど。
てんいん：小さいのはこちらです。
リー　　：どうも。

New vocabulary

Nouns

Books & Stationeries：

えんぴつ	pencil
教科書（きょうかしょ）	textbook
けしゴム	eraser
シャープペンシル	mechanical pencil
電子辞書（でんしじしょ）	electronic dictionary
はさみ	scissors
文房具(ぶんぼうぐ)／文具(ぶんぐ)	stationary
ボールペン	ball point pen
ホチキス	stapler

Foods：

ケーキ	cake
しょくりょうひん	food
飲（の）み物（もの）	drink

Clothes：

くつ	shoes/boots
靴下（くつした）	socks/stockings
シャツ	shirt
スーツ	suit
ズボン	trousers
セーター	sweater
Tシャツ	T-shirt
ふく	clothes
ワンピース	one-piece dress

Furniture：

いす	chair
インテリア	interior
かぐ	furniture
つくえ	desk
テーブル	table
ベッド	bed
本だな	book shelf

Electronic goods：

カメラ	camera
携帯電話（けいたいでんわ）	cellular phone

電気製品（でんきせいひん）	electric appliance
パソコン	personal computer

Nouns

Daily necessities：

シャンプー	shampoo
せっけん	soap
せんざい	detergent
ティッシュペーパー	tissue
日用品（にちようひん）	daily necessities

Department store：

デパート	department store
うりば	section/floor
カウンター	counter
セール	sale
地下（ちか）	basement
フロアガイド	floor map
レジ	cash register

Things/goods：

かさ	umbrella
カップ	cup
かばん／バッグ	bag
けしょうひん	cosmetics
スプーン	spoon
だいどころようひん	kitchen goods
てがみ	letter
時計（とけい）	clock/watch
花（はな）	flower
プレゼント	present

People：

男(おとこ)／男(おとこ)の人(ひと)	man
女(おんな)／女(おんな)の人(ひと)	woman
子（こ）／子（こ）ども	child/boy/girl
てんいん	shop clerk
てんちょう	manager
人（ひと）	person/human being

Shops & stores：

コーヒーショップ	coffee shop
ショッピングセンター	shopping center

Nouns	
みせ	shop/store
Others：	
いりぐち	entrance
いろ	color
こちら	this/this way/this place
デザイン	design
バレンタインデー	St. Valentine's day
Verbs	
あげます	to give
おくります	to send/to present
おしえます	to teach/to tell
かします	to lend
だします	to send
ならいます	to learn
もらいます	to receive
Adjectives	
あおい	blue
あかい	red
あつい	thick
うすい	thin
おおい	a lot/many
おもい	heavy
かるい	light
くろい	black
しろい	white
すくない	a few/a little
ながい	long
みじかい	short
若（わか）い	young
わるい	bad
しんせつ［な］	kind
ハンサム［な］	handsome

Adverbs

もうすこし　　some more/a few more/a little more

Question Words

どんな　　what kind of ～/what ～ like

Vocabulary exercises

1. Adjective words

Exercise A

Match the words to the pictures.

(a) あついです	(b) あおいです	(c) いいです	(d) おもいです
(e) ながいです	(f) みじかいです	(g) おおいです	(h) わるいです
(i) くろいです	(j) しろいです	(k) うすいです	(l) あかいです
(m) かるいです	(n) すくないです		

国語辞典

① 〔　〕⇔ ② 〔　〕 ③ 〔　〕⇔ ④ 〔　〕 ⑤ 〔　〕⇔ ⑥ 〔　〕 ⑦ 〔　〕⇔ ⑧ 〔　〕

Black　White　Blue　Red

⑨ 〔　〕 ⑩ 〔　〕 ⑪ 〔　〕 ⑫ 〔　〕　⑬ 〔　〕⇔ ⑭ 〔　〕

Exercise B

Answer each question and choose the best answer from the above list and write it as in the example. You may choose an answer more than once.

e.g. How is your Japanese textbook? … k, m

(1) How is your Japanese textbook? … ______

(2) How is your pencil or pen? … ______

(3) How is your bag? … ______

(4) How are your clothes on you now? … ______

(5) How are your socks? … ______

2. Noun words

Exercise A

Match the picture to the word as shown in the example.

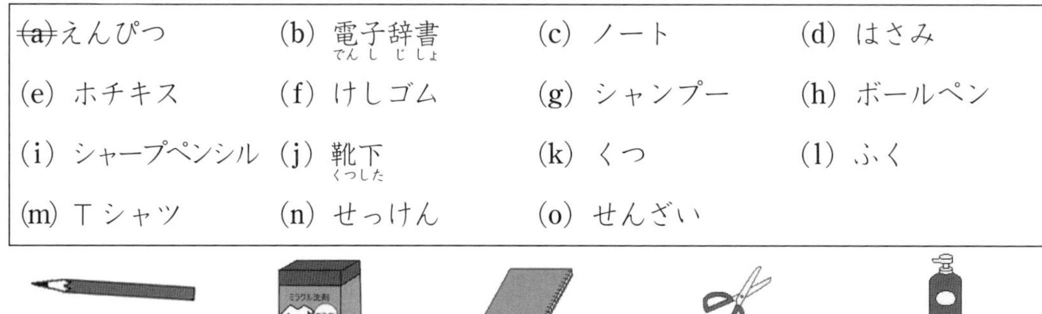

~~(a)~~えんぴつ	(b) 電子辞書(でんしじしょ)	(c) ノート	(d) はさみ
(e) ホチキス	(f) けしゴム	(g) シャンプー	(h) ボールペン
(i) シャープペンシル	(j) 靴下(くつした)	(k) くつ	(l) ふく
(m) Tシャツ	(n) せっけん	(o) せんざい	

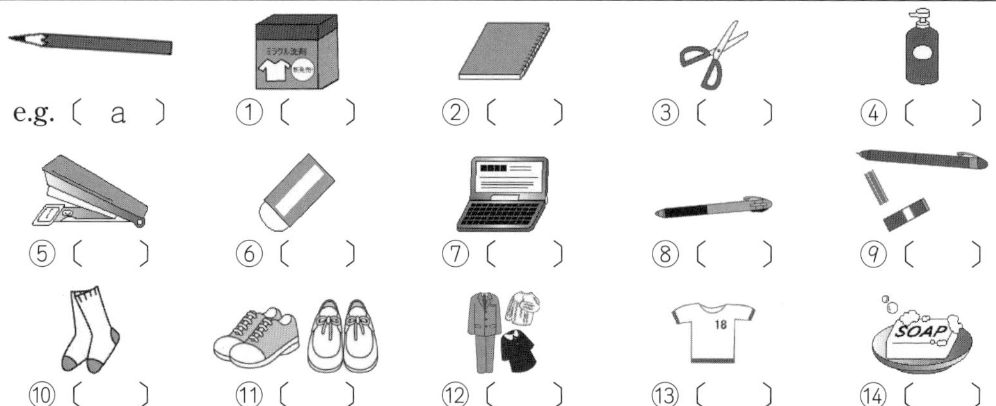

e.g.〔 a 〕 ①〔 〕 ②〔 〕 ③〔 〕 ④〔 〕

⑤〔 〕 ⑥〔 〕 ⑦〔 〕 ⑧〔 〕 ⑨〔 〕

⑩〔 〕 ⑪〔 〕 ⑫〔 〕 ⑬〔 〕 ⑭〔 〕

Exercise B

Look at the picture of the shop (ホームセンター別府(べっぷ)タウン) below. Write which section (A - G) you can find the objects above as in the example.

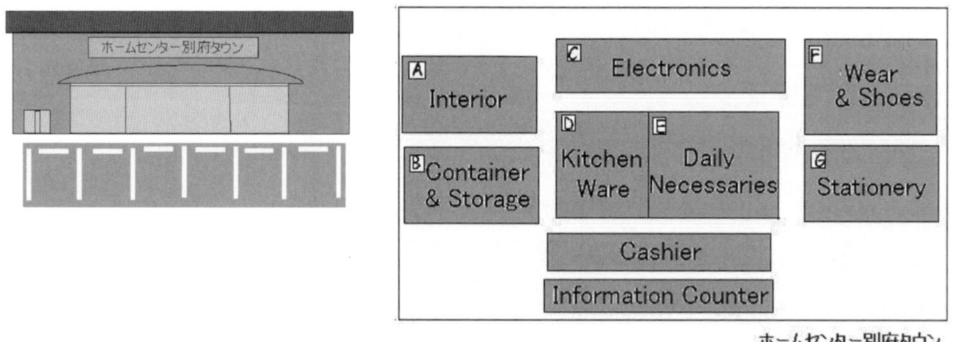

ホームセンター別府タウン

e.g. G ①_____ ②_____ ③_____ ④_____ ⑤_____ ⑥_____ ⑦_____ ⑧_____

⑨_____ ⑩_____ ⑪_____ ⑫_____ ⑬_____ ⑭_____

Grammar explanations and exercises

1. ～があります／います

① あります／います are verbs and express existence. The verb あります is used for inanimate things such as books, pens or plants. います is used for living things such as people or animals. The particle に is used to indicate the place. The particle が is used for people or things.

Place	Particle	Animals/People	Particle	Verb
みせ	に	子供(こども)	が	います。
There is a child at the store.				
Place の Location	Particle	Things/Places	Particle	Verb
えきのとなり	に	電気屋(でんきや)	が	あります。
There is an electrical appliance shop next to the station.				

② The following sentences indicate that the speaker describes where the topics are.

Topic (person)	Particle	Location	Particle	Verb
てんいん	は	レジの前(まえ)	に	います。
The shop clerk is in front of the casher.				
Topic (inanimate)	Particle	Location	Particle	Verb
文具(ぶんぐ)	は	６かい	に	あります。
The stationary is on the sixth floor.				

③ When you ask the whereabouts of things or people, use the question word どこ.

A：すみません。せっけんはどこにありますか。　Excuse me. Where is the soap?

B：日用品(にちようひん)うりばにあります。　It is at the section of daily necessities.

れんしゅう１　Choose the best answer using the following picture.

① しょくりょうひんうりばに（女の子(おんなのこ)・てんいん）が（います・あります）。

② けしょうひんうりばに（女の子(おんなのこ)・てんいん）が（います・あります）。

③ レジの（後ろ(うしろ)・前(まえ)）にだいどころようひんうりばが（います・あります）。

④ A：カップはどこ（に・で）ありますか。

　B：だいどころようひんうりば（に・で）あります。

⑤ A：文房具(ぶんぼうぐ)うりばはどこ（に・で）ありますか。

　B：日用品(にちようひん)うりば（に・の）となり（に・で）あります。

ホームセンター

れんしゅう２　Practice as in the example choosing the items and people from the above picture.

e.g.　A：せっけんはどこにありますか。　　B：日用品（にちようひん）うりばにあります。

　　　A：日用品（にちようひん）うりばはどこにありますか。B：文房具（ぶんぼうぐ）うりばのとなりにあります。

2. Adjective + Noun

Adjectives can be used to modify nouns. Place the adjective before the noun you want to modify.

い Adjective／な Adjective	Noun	
あたらしい	スーパー	new supermarket
しんせつな	てんいん	kind shop clerk

1) これはあたらしいデザインです。　　This is a new design.

2) きれいないろですね。　　It's a nice color, isn't it?

* The particle ね is added at the end of the sentence when you comment on something.

れんしゅう　Practice as in the example.

e.g.

小(ちい)さいシャツ　　大(おお)きいシャツ

①　　②　　③

white　　black

3. Adjective + Adjective くて／で

For connecting い adjectives, change い to くて, for な adjectives change な to で. Do not use the particle と for connecting two adjectives or two sentences.

1) ハンサムでしんせつなてんいんです。　（×）ハンサム㋣しんせつ

He is a handsome and kind shop clerk.

2) あかるくて広(ひろ)いかぐうりばです。　（×）あかるい㋣広(ひろ)い

It is a bright and spacious furniture section.

れんしゅう　Choose two adjectives and complete the sentences as in the example.

e.g.　コープでうすくて小(ちい)さいノートをかいました。

① デパートの１かいのコーヒーショップで＿＿＿＿＿＿＿＿ケーキをたべました。

② 昨日(きのう)、＿＿＿＿＿＿＿＿セーターをかいました。

③ 昨日(きのう)、＿＿＿＿＿＿＿＿ショッピングセンターへいきました。

④ スーパーに＿＿＿＿＿＿＿＿てんちょうがいます。

4. Question word どんな

① The question word どんな is used only before nouns. どんな is used when you ask what the characteristics of things or people are.

1) A：どんなパソコンをかいましたか。　What kind of PC did you buy?

B：かるくて小(ちい)さいパソコンをかいました。　I bought a light and small PC.

2) A：リーさんはどんな人(ひと)ですか。　What kind of person is Lee?

B：しんせつな人(ひと)です。　She is a kind person.

② どんな is also used to ask for an example or examples from a larger list. どんな can be literally translated as "what kind of".

3) A：どんなスポーツをしますか。　　B：サッカーです。
What kind of sports do you do?　　I play soccer.

れんしゅう Recommend the stores for shopping in town. Ask your classmates as in the example. If you have never been to the shop, ask what kind of shop it is.

e.g. A：どこでふくやくつをかいますか。

B：マイタウンです。

A：どんなところですか。 or 私(わたし)もマイタウンで買(か)い物(もの)をします。

B：広(ひろ)くて新(あたら)しいショッピングセンターです。

① 食(た)べ物(もの)　② 電気製品(でんきせいひん)　③ 日用品(にちようひん)　④ your choice

5. 〜がほしい

〜がほしい can describe the speaker's desire to possess things or to make friends. It is always used with nouns. The particle が is used after the object of desire. "ほしい" conjugates like い adjective.

	Affirmative	Negative
Present	ほしいです	ほしくないです

リー

1) 私(わたし)は自転車(じてんしゃ)がほしいです。　I want (to buy) a bicycle.

2) 私(わたし)は友達(ともだち)がほしいです。　I want (to have) a friend.

*(things) がほしいんですけど／が

〜んです is attached to ほしい。It is used when asking or requesting an explanation. The sentence ends with けど literally means "but" and implies to say more.

せっけんがほしいです。　I want soap. (Statement of one's wish)

せっけんがほしいんですけど。　I want soap. (Please tell me where it is.)

れんしゅう Choose the items and ask where they are. Practice as in the example.

e.g. A：すみません。かさがほしいんですけど、どこにありますか。

B：１かいにあります。

デパート

＜フロアガイド＞

５かい	
４かい	
３がい	
２かい	
１かい	
地下(ちか)１かい	

6. Adjective ／ Noun ＋の

の is a pronoun that means “one/ones” in English. It refers to something mentioned before, normally in the preceding sentence. You can replace the noun with “ の ” when it is clear what you are referring to. The same noun should not be repeated when the noun has been used once.

1）い adjective ＋の

A：どんなバイクがほしいですか。　What kind of motorbike do you want?

B：やすいのがほしいです。　I want a cheap one.

2）な adjective ＋の

A：このスプーンはきれいじゃないですね。　This spoon is not clean.

B：ここにきれいなのがあります。　Here is a clean one.

3）Noun ＋の

A：これはだれの教科書(きょうかしょ)ですか。　Whose textbook is this?

B：リーさんのです。　It’s Lee’s

れんしゅう　Ask your classmates as in the example.

e.g. A：今、何がほしいですか。　B：携帯電話がほしいです。
A：どんなのがほしいですか。　B：うすくて小さいのがほしいです。

7. Question word どの

どの is a question word to ask which one such as どのみせ (which store) or どの人 (which person).

1) A：どのみせで飲み物をかいますか。　Which shop do you buy drinks at?
B：うちのちかくのスーパーでかいます。　I buy them at the supermarket near my place.

2) A：シンさんはどの人ですか。　Which person is Shin-san?
B：山田さんのとなりの人です。　He is the person next to Yamada-san.

れんしゅう　Ask your classmates which store they usually go shopping at as in the example.

e.g. A：どの電気屋で買い物をしますか。　B：おおた電気でかいます。

① ショッピングセンター　② コンビニ　③ スーパー

れんしゅう２　Make a sentence as in the example.

e.g. Q：イラさん→イラさんはどの人ですか。　A：パクさんの左の人です。

イラ　パク　シン　チョー　プロイ

① Q：パクさん→＿＿＿＿＿＿＿＿＿＿。
A：＿＿＿＿＿＿＿＿＿＿。

② Q：プロイさん→＿＿＿＿＿＿＿＿＿＿。
A：＿＿＿＿＿＿＿＿＿＿。

③ Q：チョーさん→＿＿＿＿＿＿＿＿＿＿。
A：＿＿＿＿＿＿＿＿＿＿。

8. Particle に（from ／ to）

The particle に indicates a goal which an action is moving towards. It specifies the direction an object is going, whether it's toward a person, or away from a person.

リーさんはヨンさんにプレゼントをあげました。

ヨンさんはリーさんにプレゼントをもらいました。

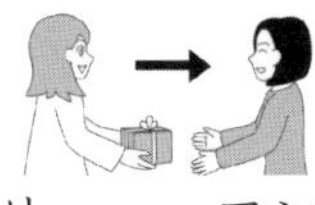

リー　　ヨン

Topic	Indirect object (people) + に	Direct object (things) + を	Verb
リーさんは	ヨンさんに	プレゼントを	あげました。
Lee-san gave a present to Yon-san.			
ヨンさんは	リーさんに	プレゼントを	もらいました。
Yon-san received a present from Lee-san.			

Other verbs using the same structure：はらいます、おくります、おしえます、ならいます、かします、かります、だします

1) 私(わたし)は友達(ともだち)に本(ほん)をかりました。　I borrowed a book from my friend.

2) リーさんはレジの人(ひと)にお金(かね)をはらいました。　Lee paid money to the cashier.

3) 山田先生(やまだせんせい)は学生(がくせい)に日本語(にほんご)をおしえます。　Mr. Yamada teaches Japanese to the students.

れんしゅう 1　Make the sentences as in the example.

e.g.　ゆり→ハンさん（本(ほん)）

ゆりさんはハンさんに本(ほん)をあげました。ハンさんはゆりさんに本(ほん)をもらいました。

① 先生(せんせい) → 学生(がくせい)（辞書(じしょ)）____________かしました。____________かりました。

② マイクさん→ハンさん（英語(えいご)）__________おしえます。__________ならいます。

③ ヤンさん→ジンさん（プレゼント）________おくります。________もらいます。

④ ジンさん→友達(ともだち)（てがみ）___________だします。____________もらいます。

れんしゅう２　Answer the following questions.

① 誕生日(たんじょうび)にだれに何(なに)をもらいましたか。

② （あなたの国(くに)で）バレンタインデーにだれに何(なに)をあげますか。

はなします　Speaking

Check the following points:

1. よ added to the statements is used to give new information to the listener.
   今、セールですⓎ。　　They have sales now.
2. もうすこし (A little more) + adjective
   もうすこし大きい／小さい　　a little bigger/a little smaller

れんしゅう１　Practice the conversation using the listening material.

れんしゅう２　〈Role play〉 Practice the conversation with your partner. One student takes role A and another student takes role B.

Situation: Choose the item that you want to buy and ask the location of the item at the store.

A ・Ask where the item that you want is.
　・Ask whether they have a different one.
　・End the conversation.

B ・Tell A the location of the item.

れんしゅう３

1. Talk about your favorite shop in the town. Describe the shop and the location.
2. Show the item and explain where you bought it.

【はなしたあとで】**After speaking** 〈Self-check〉 Evaluate your speaking.

I was able to:			
ask the location of things.	☺	😐	☹
describe the thing I want.	☺	😐	☹
say that I understood the information.	☺	😐	☹

読みます　Reading

【読むまえに】**Before reading**

① どこで買(か)い物(もの)をしますか。ネットショッピングをしますか。何をかいますか。

② Read the following shopping site on the Internet. What would you like to see?

Circle them.

≪インターネットショッピング≫

バッグ　PCソフト　MP3　くつ　自転車(じてんしゃ)　プリンター　電子辞書(でんしじしょ)　ざっし

クラシックCD　本　ヒーター　テレビ　ピアス（イヤリング）　コミック

アニメ　テニスラケット　エアコン　ジャケット　ネックレス

③ Which category do the above items belong to? Write as in the example.

category	物	category	物
書籍(しょせき)	e.g. 本	音楽(おんがく)	
スポーツ・アウトドア		パソコン	
うで時計(どけい)・ファッション		家電(かでん)・カメラ	

【読みましょう】Let's read

Recommend a store in town for each person below.

しつもん

どの店(みせ)で買(か)いますか。

ヤン

小さくてうすいテレビがほしいです。いいでんきやがありますか。どこですか。セールがありますか。何時までですか。

リー

しろいセーターがほしいです。友達(ともだち)のたんじょうびのプレゼントです。あした、友達(ともだち)にあげます。今日、じゅぎょうが7時半まであります。7時45分にバスでいきます。いいみせがありますか。どこにありますか。

ジン

カップとスプーンがほしいです。パーティーで使います。やすいみせがありますか。えきのちかくにありますか。どのみせですか。のみ物(もの)もありますか。

書きます　Writing － Shopping －

【書くまえに】Before writing

1. Put each sentence in order.

① 私は先週の土曜日にえきの前の電気屋(でんきや)へいきました。

② 明日(あした)、そのしゃしんをくにの友達(ともだち)におくります。

③ 電気屋(でんきや)にコンピュータやテレビやカメラがありました。

④ 昨日(きのう)、あたらしいデジタルカメラでクラスメートのしゃしんをとりました。

⑤ そこで私は小さくて、かるいデジタルカメラをかいました。

（ ① ）→（　　）→（　　）→（　　）→（　　）

2. Write about your shopping in Japan.

① 何をかいましたか。　② いつかいましたか。　③ どこでかいましたか。

④ どんなものですか。　⑤ どうやって使いますか。

【書きましょう】Let's write

Write about your shopping in Japan using information on the previous page.

【書いたあとで】After writing

〈For your partner's writing〉 Read your partner's writing out loud. Tell your partner if something is not clear.

〈For your writing〉 Improve your writing by including your partner's questions and comments.

〈Self-check〉 Evaluate your writing.

I was able to explain what I bought in proper order.			

Cultural Challenge

> Things in Japan are expensive. I need to find cheap places to shop.

Your challenge: Find a sale at a shopping center, check the prices and then report your experiences to your classmates.

Additional information

1. When you change or return things you bought, the following expressions are used: 換(か)える to change, and 返品(へんぴん)する to return. If it's on sale, you may not be able to exchange or return it. Make sure to bring the receipt.
2. When you buy clothes, sizes are labeled S (small) "*esu*", M (medium) "emu", L (large) "*eru*" or LL (extra large) "*erueru.*" Numbers are also used: 9号(ごう) (medium), 11号(ごう) (large), 13号(ごう) (extra large). Shoes are measured in centimeter like 23 cm "*nijuusansenchi.*"
3. Praise the belongings of your classmates. Place " ね " at the end of the sentence.

   いいですね。It looks good.　すてきですね。It looks nice.

   かわいいですね。It looks pretty.　かっこいいですね。It looks cool.

Topic 7　何が好(す)きですか

Objectives:

In this lesson, you will learn how to:

1. Ask someone to do activities together.
2. Express your preference for food, a thing or a person.
3. Order meals at a restaurant.
4. Read menus and recipes.
5. Write about your favorite food.

Introduction:

1. Listen to the vocabulary and match it to the pictures on the page 99.
2. Watch two videos. If the statement is correct, write a ○. If the statement is wrong, write an ×.

1st video：

① リーさんは肉(にく)が好(す)きです。　(　　)

② リーさんはお好(この)み焼(や)きの作(つく)り方(かた)をならいました。　(　　)

2nd video：

① リーさんはそばやへいきました。　(　　)

② リーさんはそばとやさいのてんぷらを食(た)べました。　(　　)

③ 1人(ひとり)2750円でした。　(　　)

Eating at the restaurant

1. Yoshida asks Lee about food.

吉田(よしだ)：リーさん、土曜日いっしょに食事(しょくじ)をしませんか。
リー：いいですねえ。しましょう。
吉田(よしだ)：リーさんは何が好(す)きですか。
リー：やさいや果物(くだもの)が好(す)きです。ベジタリアンなんです。
吉田(よしだ)：そうですか。日本料理(にほんりょうり)はどうですか。
リー：とても好(す)きです。ときどき作(つく)ります。先週、友達(ともだち)にお好(この)み焼(や)きの作(つく)り方(かた)をならいました。
吉田(よしだ)：どうでしたか。
リー：かんたんでおいしかったです。

2. Lee and Yoshida went to a Soba restaurant and ordered some food.

そばや：いらっしゃいませ。何めいさまですか。
吉田(よしだ)　：２人です。
そばや：どうぞこちらへ。

・・・・・・・・・・・・・・・・・・・・・・・・・・・・・・

吉田(よしだ)　：リーさん、何にしますか。
リー　：私はざるそばが食(た)べたいです。
吉田(よしだ)　：ぼくもざるそばにします。やさいのてんぷらもどうですか。
リー　：いいですねえ。
吉田(よしだ)　：すみません、おねがいします。
リー　：ざるそばを２つとやさいのてんぷらを２つください。

・・・・・・・・・・・・・・・・・・・・・・・・・・・・・・

吉田(よしだ)　：ごちそうさまでした。
そばや：ごいっしょですか。

吉田(よしだ)　：はい。
そばや：ぜんぶで2750円です。

New vocabulary

Verbs

あらいます	to wash
きります	to cut
ご飯（はん）をたきます	to cook rice
注文（ちゅうもん）します	to order
作（つく）ります	to make
りょうりします	to cook
りょこうします	to travel

Adjectives

あつい	hot
あまい	sweet
からい	hot
さむい	cold (weather)
しおからい	salty
つめたい	cold (to touch)
すっぱい	sour
きらい［な］	dislike
好（す）き［な］	like

Nouns

Food：

果物（くだもの）	fruit
牛肉（ぎゅうにく）	beef
魚（さかな）	fish
たまご	egg
鳥肉（とりにく）	chicken
肉（にく）	meat
にんじん	carrot
ピーマン	green pepper
豚肉（ぶたにく）	pork
やさい	vegetable
りんご	apple

Nouns

Other food：

アイスクリーム	ice cream
うどん	Japanese wheat-based noodle
お好（この）み焼（や）き	Japanese pizza
おにぎり	rice ball
からあげ	fried chicken
カレー	curry
キャンディー	candy
紅茶（こうちゃ）	English tea
ご飯（はん）	cooked rice/meal
コーラ	coke
サラダ	salad
サンドイッチ	sandwiches
すし	sushi
そば	Japanese noodle made from buck-wheat
チョコレート	chocolate
つけもの	pickles
定食（ていしょく）	set menu
てんぷら	tempura
なっとう	fermented beans
ハンバーガー	hamburger
パスタ	pasta
ピザ	pizza
みそしる	miso soup
ラーメン	Chinese noodles (in soup)

Seasoning：

調味料（ちょうみりょう）	seasoning
こしょう	pepper
さとう	sugar
しお	salt
しょうゆ	soy sauce

Nouns

みそ	miso
みりん	sweet sake
Others：	
アルバイト	part-time job
居酒屋（いざかや）	Japanese pub
いっしょ［に］	together
かいてんずし	fast-food sushi
ざいりょう	ingredients
さら	plate/dish
ぜんぶ	all
テレビゲーム	video game
電子（でんし）レンジ	microwave oven
はし	chopsticks
ベジタリアン	vegetarian
まんが	cartoon
物（もの）	things

counters

本（ほん／ぼん／ぽん）	counter for long things
めい	counter for people

Vocabulary exercises

1. Noun words: Food

Exercise A

Match the word to the picture.

(a) 肉(にく)	(b) やさい	(c) 魚(さかな)	(d) 果物(くだもの)
(e) 定食(ていしょく)	(f) 鳥肉(とりにく)	(g) チョコレート	(h) 豚肉(ぶたにく)
(i) にんじん	(j) ご飯(はん)	(k) みそしる	(l) アイスクリーム
(m) たまご	(n) ピーマン	(o) 牛肉(ぎゅうにく)	(p) キャンディー
(q) てんぷら			

Exercise B

Write the name of food you like or dislike. Choose the food from the above list.

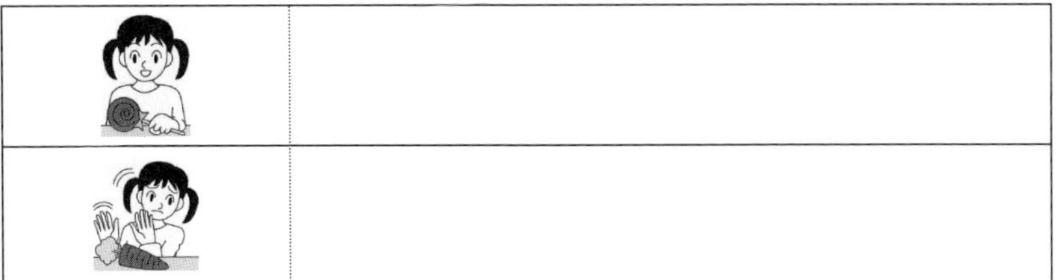

2. Adjective Words

Exercise A

Match the picture to the word.

(a) 好きです	(b) さむいです	(c) きらいです	(d) すっぱいです
(e) あついです	(f) からい／しおからいです		(g) あまいです

①〔　　〕　②〔　　〕　③〔　　〕　④〔　　〕

⑤〔　　〕　⑥〔　　〕　⑦〔　　〕

Exercise B

Write the name of the food that you know and check the comment about it as in the example.

e.g. 日本のりょうり：[　　てんぷら　　　　　]

☑好きです　□きらいです　□わかりません

(1) 日本のりょうり：[　　　　　　　　　　　]

□あまいです　□からいです　□すっぱいです　□わかりません

(2) くにのりょうり：[　　　　　　　　　　　]

□あまいです　□からいです　□すっぱいです　□わかりません

3. 調味料 (seasoning)

These are Japanese seasonings. Write the name and describe the taste of seasonings you use in your country.

日本　：さとう・しお・こしょう・しょうゆ・みりん・みそ

私のくに：＿＿＿＿＿＿＿＿＿＿＿＿＿＿＿＿

味　：□あまい　□からい　□すっぱい　□＿＿＿＿

Grammar explanations and practice

1. ～ませんか／ましょう

The present negative question form with a verb is used for suggesting something be done together. It means "won't you~ or why don't we~". いっしょに means "together" and is often used with invitation phrases. A common expression for accepting an invitation is ええ、verb stem ＋ましょう. If you decline an invitation, you use the phrases like あのう、すみません。今日は、ちょっと (＋ reason).

A：(いっしょに) ご飯を食べませんか。　Why don't we eat lunch together?

B：いいですね。食べましょう。　Yes, let's eat.

or

B：すみません、ちょっと…。　Sorry, it's a little inconvenient.
今日、アルバイトがあります。　I will have a part time job today.

れんしゅう Practice as in the example. If your invitation is accepted, write a ○. if it is not accepted, write an ×.

e.g. A：いっしょに昼(ひる)ご飯(はん)を食(た)べませんか。 B：いいですね。食(た)べましょう。(○)

C：すみません、ちょっと…。(×)

名前(なまえ)	さん	さん	さん
お茶(ちゃ)を飲(の)みます。			
パーティーにいきます。			
(Your own invitation)			

2. 好(す)きです／きらいです

好(す)き and きらい are used to express likes and dislikes. 好(す)き and きらい are な-adjective and can be used before nouns. The object is indicated by が not を. きらい sounds like a very strong word, so you should avoid using it to answer a question.

1) 私(わたし)は魚(さかな)がとても好(す)きです。 I like fish very much.

2) オンさんは魚(さかな)があまり好(す)きじゃないです。 On-san doesn't like fish very much.

れんしゅう Ask your classmates.

① どんな音楽(おんがく)が好(す)きですか。 ② どの授業(じゅぎょう)が好(す)きですか。

③ 何(なに)いろが好(す)きですか。 ④ your choice

3. Past and negative form of adjectives

When an adjective changes to a past form, い-adjectives and な-adjectives change differently.

	Present	Past	Past Negative
い-Adjective	あまいです	あまかったです	あまくなかったです
な-Adjective	べんりです	べんりでした	べんりじゃなかったです

れんしゅう 1　Fill in the blanks as in the example.

e.g.	つめたいです	つめたかったです	つめたくなかったです
	あついです		
	おいしいです		
	まずいです		
	すっぱいです		
	からい／しおからいです		
	あまいです		

れんしゅう 2　Interview your classmates as in the example, then fill in the blanks.

e.g.　A：昨日の夜、何を食べましたか。　B：カレーを食べました。
A：どこで食べましたか。　B：食堂で食べました。
A：どうでしたか。　B：とてもおいしかったです。

なまえ	どこで	何を	どうでしたか

4. いつも、よく、ときどき、あまり、ぜんぜん

いつも、よく、ときどき、ぜんぜん、are adverbs of frequency. いつも means "always". よく means "often". ときどき means "sometimes". あまり means "not often" and ぜんぜん means "not at all". あまり and ぜんぜん are used with negative forms.

1) 私はいつもいえでりょうりします。　I always cook at home.
2) チンさんはよくコーラを飲みます。　Chin often drinks coke.
3) 私はときどきピザを注文します。　I sometimes order pizza.
4) 私はぜんぜん肉を食べません。　I don't eat meat at all.

れんしゅう　Answer the following questions using the scale below as in the example.
Then ask your classmates and compare their answers with yours.

いつも－５　よく－４　ときどき－３　あまり－２　ぜんぜん－１

e.g.　からい物(もの)を食(た)べますか。（３）

①りょうり を作(つく)りますか。（　）　②コーヒーを飲(の)みますか。（　）
③あまい物(もの)を食(た)べますか。（　）　④新聞(しんぶん)を読(よ)みますか。（　）
⑤テレビを見(み)ますか。（　）　⑥図書館(としょかん)で本(ほん)をかりますか。（　）

5. ～たいです（Verb stem ＋たいです）

たいです can describe the speaker's desire to do something. It is always used with a verb stem. It can be used to express one's own desire, but not someone else's desire. The particle for the object can be が or を. たい conjugates like an い adjective: いきます＋たい → いきたいです.

	Affirmative	Negative
Present	食(た)べたいです	食(た)べたくないです
Past	食(た)べたかったです	食(た)べたくなかったです

1）すしが食(た)べたいです。　I want to eat sushi.
2）さらをあらいたくないです。　I don't want to wash dishes.

れんしゅう１　Ask your classmates as in the example.

e.g.　A：何(なに)が飲(の)みたいですか。　B：水(みず)が飲(の)みたいです。

ジュース

コーヒー

お茶(ちゃ)

水(みず)

コーラ

ラーメン

からあげ

ハンバーガー

れんしゅう２　Ask your classmates what they want to eat and recommend the place to eat as in the example. Then fill in the blanks.

e.g.　A：何(なに)が食(た)べたいですか。　B：すしが食(た)べたいです。
　A：かいてんずしにいきませんか。　B：いいですね。いきましょう。

	何(なに)	どこ
さん		
さん		

6. Noun ＋にします

します usually means to do but します in the expression "Noun ＋にします" means to decide.

A：何にしますか。　　What would you like to have?

B：コーヒーにします。　　I will have a cup of coffee.

れんしゅう　Practice as in the example. Choose the food from the menu.

e.g.　リー：ヨンさん、何にしますか。　　ヨン：コーヒーにします。

メニュー

食事						飲み物	
パスタ	¥700	ハンバーグ	¥600	ピザ	¥600	コーヒー	¥300
サラダ	¥500	カレー	¥700	定食	¥800	紅茶	¥300
そば	¥500	ラーメン	¥600	うどん	¥500	ジュース	¥300

7. Word order with numbers

① When you use a number with a price, the number comes before the price. Numbers do not require a particle.

りんごは１つ50円です。　　One apple is 50 yen.

② With an object：Noun を／が＋ number ＋ counter

1) コープでパンを４つかいました。　　I bought four pieces of bread at COOP.

2) ハンバーガーを２つください。　　Please give me two hamburgers.

3) 居酒屋にアルバイトの学生が２人います。　　There are 2 students working part-time at the Japanese pub.

れんしゅう１　Practice as in the example.

e.g.　コーラを３本ください。

れんしゅう２ Make a sentence by putting the words in the proper order. Provide the appropriate particles.

①２はい・飲(の)みました・コーヒー　②ケーキ・へや・食(た)べました・２つ・昨日(きのう)

③やすい・１つ・かいました・りんご・生協(せいきょう)

8. Numbers/quantity + particle で

When you use で after a number or a word, it expresses quantity. で also indicates the extent.

	Number ／ Quantity ＋で	Statement
りんごは	３つ　＋　で	400円(えん)です。
たまごは	ぜんぶで	８つあります。
留学生(りゅうがくせい)は	ぜんぶで	100人(にん)います。

れんしゅう How much? Ask your classmate as in the example.

e.g. りんごは１つ120円(えん)です。３つでいくらですか。→３つで360円(えん)です。

①アイスクリーム　150円(えん)　→５つ？　②たまご　20円(えん)　→７つ？

③ハンバーガー　280円(えん)　→３つ？　④ホテル１人(ひとり)　8000円(えん)→２人(ふたり)？

⑤学生(がくせい)　男(おとこ)の人(ひと)12人(にん)と女(おんな)の人(ひと)10人(にん)　→ぜんぶ？

9. Verb stem ＋方(かた)（how to）

Adding "かた" after a verb stem makes a phrase meaning "how to do things" or "the way of doing things". The phrase of the verb stem ＋かた is a noun phrase so that the particle in a sentence is changed.

りょうり[を]作(つく)ります → りょうり[の]作(つく)り方(かた)をならいました

I cook. → I learned how to cook.

The particles of を and が in a sentence are changed to の in the phrase, but other particles such as へ, で and と remain and "の" is added after the particles.

レストランへいきます。→レストラン[への]いき方(かた)がわかりません。

I go to the restaurant. → I don't know how to go to the restaurant.

れんしゅう　Change the sentences as in the example then choose what you did and what you want to do.

e.g. やさいカレーを作ります。→ やさいカレーの作り方をならいました。

① はしを使います。　② すしを食べます。　③ 日本料理を作ります。

④ ご飯をたきます。　⑤ 電子レンジを使います。　⑥ your own choice

はなします　Speaking

Check the following points:

1. Accept the invitation: いいですねえ。　Let's do that.
2. Decline the invitation: じゃあ、またこんど／じゃあ、またいつか　Let' s do it some other time.
3. Give the reason not to eat certain food: アレルギーです (allergy), ダイエット中です (on diet), イスラム教徒です (Moslem).
4. Order something: (thing) (を) + (number) + おねがいします
   おねがいします is a useful expression to use when asking someone to give you something or do something for you. おねがいします follows something which you want.
   e.g. からあげ (を) 1つおねがいします。　Please give me one fried chicken.
5. Pay separately: べつべつです。

れんしゅう 1　Practice the conversation using the listening material.

れんしゅう 2　〈Role play〉 Practice the conversation with your partner. Two students take role A and one student takes role B.

Situation: You and your friend order meals at the restaurant looking at the menu on the page 104.

A (you and your friend)	B (waiter or waitress)
· Tell the number of people.	· Ask the number of people.
· Order dishes and drinks.	· Take orders.
· Pay separately.	· Tell how much it is.
· End the conversation	· Ask how to pay.

れんしゅう３ Discuss what you can't eat. Explain the reason.

れんしゅう４ Share a recipe with your classmates. Bring a picture of the food and explain what it is using the following format.

Steps：1. これは私のくにのりょうりです。　2. 名前(なまえ)は＿＿＿＿＿＿

3. （ざいりょう）＿＿と＿＿で作ります。　4. （味）とても＿＿＿＿＿

【はなしたあとで】After speaking 〈Self-check〉 Evaluate your speaking.

I was able to:			
order meals.	☺	😐	☹
explain about the food in my country.	☺	😐	☹

読みます　Reading

【読むまえに】Before reading

1. Read the following food words and answer the questions.

① 何を食べましたか。

② どれが好きですか。

③ Explain about the food you have eaten so far in Japan to your classmates who have never tried the dishes before.

ハンバーグ　パスタ　カレー　ハヤシライス　そば　うどん　ラーメン
お好(この)み焼(や)き　焼(や)き肉　とんかつ　みそしる　牛丼(ぎゅうどん)　すし　さしみ　おべんとう
おにぎり　つけもの　てりやき

2. あたらしいことば

ざいりょう ingredients　こむぎこ flour　いか squid　あぶら oil
かけます pour

【読みましょう】Let's read

Read the following recipe and choose the correct picture from A ～ E. Write the answer in（　　）.

本文

＜お好み焼きの作り方＞

【ざいりょう】

こむぎこ－１カップ	水－ 1/2 カップ	たまご－２こ
いか or えび or ぶた肉－ 100g	キャベツ－３まい	あぶら－すこし

【作り方】

① キャベツをきります。（　　）

② こむぎことキャベツとたまごと水をいっしょにまぜます。（　　）

③ フライパンにあぶらをいれます。（　　）

④ ぶた肉といっしょにやきます。（　　）

⑤ ソースをかけます。（　　）

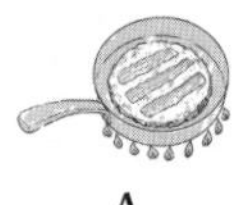
A

B

C

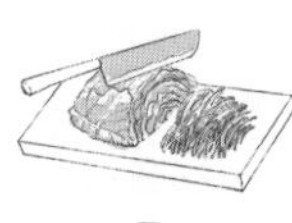
D

E

書きます　Writing － My favorite food －

【書くまえに】Before writing

1. What is your favorite food?
2. Answer the following questions about your favorite food.

① どんな味ですか。　② ざいりょうは何ですか。　③ どこで食べますか。
④ そのりょうりをよく食べますか。　⑤ あなたはそのりょうりを作りますか。

【書きましょう】Let's write

Write about your favorite food including the above information.

【書いたあとで】After writing

〈For your partner's writing〉 Read your partner's writing out loud. Tell your partner if something is not clear.

〈For your writing〉 Improve your writing by including your partner's questions and comments.

〈Self-check〉 Evaluate your writing.

My explanation about my favorite food was clear enough to make others understand.   

Cultural Challenge

How do Japanese people eat Soba? What does the slurping mean?

1. Personal culture notes: Write about what surprises you about Japanese eating habits, such as taste, manners and so on. What do you think?
2. Your challenge: Go out and eat something new then report your experiences to your classmates.

Additional information

1. It is customary to say いただきます (lit. "I shall receive") before starting to eat a meal, and ごちそうさまでした (lit. "That was a feast") to the host after the meal and to the restaurant staff when leaving.
2. Eating etiquette: Chopsticks are never left sticking vertically in the rice, as this is how they are ritually offered to the dead. Using chopsticks to stick into food, to point, or to pass food to someone else's chopsticks is also frowned upon. It is also very bad manners to bite on your chopsticks.
3. Popular lunch menu: Bento (べんとう) is a single-portion takeout or home-packed meal. When you take it to the register, the cashier may ask you, for example:
   あたためましょうか。　Shall I warm it up?
   おはしをおつけしましょうか。　Do you need chopsticks?
   If your answer is "Yes", you say: おねがいします。　Please.
   If your answer is "No", you say: けっこうです。　No thank you.
4. Asking whether the food contains an ingredient a person can't eat:
   ぶた肉ははいっていませんか。　Does this contain pork?
5. Useful expressions:
   おなかがへりました。　I'm hungry.
   おなかがいっぱいです。　I'm full.
   のどがかわきました。　I'm thirsty.

Topic 8　本をかりることができますか

Objectives:

In this lesson, you will learn how to:

1. Ask to borrow library resources.
2. Scan titles of books and audio materials.
3. Read about library information.
4. Write comments about the book or audio materials.

Introduction:

1. Listen to the vocabulary and match it to the pictures on the page 115-116.
2. Watch two videos. If the statement is correct, write to a ○ . If the statement is wrong, write an × .

1st video：

① ダナさんは日本のアニメが好きです。（　）

② ダナさんとリーさんはいっしょにDVDを見ます。（　）

2nd video：

① リーさんは本を６さつかります。（　）

② 図書館でざっしを読みます。（　）

At the library

1. Lee and Dana talk about the DVD at the library

リー：ダナさん、べんきょうですか。
ダナ：日本のアニメの DVD を見に来(き)ました。
リー：アニメが好きですか。
ダナ：ええ。私の趣味(しゅみ)はアニメの DVD を見ることです。
リー：そうですか。どんなアニメが好きですか。
ダナ：そうですねえ。たくさんあります。ファンタジーや SF をよく見ます。
リー：私もファンタジーが好きです。図書館(としょかん)にいいのがありますか。
ダナ：ありますよ。リーさんも今から見ますか。
リー：これからじゅぎょうがありますから、帰(かえ)るまえに見に来(き)ます。
ダナ：そうですか。じゃあ、また。

2. Lee borrows some books.

リー：すみません。この本をかりたいんですけど。
としょかんいん：3 さつですか。
リー：はいそうです。
としょかんいん：学生証(がくせいしょう)をおねがいします。1 さつしかかしだすことができませんけど。
リー：どうしてですか。
としょかんいん：これはざっしですから、図書館(としょかん)でしか読むことができません。
リー：そうですか。本はいつまでかりることができますか。
としょかんいん：来月(らいげつ)の 10 日までです。
リー：わかりました。

New vocabulary

Verbs

あずけます	Ⅱ	to leave a thing with a person
あそびます	Ⅰ	to play
いれます	Ⅱ	to put in
歌（うた）います	Ⅰ	to sing
うんてんします	Ⅲ	to drive
おぼえます	Ⅱ	to memorize
泳（およ）ぎます	Ⅰ	to swim
おろします	Ⅰ	to withdraw
かえします	Ⅰ	to return
かきます	Ⅰ	to draw
かしだします	Ⅰ	to loan
聞（き）きます	Ⅰ	to ask
けんさくします	Ⅲ	to search
こたえます	Ⅱ	to answer
さがします	Ⅰ	to look for
しらべます	Ⅱ	to research/to investigate
せつめいします	Ⅲ	to explain
そうじします	Ⅲ	to clean
だします	Ⅰ	to submit/to hand in (an assignment)
できます	Ⅱ	to be able to
とります	Ⅰ	to pick up/to take
（しゃしんを）とります	Ⅰ	to take a picture
のぼります	Ⅰ	to climb
のります	Ⅰ	to get on/to ride
はこびます	Ⅰ	to carry
はしります	Ⅰ	to run
はっぴょうします	Ⅲ	to give a presentation
ひきます	Ⅰ	to play (music instrument)
まちます	Ⅰ	to wait
見（み）せます	Ⅱ	to show
むかえます	Ⅱ	to go and meet
りようします	Ⅲ	to make (good) use of
わすれます	Ⅱ	to forget

Nouns

歌（うた）	song
絵（え）	drawing/painting
学生証（がくせいしょう）	student ID
コピー機（コピーき）	copy machine
じこしょうかい	self-introduction
しりょう	material
小説（しょうせつ）	novel
スキー	skiing
先輩（せんぱい）	senior
DVD	DVD
ダンス	dance
びじゅつかん	museum of art
ビデオ	video
プール	pool
ホームページ	homepage
メール	email
ヨガ	yoga
ロシア語（ご）	Russian

Phrases

おなかがすきます	to be hungry
のどがかわきます	to be thirsty

Vocabulary exercises

1. Verb words

Exercise A

Match the verbs to the pictures.

(a) あそびます	(b) まちます	(c) かります	(d) (ピアノを) ひきます
(e) うんてんします	(f) おぼえます	(g) しらべます	(h) 聞きます
(i) せつめいします	(j) 歌(うた)います	(k) かします	(l) (絵を) かきます
(m) かえします	(n) わすれます	(o) おくります	(p) あずけます
(q) おろします	(r) だします	(s) 泳(およ)ぎます	(t) むかえます
(u) 注文(ちゅうもん)します	(v) さがします		

①〔　　〕 ②〔　　〕 ③〔　　〕 ④〔　　〕

⑤〔　　〕 ⑥〔　　〕 ⑦〔　　〕 ⑧〔　　〕

⑨〔　　〕 ⑩〔　　〕 ⑪〔　〕 ⑫〔　〕 ⑬〔　　〕

⑭〔　　〕 ⑮〔　　〕 ⑯〔　　〕 ⑰〔　　〕

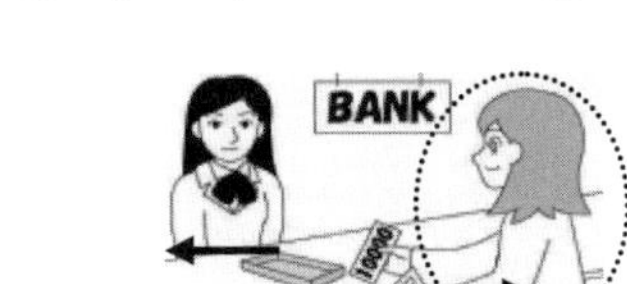

⑱〔　　〕 ⑲〔　　〕 ⑳〔　　〕 ㉑〔　　〕 ㉒〔　　〕

Exercise B

What do you do at the places below? Choose the verb from (a)-(v) on the previous page and fill in the chart below using the appropriate letter. You may use each number more than once.

カラオケ		くうこう		食堂（しょくどう）		こうえん	
プール		銀行（ぎんこう）		図書館（としょかん）		郵便局（ゆうびんきょく）	

Exercise C

Check what you can do.

☐	☐	☐	☐
☐	☐	☐ 10km	☐
☐	☐	☐	☐

2. 図書館（としょかん）

Answer the questions about the library.

(1) よく図書館（としょかん）へ行（い）きますか。　□よく　□ときどき　□あまり　□ぜんぜん

(2) 図書館（としょかん）にどんなDVDやCDがありますか。タイトルを書（か）きましょう。

本

e.g. Japanese History

DVD

CD

(1)________________

(2)________________

Grammar explanations and exercises

1. Dictionary form of verbs (Plain Present Affirmative Form)

ます-form verbs are the polite form of verbs. There are plain forms corresponding with these ます-form verbs. The plain present affirmative form is called "Dictionary form" which is listed in the dictionary with the ます-form.

Japanese verbs are divided into three groups based on the way of conjugation.

Group 1

The ます-form of all the Group 1 verbs has an " i "sound before ます. The part of a verb before ます is called a verb stem. To make the dictionary form, change the end of the verb stem " i " sound to an "u"sound.

ます-Form	Verb-Stem	i → u	Dictionary Form
歌(うた)います	uta**i**	uta**i** → uta**u**	歌(うた)う
かえします	kaesh**i**	kaesh**i** → kaes**u**	かえす
まちます	mach**i**	mach**i** → mats**u**	まつ

Group 2

The ます-form of most of the Group 2 verbs has an "e" sound before ます. Drop ます and add る.

ます-Form	Verb-stem	+ **ru**	Dictionary Form
こたえます	kotae	kotae + **ru**	こたえる
見(み)せます	mise	mise + **ru**	見(み)せる
わすれます	wasure	wasure + **ru**	わすれる

There are Group 2 verbs which have an " i " sound before ます. Remember these verbs and do not confuse them with the Group 1 verbs.

ます-Form	Verb-Stem	+ **ru**	Dictionary Form
見(み)ます	mi	mi + **ru**	見(み)る
おきます	oki	oki + **ru**	おきる
います	**i**	**i** + **ru**	いる

Group 3

Group 3 verbs are irregular verbs. There are two verbs in group 3.

	Dictionary Form
きます	くる
します	する
べんきょうします	べんきょうする

れんしゅう　Write the dictionary form and the group number.

ます -Form	Dictionary Form	Group	ます -Form	Dictionary Form	Group
あずけます			いれます		
だします			のぼります		
はこびます			さがします		
せつめいします			のります		

2. Dictionary form verb ＋こと／ことができます

① When こと is added to the dictionary form of a verb, the verb becomes a noun.

読(よ)む（read）→読(よ)むこと（reading）

聞(き)く（listen）→聞(き)くこと（listening）

e.g.（私(わたし)の）趣味(しゅみ)は本(ほん)を読(よ)むことです。　My hobby is reading books.

れんしゅう 1　Make a sentence as in the example.

e.g.　趣味(しゅみ)は買(か)い物(もの)することです。

①
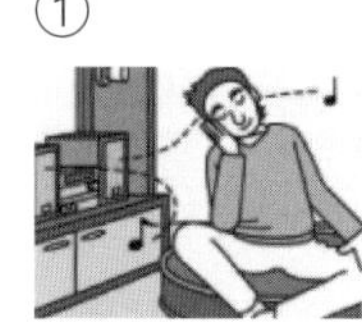
②

③

④

⑤

れんしゅう 2　Talk about your hobby as in the example.

e.g.　私(わたし)の趣味(しゅみ)は本(ほん)を読(よ)むことです。よく図書館(としょかん)で小説(しょうせつ)をかります。
日本語(にほんご)がよくわかりませんから、英語(えいご)の小説(しょうせつ)をかります。

②ことができます is added to a dictionary form of a verb to express a person's ability or possibilities. It means "be able to".

1) タンさんはロシア語(ご)を話(はな)すことができます。(ability)　　Tan can speak Russian.

2) 図書館(としょかん)でコンピューターを使(つか)うことができます。(possibility)　　You can use a computer at the library.

③ことができます is used with する verbs. In this case, ～をすること is dropped. The particle を changes to の.

1) しりょう(を)けんさくすることができます。　　I can search the materials.

→しりょう(の)けんさくができます。

2) テニスをすることができます。　　I can play tennis.

→テニスができます。

Exception：A verb is omitted. The particle を changes to が。

3) ジンさんは中国語(ちゅうごくご)(を)話(はな)すことができます。　　Jin can speak Chinese.

→ジンさんは中国語(ちゅうごくご)(が)できます。

* できます conjugates as follows.

Affirmative	Negative	Past	Past negative
できます	できません	できました	できませんでした

れんしゅう３　What can you do using Japanese? If you can, write a ○, if you can't, write an ×. Ask your classmates and compare answers.

① じこしょうかいができます。　(　　)

② ホームページを作(つく)ることができます。(　　)

③ メールを書(か)くことができます。　(　　)

④ 時間(じかん)を聞(き)くことができます。　(　　)

⑤ Your choice　(　　)

3. ～するまえに／～のまえに

Nの／V1（dictionary form）＋まえに＋V2

まえ indicates the action of V2 occurs before the action of V1. V1 is the dictionary form. When まえ follows the noun, the particle の is used between the noun and まえ.

1）うちに帰(かえ)るまえに図書館(としょかん)にDVDを見(み)に来(き)ます。　I will come to the library to see the DVD before I go home.

2）はっぴょう**の**まえにしりょうを作(つく)ります。　We will prepare handouts before the presentation.

れんしゅう　Complete the following sentences as in the example.

e.g. じゅぎょうに行(い)くまえに<u>図書館(としょかん)でしゅくだいをします。</u>

① 友達(ともだち)の家(いえ)に行(い)くまえに＿＿＿＿＿＿＿＿＿　② 日本(にほん)へ来(く)るまえに＿＿＿＿＿＿＿＿＿

③ うちに帰(かえ)るまえに＿＿＿＿＿＿＿＿＿　④ 旅行(りょこう)のまえに＿＿＿＿＿＿＿＿＿

4. Verb stem ＋に行(い)きます／来(き)ます

Verb stem ＋に＋行(い)きます・来(き)ます・帰(かえ)ります means "for the purpose of" doing some action for going or coming.

Place ＋へ／に	Object ＋を	Purpose（Verb stem）＋に	行(い)きます／来(き)ます／帰(かえ)ります
図書館(としょかん)へ／に	本(ほん)を	かりに	行(い)きます。
I'll go to the library（for the purpose of）borrowing the book.			
うちへ／に	しゅくだいを	とりに	帰(かえ)りました。
I went home to pick up my homework.			

＊ With some activities such as 買(か)い物(もの)をする，べんきょうをする，スキーをする，する can be omitted and the noun is used in this expression.

1）デパートへ<u>買(か)い物(もの)</u>(noun)に行(い)きます。　I will go to a department store to do shopping.

2）北海道(ほっかいどう)へ<u>スキー</u>(noun)に行(い)きます。I will go skiing to Hokkaido.

＊ When the noun べんきょう is used, pay attention to the change. The particle を becomes の.

日本(にほん)へ日本語(にほんご)**の**べんきょうに来(き)ました。I came to Japan to study Japanese.

れんしゅう Answer the questions as in the example. Choose the appropriate words from the list and give your own answers based on your experiences .

しつもん:あなたは図書館(としょかん)へ何(なに)をしに行(い)きますか。　e.g. べんきょうしに行(い)きます。

本(ほん)、レポート、ざっし、CD、しりょう、ビデオ、国(くに)の新聞(しんぶん)、コンピューター、DVD、your choice	かります、読(よ)みます、書(か)きます、使(つか)います、べんきょうします、見(み)ます、かえします、さがします、your choice

5. Sentence 1 ＋から＋ Sentence 2（reason）

から is a particle which connects two sentences and indicates a reason. Sentence 1 is the reason for Sentence 2.

Sentence 1（reason）		Sentence 2
これはざっしです	から	かりることができません。
This is a magazine that's why I can't borrow it.		
お金(かね)がありません	から	アルバイトをしたいです。
I want to work part time because I don't have money.		

れんしゅう１ Match the sentences.

① 学生証(がくせいしょう)がありませんから　・　　・ そうじをします。
② 漢字(かんじ)がわかりませんから　・　　・ おなかがすきました。
③ コーヒーにさとうをいれましたから　・　　・ 新聞(しんぶん)を読(よ)むことができません。
④ 朝(あさ)ご飯(はん)を食(た)べませんでしたから　・　　・ あまいです。
⑤ 友達(ともだち)があそびに来(き)ますから　・　　・ 本(ほん)をかりることができません。

れんしゅう２ Complete the sentences.

① ________から、とりに行(い)きます。　② ________から、英語(えいご)で話(はな)します。

③ 明日(あした)友達(ともだち)の誕生日(たんじょうび)ですから、________　④ のどがかわきましたから、________

6. どうして／なぜ

どうして is a question word to ask a reason. In the answer, から is attached to the sentence to give the reason as shown below.

A：休(やす)みにどうして国(くに)へ帰(かえ)りませんか。	Why won't you go back home during the holiday?
B：アルバイトをしたいですから、帰(かえ)りません。	I won't go back home because I want to work part time.

れんしゅう　Answer each question as in the example then ask your classmates.

e.g. A：教科書(きょうかしょ)を買(か)いましたか。　B：いいえ。

A：どうして買(か)いませんか。　B：先輩(せんぱい)にもらいますから。

① いつもどこで買(か)い物(もの)をしますか。どうしてですか。

② いつもどこで食事(しょくじ)をしますか。どうしてですか。

7. ～しか～ません

しか～ません indicates the limit, meaning "only" and "~no more than". しか is used with the negative form of verbs. しか implies a negative nuance of only and nothing else. It is placed after a noun or a particle except the particles が , は , を .

1) 1さつしかかりません。	I borrow only one book.
2) ざっしは図書館(としょかん)でしか読(よ)むことができません。	You can read magazines only at the library.

れんしゅう　Write as in the example using the pictures.

e.g. A：辞書(じしょ)は何(なん)さつありますか。　B：1さつしかありません。

①A：何(なん)さつ本(ほん)をかりることができますか。　B：

②A：びじゅつかんに人(ひと)は何人(なんにん)いますか。　B：

③A：スーパーで何(なに)を買(か)いましたか。　B：

④A：お金(かね)はいくらありますか。　B：

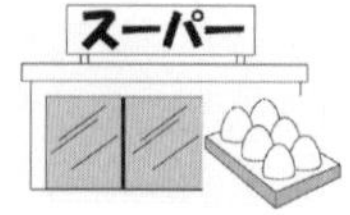

話(はな)します　Speaking

Check the following points:

1. Giving information by adding よ at the end of the sentence.
2. Asking the length of the book loan.

何日間かりることができますか。	How long can I borrow it?
いつまでかりることができますか。	When is the due date?

れんしゅう１　Practice the conversation using the listening material.

れんしゅう２　〈Role play〉 Practice the conversation with your partner. You take role A and your partner takes role B.

Situation: You go to the library service counter to borrow books.

A ・Ask to borrow books.
・Ask the reason why he/she can't lend the books.
・Ask the length of the book loan.
・End the conversation.

B ・Ask to see the ID card.
・Tell that the book loan is not available.
・Tell the length of the book loan.

れんしゅう３　Borrow some materials at the library and talk about the title, the author and the reason why you borrowed it.

【話(はな)したあとで】After speaking 〈Self-check〉 Evaluate your speaking.

I was able to:

ask the length of the book loan and the reasons not to be lent.	☺	😐	☹
talk about the book I read.	☺	😐	☹

読みます　Reading

【読むまえに】Before reading

あたらしいことば　個室(こしつ)　individual room

【読みましょう】Let's read

しつもん

Read the following information about the library and answer the questions, 1 and 2.

1. If the statement is correct, write a ○ . If the statement is wrong, write an × .

①（　）１げんめ（8：45～）のじゅぎょうのまえに、新聞を読むことができます。

②（　）CD や DVD しかかりることができません。

③（　）本を２週間かりることができます。

④（　）クラスメートといっしょに図書館の部屋を使うことができます。

⑤（　）コンピューターの辞書を使うことができます。

2. しろくろコピーを９まい、カラーコピーを３まいしました。ぜんぶでいくらですか。

本文

図書館サービス

1. 利用時間：月～金（平日）8：45 ～ 21：30　土、日、祝 9：30 ～ 17：15
2. 館内利用：新聞、ざっし、CD、ビデオ、DVD （かし出しはできません。）
   オンライン辞書、電子ジャーナルを使うことができます。
3. かし出し：本５さつ　14 日間
4. コピー：しろくろ１まい　10 円、カラー１まい　50 円
5. 部屋：グループの部屋と個室が利用できます。

Ⅱ.【読むまえに】Before reading

1. Guess the meaning of the Katakana words below and choose the words relating to each picture.

A

B

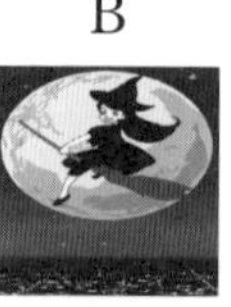

C

ロマンチック、ラブストーリー、SF、ファンタジー、ハッピーエンド
コメディー、アクション、サスペンス、ホラー、ロボット

2. あなたはどのアニメが見たいですか。

3. あたらしいことば

文化(ぶんか) culture　テーマソング theme song　ふきかえ stand-in　字幕(じまく) subtitle

【読みましょう】 Read the passage and answer the questions.

しつもん

① 日本のアニメから何をべんきょうすることができましたか。

② どんなアニメが好きですか。

③ アニメはどうしてむずかしかったですか。

本文

私の趣味(しゅみ)

　私の趣味(しゅみ)は日本のアニメを見ることです。日本へ来るまえに、国でよく日本のアニメを見ました。日本のアニメから日本の文化(ぶんか)や日本語をべんきょうしました。テーマソングもおぼえました。下手(へた)ですが、日本語で歌うことができます。

　今、日本でテレビアニメをよく見ますが、アクションやホラーが好きじゃないです。ファンタジーやコメディーが好きです。

　先週、ラブコメディーを見ました。タイトルは『マリーの絵』です。18さいの大学生のストーリーです。ふきかえや字幕(じまく)がありませんから、むずかしかったですが、おもしろかったです。

【読んだあとで】After reading

あなたは日本のアニメやドラマを見ますか。どうですか。

 書きます　Writing － Using the library －

【書くまえに】Before writing

1. Make a list of books and DVDs that you want to read or watch.
2. Borrow a book or see a DVD in the library and write down the title, story, and your comments.

【書きましょう】Let's write

Write a summary about the book or DVD that you read or watched.

Writing tip Use『　』for the title.

【書いたあとで】After writing

〈For your partner's writing〉 Read your partner's writing out loud. Tell your partner if something is not clear.

〈For your writing〉 Improve your writing by including your partner's questions and comments.

〈Self-check〉 Evaluate your writing.

My writing included the title and the comments about the material.	 

Cultural challenge

I learn Japanese from Japanese songs and anime.

Your challenge: Let's find Japanese materials to learn Japanese for fun, then report how to find them and what they are (for example, manga, animation and so on).

Additional Information

How to use the library and borrow the materials

1. The following words are important to search for a book:

   書名(しょめい) book title　著者名(ちょしゃめい) author　出版社(しゅっぱんしゃ) publisher

   出版年(しゅっぱんねん) year of publishing　請求番号(せいきゅうばんごう) call number

   百科事典(ひゃっかじてん) encyclopedia　参考文献(さんこうぶんけん) reference material

   白書(はくしょ) whitepaper　予約(よやく) requesting

2. Corner/Sections:

   コピーコーナー copy corner　リザーブセクション reserved section

   レファレンスコーナー reference corner

3. Study room:

   個室(こしつ) individual study room　AV ブース AV booth

   グループ学習室(がくしゅうしつ) group studying room

4. Library fine:

   延滞金(えんたいきん) (late charge)

5. If books are not available at the library, you can request for the book to be sent from another library.

Topic 9　かしてください（りょうで）

Objectives:

In this lesson, you will learn how to:

1. Request someone to do something or not to do something politely.
2. Ask another person for permission to do something.
3. Apologize for a mistake.
4. Read the rules of the dormitory.
5. Write about your life at the dormitory.

Introduction:

1. Listen to the vocabulary and match it to the pictures on the page 133-134.
2. Watch two videos. If the statement is correct, write a ○. If the statement is wrong, write an ×.

1st video：

①リーさんはそうじきをかります。（　）

②そうじきは３時までかりることができます。（　）

2nd video：

①リーさんは部屋の前にごみをだします。（　）

②リーさんは午後 10 時 45 分にごみをすてることができます。（　）

At the dormitory

1. Lee asks the caretaker if she can borrow a vacuum cleaner at the dormitory.

リー　：すみません。そうじきをかしてください。

管理人(かんりにん)：ここに、名前(なまえ)と部屋(へや)番号(ばんごう)と時間を書いてください。

リー　：これでいいですか。

管理人(かんりにん)：はい、けっこうです。

このかぎで、ロッカーをあけて、そうじきをとってください。

リー　：わかりました。

管理人(かんりにん)：学生証(がくせいしょう)をあずかります。3時までにそうじきをもどして、

かぎをかえしてください。

リー　：はい。わかりました。

2. The student assistant gives Lee instructions on the proper way to throw out the garbage in a dormitory.

アシスタント：リーさん、ドアの前にごみを出(だ)さないでください。

リー　：すみません。きをつけます。今、ごみ置(お)き場(ば)にすてて

てもいいですか。

アシスタント：すててはいけません。夜、すててください。

毎晩10時半から11時までゴミ置(お)き場(ば)をあけます。

リー　：わかりました。

New vocabulary

Verbs

あけます	II	to open
あずかります	I	to keep
（シャワーを）あびます	II	to take a shower
おきます	I	to place/to put down
おくれます	II	to be late
（ペットを）かいます	I	to keep (a pet)
かえます	II	to change
（かぎを）かけます	II	to lock
（でんわを）かけます	II	to make a phone call
（でんきゅうが）きれます	II	The electric bulb burns out
きをつけます	II	to be careful
けします	I	to turn off
しにます	I	to die/to pass away
しめます	II	to close
じろじろ見（み）ます	II	to stare at
（たばこを）すいます	I	to smoke
すてます	II	to dump/to throw away
すわります	I	to sit down
洗濯（せんたく）します	III	to do the laundry
出（だ）します	I	to take out
たちます	I	to stand up
つけます	II	to turn on (a light)
とめます	II	to park (a car)/to take a person in
とりかえます	II	to change/to replace
（はを）みがきます	I	to brush one's teeth
もどします	I	to return
れんしゅうします	III	to practice
れんらくします	III	to contact

Nouns

Places：

そうこ	storage
台所（だいどころ）／キッチン	kitchen
駐車場（ちゅうしゃじょう）	parking
駐輪場（ちゅうりんじょう）	parking for motor cycle
ランドリー	laundry

Bedding：

シーツ	sheets
まくらカバー	pillow case

Garbage：

かん	can
ごみ	garbage
ごみ置（お）き場（ば）	garbage dumping area
ごみばこ	trashcan
生（なま）ごみ	kitchen garbage
びん	glass bottles
プラスチック	plastic
ペットボトル	PET（plastic）bottle

Room：

かべ	wall
洗面台（せんめんだい）	washing stand
電気（でんき）	electricity
電球（でんきゅう）	light bulb
ドア	door
まど	window
浴室（よくしつ）／おふろ	bathroom
れいぞうこ	refrigerator

Dormitory：

アイロン	iron
アイロンだい	ironing board
アシスタント	assistant
かぎ	key
そうじき	vacuum cleaner

Nouns

ふとん	Futon
ふとんかんそうき	Futon dryer
部屋番号（へやばんごう）	room number
ロッカー	locker
管理人（かんりにん）	caretaker
ふくろ	bag/sack

Others

いぬ	dog
家族（かぞく）	family
けっこうな	fine/excellent
国際電話（こくさいでんわ）	international phone call
作文（さくぶん）	writing/composition
自分（じぶん）	oneself
しめきり	deadline
ちょっと	for a moment/a little
て	hand
ドル	dollar
荷物（にもつ）	luggage
ねこ	cat
ほか	other

Vocabulary exercises

1. Noun words：りょう

Exercise A

Find the right place for each picture and write the answer in the〔　　〕.

(a) 浴室(よくしつ)	(b) キッチン／台所(だいどころ)	(c) ごみ置(お)き場(ば)	(d) 駐車場(ちゅうしゃじょう)／駐輪場(ちゅうりんじょう)
(e) そうこ	(f) 管理人室(かんりにんしつ)	(g) 部屋(へや)	(h) ランドリー(ルーム)

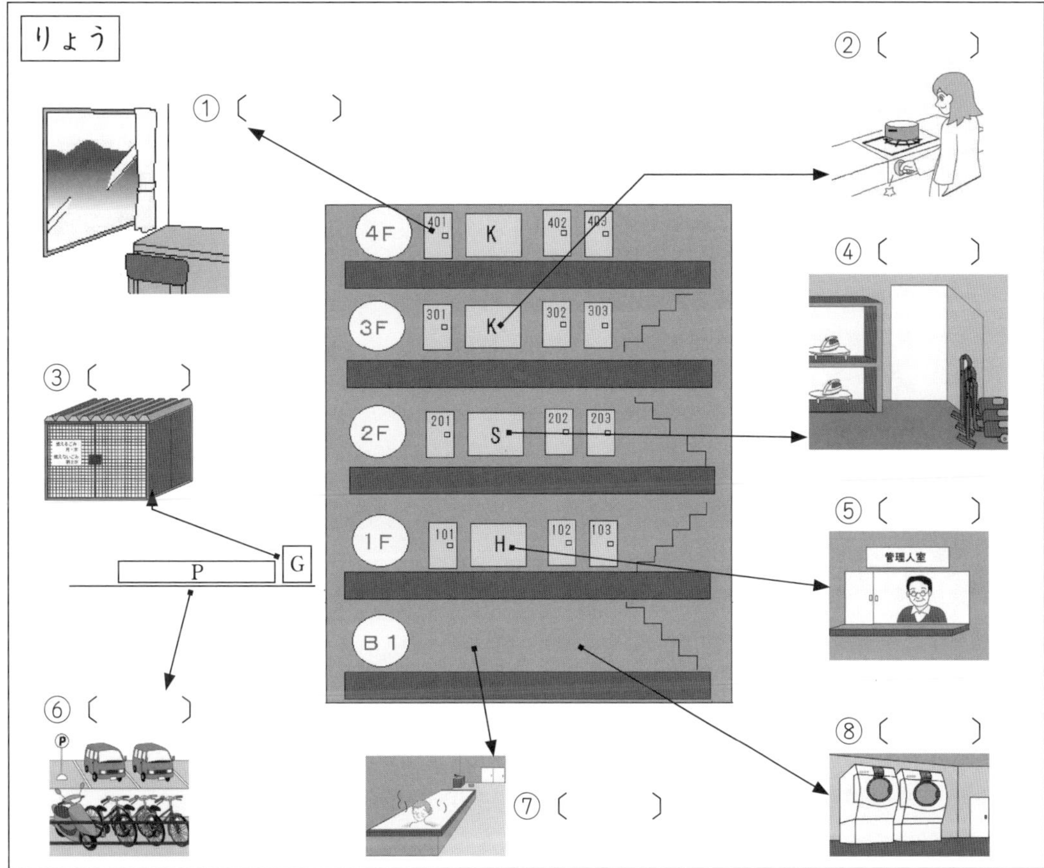

Exercise B

Where can you find the following things? Choose the place from the list in Exercise A above. You may use a word more than once.

生(なま)ごみ ＿＿	アイロン ＿＿	シーツ ＿＿	ふとん ＿＿
本だな ＿＿	そうじき ＿＿	れいぞうこ ＿＿	ごみばこ ＿＿
自転車(じてんしゃ) ＿＿	洗面台(せんめんだい) ＿＿	そうこのかぎ＿＿	

2. Verb words：りょうですること

Exercise A

Choose the best answer for each picture and write it in the〔　　〕.

~~(a)~~　すてます	(b)　つけます	(c)　おきます	(d)　とめます
(e)　あけます	(f)　（ごみを）出(だ)します	(g)　けします	(h)　もどします
(i)　しめます	(j)　そうじします	(k)　洗濯(せんたく)します	(l)　かります
(m)　あずけます	(n)　あずかります	(o)　（たばこを）すいます	
(p)　かえします	(q)　とります		

Exercise B

Match the expressions on the left to their appropriate ending.

(1) ごみを	・	・	そうじします。
(2) 自転車(じてんしゃ)を	・	・	あずけます。／あずかります。
(3) 電気(でんき)を	・	・	すてます。／出(だ)します。
(4) ドア／まどを	・	・	とめます。
(5) 部屋(へや)を	・	・	かります。／かえします。
(6) ふくを	・	・	つけます。／けします。
(7) たばこを	・	・	洗濯(せんたく)します。
(8) 荷物(にもつ)を	・	・	あけます。／しめます。
(9) そうじきを	・	・	すいます。

Grammar explanations and practices

1. Verb て -form

There is a conjugation of verbs called the て-form. The て-form is very important because this is used for many useful expressions such as making requests and giving and asking for permission. Japanese verbs are divided into three groups based on their conjugation patterns.

Group 1

There are five different rules for conjugating group 1 verbs to the て-form. For this group, conjugate according to the last sound of the verb-stem.

ます -form	て -form	ます -form	て -form
き→いて（ぎ→いで）		に・び・み→んで	
聞(き)きます	聞(き)いて	しにます	しんで
書(か)きます	書(か)いて	あそびます	あそんで
泳(およ)ぎます	泳(およ)いで	飲(の)みます	飲(の)んで
き→って (exception)		い・ち・り→って	
行(い)きます	行(い)って	買(か)います	買(か)って
し→して		まちます	まって
話(はな)します	話(はな)して	帰(かえ)ります	帰(かえ)って

Group 2

The て-form attached to the verb-stem.

ます -form	て -form	ます -form	て -form
食(た)べます	食(た)べて	すてます	すてて
見(み)ます	見(み)て	あびます	あびて

Group 3

Irregular verbs with no set rules.

ます -form	て -form
来(き)ます	来(き)て
します	して

れんしゅう Write the て-form and the group as in the example.

e.g. 読(よ)みます →読(よ)んで（1）

① すわります →＿＿＿＿（　）　② おきます →＿＿＿＿（　）

③ かります →＿＿＿＿（　）　④ 使(つか)います →＿＿＿＿（　）

⑤ おくります →＿＿＿＿（　）　⑥ れんしゅうします →＿＿＿＿（　）

2. ～てください

て-form verbs together with ください make the request polite, but it is not polite enough to use towards elders or people with a higher position. Later we will learn how to make requests towards elders or people in a higher position. For now, let's learn the general way to make a polite request.

1) 電球(でんきゅう)がきれましたから、とりかえてください。　The electric bulb has burnt out. Please change it.

2) ごみ置(お)き場(ば)にごみをすててください。　Please dump the garbage in the garbage dumping area.

3) ちょっとまって（ください）！　Please wait a moment!

れんしゅう１ Make a sentence as in the example.

e.g. アイロンをかします→アイロンをかしてください

① かぎをかえしに来(き)ます→　② 洗面台(せんめんだい)の電球(でんきゅう)をとりかえます→

③ ふとんかんそうきをかします→　④ シーツとまくらカバーを洗(あら)います→

れんしゅう２ Complete each blank as in the example.

れんしゅう3 Ask your partner to do an action as in the example.

e.g. 日本語(にほんご)で話(はな)します→ 日本語(にほんご)で話(はな)してください

① いすの後(うし)ろにたちます→ ② すわります→ ③ 名前(なまえ)をノートに書(か)きます→

④ クラスメートにけしゴムをかります→ ⑤ your choice

3. ～て、～て

て-form verbs can describe:

① A sequence of events or actions by combining two or more verbs

1) 管理人室(かんりにんしつ)へ行(い)ってそうこのかぎをかえしてください。 Please go to the caretaker's office then return the storage key.

2) 学生証(がくせいしょう)をあずけてそうじきをかります。 I will leave my student ID at the office then borrow the vacuum cleaner.

② Two actions which take place simultaneously, where the first action is the means to do the second action

3) 漢字(かんじ)を書(か)いておぼえます。 I memorize Kanji by writing.

れんしゅう Make a sentence as in the example.

e.g. 朝(あさ)おきます→朝(あさ)おきて、コーヒーを飲(の)みます。

コンピュータを使(つか)います→コンピュータを使(つか)って、レポートを書(か)きます。

① 管理人室(かんりにんしつ)へ行(い)きます。→ ② 学生証(がくせいしょう)をあずけます。→

③ 日本語(にほんご)の CD を聞(き)きます。→ ④ うちで晩(ばん)ごはんを作(つく)ります。→

⑤ 電子(でんし)レンジを使(つか)います。→ ⑥ そうじきをかります。→

4. ～てもいいですか

て-form verbs, together with もいいです means to grant permission. "てもいいですか" is an expression used to ask for permission.

1) 台所(だいどころ)のごみばこにびんをすててもいいですか。 May I put glass bottles in the kitchen trashcan?

2) 駐車場(ちゅうしゃじょう)に自転車(じてんしゃ)をとめてもいいですか。 May I park my bicycle in the car park?

れんしゅう１　Write a ○ if you're allowed to do the following in your room. Write an × if you're not allowed to do it in your room.

① たばこをすってもいいです。（　　）② 料理(りょうり)をしてもいいです。（　　）

③ いぬやねこをかってもいいです。（　　）④ ほかの人(ひと)をとめてもいいです。（　　）

⑤ かべのいろをかえてもいいです。（　　）

れんしゅう２　Ask your teacher. Practice as in the example.

e.g. 部屋(へや)の中(なか)はあついですから、まどをあけたいです。→ まどをあけてもいいですか。

① 先生(せんせい)といっしょにしゃしんがとりたいです。　② トイレに行(い)きたいです。

③ しゅくだいをわすれました。明日(あした)出(だ)したいです。

④ えんぴつがありません。ペンで書(か)きたいです

⑤ 日本語(にほんご)で説明(せつめい)することができません。英語(えいご)で話(はな)したいです。

5. ～てはいけません

"てはいけません" is used when you express prohibition, or a strong negative command. This form should be avoided when you talk to your superiors.

1) 部屋(へや)の外(そと)にごみをすててはいけません。　You must not leave garbage outside your room.

2) 生(なま)ごみとペットボトルをいっしょにふくろに入(い)れてはいけません。　You must not put kitchen garbage together with plastic bottles in a garbage bag.

れんしゅう１　See the れんしゅう１ above in 4 and say what is prohibited.

れんしゅう２　Practice as in the example.

e.g. 何(なに)をしてはいけませんか。　びじゅつかん → しゃしんをとってはいけません

① 図書館(としょかん)→　② びょういん→　③ 電車(でんしゃ)の中(なか)→　④ 日本語(にほんご)のじゅぎょう→

6. Noun (method) ＋で

The particle で indicates methods or means of action. Transportation methods can also be included in this category.

Topic	Methods	Particle	Action
(私(わたし)は)	このかぎ	で	ロッカーをあけます。
I open the locker with this key.			
インドの人(ひと)は	て	で	食(た)べます。
Indian people eat by hands.			
友達(ともだち)と	日本語(にほんご)	で	話(はな)します。
I speak with my friends in Japanese.			

れんしゅう Ask your classmates.

① どうやって家族(かぞく)とれんらくしますか。
② どうやって漢字(かんじ)の読(よ)み方(かた)をしらべますか。
③ 友達(ともだち)と何語(なにご)で話(はな)しますか。
④ どうやって自分(じぶん)の国(くに)の料理(りょうり)を食(た)べますか。

7. Verb ない -form

The ない-form expresses negative meaning. The ない-form is used for many useful expressions such as making negative requests and giving advice not to do something.

Group 1

The ます-form of all the group1 verbs has an "i" sound before ます. To make the ない-form, change the "i" sound to an "a" sound and add ない. かいます and あいます which end with the verb stem い are exceptions, and their ない-forms are *かわない／あわない. The ない-form of あります is simply ない.

ます -form	ない -form	ます -form	ない -form
書(か)きます	書(か)かない	読(よ)みます	読(よ)まない
話(はな)します	話(はな)さない	買(か)います	*買(か)わない

Group 2

ない follows the verb stem.

ます -form	ない -form	ます -form	ない -form
おくれます	おくれない	かります	かりない

Group 3

Change します to しない、きます to こない.

ます -form	ない -form	ます -form	ない -form
します	しない	きます	こない

れんしゅう　Write ない-form as in the example.

e.g. 食(た)べます→食(た)べない

① 聞(き)きます→　② 作(つく)ります→　③ 使(つか)います→　④ きます→

⑤ 見(み)せます→　⑥ けします→　⑦ わすれます→　⑧ 行(い)きます→

8. ～ないでください

ない -form verbs together with でください make a negative request. "～ないでください" expresses "don't do something". It is not polite enough to use towards elders or people with a higher position. If you omit ください, it becomes more casual.

1) ドアの前(まえ)にごみを出(だ)さないでください。　Please do not put the garbage in front of the door.

2) じろじろ見(み)ないでください。　Please do not stare at me.

れんしゅう　Make a sentence as in the example.

e.g.

しゅくだいをわすれないでください。

① ② ③ ④

9. 〜までに

まで expresses the finishing time. までに expresses the time limit by when an action should be done.

アイロンとアイロンだいを 6時(じ)までにもどしてください。	Please return the iron and ironing board by 6 o'clock.

れんしゅう　Choose the best answer.

① 明日(あした)の朝(あさ)10時(じ)（まで・までに）ゴミを出(だ)してください。

② この本(ほん)を水曜日(すいようび)（まで・までに）かえしてください。

③ 4月(がつ)（まで・までに）じゅぎょうがありません。

④ 土曜日(どようび)でしたから、午前(ごぜん)2時(じ)（まで・までに）テレビを見(み)ました。

話します　Speaking

Check the following points:

1. Asking if one's writing is correct: これでいいですか。	Is it correct?
2. Accepting one's task: けっこうです。	It's all right.
3. Apologizing for a mistake: すみません。きをつけます。	Sorry, I will be careful.

れんしゅう１　Practice the conversation using the listening material.

れんしゅう２　〈Role play〉 Practice the conversation with your partner. You take role A and your partner takes role B.

① *Situation*: Today is Tuesday. You put burnable garbage out by mistake.

A	B (resident assistant)
・Apologize for putting the garbage outside the door. ・Ask the date to put out the garbage.	・Tell the person not to put the garbage outside the door. ・Explain the garbage collection calendar.

8／1（月）	8／2（火）	8／3（水）	8／4（木）	8／5（金）
もえるごみ burnable	もえないごみ non burnable		もえるごみ burnable	しげんごみ recyclable

② *Situation*: You borrow the ping-pong rackets and the balls in a dormitory.

A	B (manager)
・Ask to borrow the ping-pong rackets and the balls. ・Ask if the form is filled correctly.	・Ask to write his/her name, room number, and time. ・Tell that his/her writing is correct. ・Explain how to take out the rackets and balls. ・Ask to keep his/her ID card and return the key by 3 o'clock.

れんしゅう３　What do you have in your room? Describe your room.

あなたの部屋(へや)はどんな部屋(へや)ですか。

【話したあとで】After speaking 〈Self-check〉 Evaluate your speaking

I was able to:			
borrow things.	☺	😐	☹
ask to return things by a certain day and time.	☺	😐	☹
apologize.	☺	😐	☹
ask about the garbage collection calender.	☺	😐	☹
describe my room.	☺	😐	☹

読みます　Reading

【読むまえに】Before reading

1. あなたの国ではどうやってごみをすてますか。もえるごみともえないごみをいっしょにすてますか。

2. 新しいことば

もえるごみ burnable garbage　もえないごみ non burnable garbage　第(だい)1 first　第(だい)2 second　第(だい)3 third　第(だい)4 fourth　〜など and so on　リサイクル recycle　ろうか hallway　わけます to separate

【読みましょう】Let's read

Read the following rules, then answer the questions.

しつもん

1. Mark the following days on the calendar.

① いつ、シーツやまくらカバーを出しますか。　: Mark △

② いつ、もえるごみを出しますか。　: Mark ◇

③ いつ、もえないごみを出しますか。　: Mark □

④ リサイクルの日はいつですか。　: Mark ×

11月

月	火	水	木	金	土	日
			1	2	3	4
5	6	7	8	9	10	11
12	13	14	15	16	17	18
19	20	21	22	23	24	25
26	27	28	29	30		

2. Some of the following statements do not follow the rules on the next page. Mark (×) next to the statements that do not follow the rules.

① シーツを第(だい)1月曜日、朝9時半に出します。　(　　)

② もえるごみを木曜日の朝7時にごみ置(お)き場に出します。　(　　)

③ もえないごみを第(だい)3水曜日の朝7時に出します。　(　　)

④ 午前2時に台所(だいどころ)を使います。　(　　)

⑤ 自転車(じてんしゃ)は駐車場(ちゅうしゃじょう)にあります。　(　　)

本文

りょうのルール

1. シーツ、まくらカバーは第（だい）1・3月曜日にふくろにいれて、朝9時までにろうかに出してください。
2. もえるごみ（毎週火曜日・木曜日）、もえないごみ（毎月第（だい）1・3金曜日）、リサイクルできるもの（毎月第（だい）2・4水曜日）に分けて、ふくろに入れて、朝8時30分までにごみ置（お）き場（ば）に出してください。
3. ① 料理（りょうり）は1かいの台所（だいどころ）でしてください。
   ② 午前12時から午前6時まで、台所（だいどころ）を使わないでください。
4. 自転車（じてんしゃ）は駐輪場（ちゅうりんじょう）にとめて、かぎをかけてください。

【読んだあとで】After reading

What do you think about the rules in the dormitory?

書きます　Writing －Living in the dormitory / apartment－

【書くまえに】Before writing

Write about your life in the dormitory/apartment.

① りょうやアパートでできることやできないこと、してもいいことを書いてください。

② りょうやアパートの生活（せいかつ）で、何がいいですか。何がよくないですか。

③ あなたはりょうやアパートの生活（せいかつ）が好きですか。きらいですか。どうしてですか。

【書きましょう】Let's write

Write your opinion about life in the dormitory/apartment and give reasons.

【書いたあとで】After writing

〈For your partner's writing〉 Read your partner's writing out loud. Tell your partner if something is not clear.

〈For your writing〉 Improve your writing by including your partner's questions and comments.

〈Self-check〉 Evaluate your writing.

I explained my life in the dormitory/apartment.	☺	😐	☹
I wrote my opinion about my dormitory/apartment life at the end.	☺	😐	☹

Cultural challenge

It is very interesting to live with people from different countries!

Your challenge: Do you have any difficulties living in a dormitory or an apartment? Let's share how to make your own living comfortable.

Additional information

1. Separating garbage into three types:

① もえるごみ：はっぽうスチロール polystyrene, アルミはく aluminum foil, カセットテープ cassette tapes, etc.

② もえないごみ：乾電池(かんでんち) dry batteries, 電球(でんきゅう) light bulbs, 金属製品(きんぞくせいひん) metal items, ガラス glassware, かん cans, etc.

③ リサイクルできるごみ：ペットボトル PET bottles, びん glass bottles, etc.

*The way of separating garbages is different depending on where you live.

2. Japanese apology すみません

Saying "すみません" is translated as "I'm sorry", but Japanese people often use すみません for the situations that English speakers would say "thank you".

Topic 10　どうしましたか

Objectives:

In this lesson, you will learn how to:

1. Express physical ailments and illness.
2. Give suggestions and advice to others.
3. Read a short paragraph about diet.
4. Write advice for others about staying healthy.

Introduction:

1. Listen to the vocabulary and match it to the pictures on pages 151-152.
2. Watch two videos. If the statement is correct, write a ○ . If the statement is wrong, write an × .

1st video：

① リーさんはねつがありません。　　(　　)

② リーさんはアレルギーがありません。　　(　　)

2nd video：

① リーさんはつかれました。　　(　　)

② 吉田（よしだ）さんは休みにサークルのかつどうをします。　　(　　)

Ⅰ. At the clinic

Lee goes to the clinic and talks to the nurse.

かんごし：どうしましたか。
リー　　：今朝から、あたまが痛(いた)くて、はき気(け)がするんです。
かんごし：ねつはどうですか。
リー　　：あります。
かんごし：はかってみましょう。
リー　　：はい。
かんごし：38 どですねえ。ほかにしょうじょうはありませんか。
りー　　：のども痛(いた)いです。
かんごし：口(くち)を大きくあけてください。ちょっとあかいですねえ。
　　　　　うがいをして、薬(くすり)を飲んでください。
　　　　　アレルギーはありませんか。
リー　　：大丈夫(だいじょうぶ)です。
かんごし：今日は、水分をたくさんとって、休んでくださいね。
りー　　：はい。
かんごし：お大事(だいじ)に。

Ⅱ. In classroom

Yoshida asks Lee about his/her well being.

吉田(よしだ)：さいきん、元気(げんき)がありませんね。
リー：ええ。毎日、おそくまでべんきょうしているので、つかれました。
吉田(よしだ)：そうですか。すこし休んだほうがいいですよ。
リー：吉田(よしだ)さんはどうやってストレスをかいしょうしますか。
吉田(よしだ)：ぼくは友達(ともだち)と話したり、サークルかつどうをしたり、旅行(りょこう)したりします。今度(こんど)、休みに家(いえ)に帰るのであそびに来ませんか。
リー：ありがとうございます。

New vocabulary

Verbs

うんどうします	Ⅲ	to do physical exercise
〈ストレスを〉かいしょうします	Ⅲ	to get rid of stress
さんぽします	Ⅲ	to take a walk
つかれます	Ⅱ	to get tired
もちます	Ⅰ	to hold/to have
ふとります	Ⅰ	to gain weight
やせます	Ⅱ	to loose weight

Wearing：

〈めがねを〉かけます	Ⅱ	to wear (glasses)
〈ぼうしを〉かぶります	Ⅰ	to put on (a cap/hat)
〈ふくを〉きます	Ⅱ	to get dressed
〈めがねを〉とります	Ⅰ	to take off (one's glasses)
〈ふくを〉ぬぎます	Ⅰ	to take off (one's clothes)
〈ズボンを〉はきます	Ⅰ	to put on (trousers)

Adjectives

痛（いた）い	ache/sore/pain
おそい	slow/late
はやい	fast/early
元気（げんき）[な]	healthy/being well
まじめ [な]	serious

Nouns

Body：

あたま	head
足（あし）	leg/foot
おなか	stomach
かた	shoulder
体（からだ）	body
口（くち）	mouth
こし	waist/hip
背中（せなか）	back

Nouns

のど	throat
歯（は）	tooth
はな	nose
ひざ	knee
耳（みみ）	ear
むね	chest
目（め）	eye
People：	
医者（いしゃ）	doctor
かんごし	nurse
歯医者（はいしゃ）	dentist
目医者（めいしゃ）	eye doctor
Wearing：	
コート	coat
スカート	skirt
帽子（ぼうし）	hat/cap
めがね	glasses
Others：	
エアコン	air conditioner
おんせん	hot spring
けんこう	health
さいきん	recently
トマト	tomato
病気（びょうき）	illness
ホームシック	homesick

Adverbs

ゆっくり	slowly
もう一度（いちど）	one more time

Counters

～ど	counter for temperature/degree

Useful expressions

Symptoms and injures

アレルギーがあります	to be allergic to ～
しょうじょうがあります	to have symptom of ～

かぜをひきます	to catch a cold
Useful expressions	
気分（きぶん）がわるいです	to feel ill
けがをします	to be injured
ころびます	to fall down
食欲（しょくよく）がありません	to have poor appetite
ストレスがたまります	to be under stress
せきが出（で）ます	to cough
ねつがあります	to have a fever
はき気（け）がします	to feel like vomiting
ほねをおります	to break bones
むしばがあります	to have a cavity
Treatments：	
うがいをします	to gargle
薬（くすり）を飲（の）みます	to take medicine
水分（すいぶん）をとります	to drink fluids
ちゅうしゃをします	to inject
ねつをはかります	to take one's temperature
マスクをします	to put on a mask
Phrases：	
お大事（だいじ）に	take care

Vocabulary exercises

1. Noun words： 体(からだ)

Exercise A

Read the each word (a) to (p). Then match the pictures to the words.

(a) 目(め)	(b) 口(くち)	(c) はな	(d) は
(e) 耳(みみ)	(f) のど	(g) 足(あし)	(h) ひざ
(i) むね	(j) かた	(k) こし	(l) おなか
(m) 体(からだ)	(n) あたま	(o) 背中(せなか)	(p) 手(て)

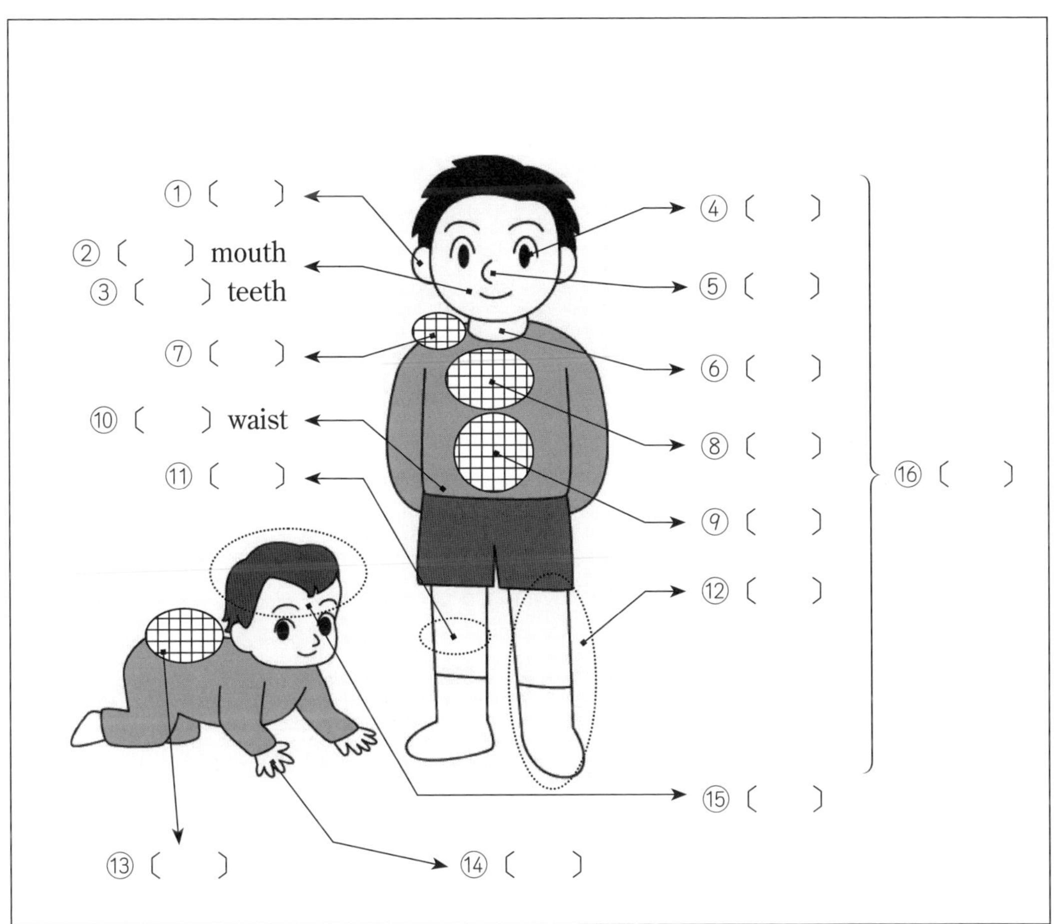

2. Idiomatic expressions：病気(びょうき)とけが

Exercise A-1

Read the sentences (a) to (l). Then match the sentences to the pictures.

(a) ねつがあります	(b) のどが痛(いた)いです	(c) かぜをひきます
(d) せきが出ます	(e) けがをします	(f) はき気(け)がします
(g) 手(て)をきります	(h) つかれます	(i) ストレスがたまります
(j) 食欲(しょくよく)がありません	(k) 気分(きぶん)がわるいです	(l) ほねをおります

Exercise A-2

Read the sentences (a) to (e). Then match the sentences to the pictures.

(a) 薬(くすり)を飲みます	(b) うがいをします	(c) ねつをはかります
(d) ちゅうしゃをします	(e) 水分をとります	

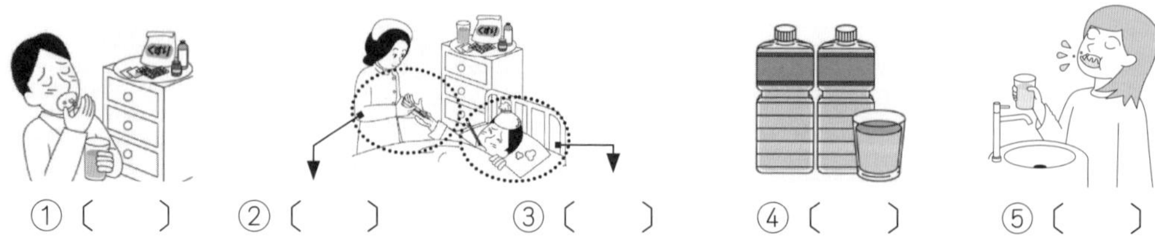

3. Verb words：ふく

Read each words (a) to (g). Then match the words to the pictures. You can use the same word more than once.

(a) きます	(b) はきます	(c) かぶります	(d) かけます
(e) とります	(f) ぬぎます	(g) つけます	

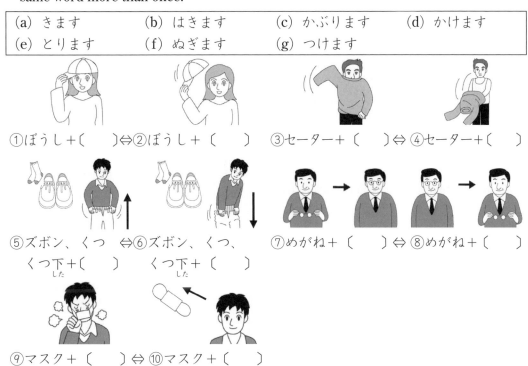

①ぼうし+〔　　〕⇔②ぼうし+〔　　〕　③セーター+〔　　〕⇔④セーター+〔　　〕

⑤ズボン、くつ、くつ下(した)+〔　　〕⇔⑥ズボン、くつ、くつ下(した)+〔　　〕　⑦めがね+〔　　〕⇔⑧めがね+〔　　〕

⑨マスク+〔　　〕⇔⑩マスク+〔　　〕

4. Exercises：病気(びょうき)の時

What do you do when you get sick? Choose the best answer from a-r. You can choose the same answer more than once.

(1) ねつがあります …__________　(2) のどが痛(いた)いです …__________

(3) せきが出ます …__________　(4) 食欲(しょくよく)がありません …__________

(5) はき気(け)がします …__________　(6) 気分(きぶん)がわるいです …__________

clothes	a. セーターをきます	b. くつ下をはきます	c. ズボンをはきます
	d. ぼうしをかぶります	e. セーターをぬぎます	f. くつをぬぎます
	g. ズボンをぬぎます	h. マスクをします	i. めがねをとります
medical	j. 薬(くすり)を飲みます	k. ちゅうしゃをします	l. ねつをはかります
	m. うがいをします	n. 水分をとります	o. ねます
	p. 果物(くだもの)を食べます	q. 病院(びょういん)へ行きます	r. 何も食べません

Grammar explanations and practice

1. Verb たり、Verb たりする

① This expression verb 1 たり、verb 2 たりする indicates a range of activities of which activity 1 and activity 2 are examples. This expression gives the impression that there are more actions other than activity 1 and activity 2.

A：どうやってストレスをかいしょうしますか。　How do you get rid of stress?

B：友達(ともだち)と話(はな)したり、旅行(りょこう)をしたりします。　I often do something with my friends such as chatting and travelling.

② The following expressions indicates that two actions are taking place alternately.

・行(い)ったり、来(き)たり：go back and forth from one place to another repeatedly.

・たったり、すわったり：stand up and sit down repeatedly.

③ The ～たり expression can also be used with only one verb. This indicates that the action consists of more than one action, even though you only mention one.

・日曜日(にちようび)はそうじしたりします。　I clean my room and do other things on Sunday.

The form is verb た-form ＋ り ＋ します. Verb た-form is plain past affirmative. た is replace て／で of the て-form with た／だ.

.	ます form	て form	た form	た form ＋ り
グループ1	行(い)きます	行(い)って	行(い)った	行(い)ったり
	話(はな)します	話(はな)して	話(はな)した	話(はな)したり
	読(よ)みます	読(よ)んで	読(よ)んだ	読(よ)んだり
	買(か)います	買(か)って	買(か)った	買(か)ったり
グループ2	見(み)ます	見(み)て	見(み)た	見(み)たり
グループ3	します	して	した	したり
	来(き)ます	来(き)て	来(き)た	来(き)たり

れんしゅう 1　Change the form as in the example.

e.g. すてます　→　すてた

①しめます　→　②けします　→　③すわります　→

④あびます　→　⑤のります　→　⑥説明(せつめい)します　→

⑦かします　→　⑧会(あ)います　→　⑨あらいます　→

れんしゅう 2　Answer the following questions using ～たり～たり

① 日曜日(にちようび)に何(なに)をしますか。　② 日本語(にほんご)のじゅぎょうで何(なに)をしますか。

れんしゅう 3　Write as in the example.

e.g.　たったり、すわったりします

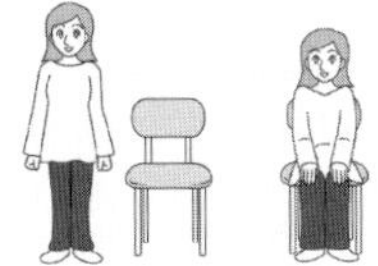

①
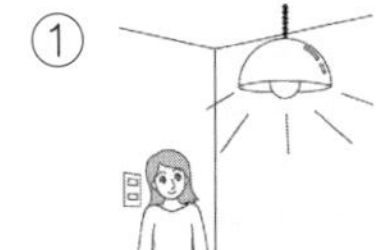

②

③

④

⑤
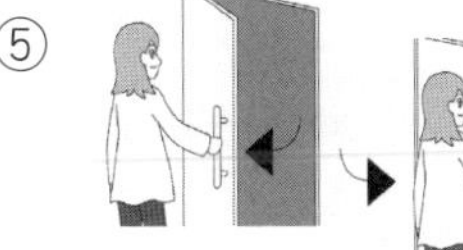
⑥

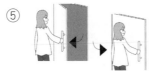

2. ～んです（どうしたんですか）

The expressions どうしましたか or どうしたんですか are used to ask what happened or what the problem is. ～んです is used to ask or give an explanation. Before ～んです, plain form is used.

A：どうしたんですか。　What happened to you?

B：ゆうべから、おなかが痛(いた)いんです。　I've had a stomachache since last night.

Plain form：

	Present		Past	
	Affirmative	Negative	Affirmative	Negative
Verb	読(よ)む 食(た)べる 来(く)る する	読(よ)まない 食(た)べない 来(こ)ない しない	読(よ)んだ 食(た)べた 来(き)た した	読(よ)まなかった 食(た)べなかった 来(こ)なかった しなかった
い Adjective	大(おお)きい	大(おお)きくない	大(おお)きかった	大(おお)きくなかった
な Adjective	ひまだ	ひまじゃない	ひまだった	ひまじゃなかった
Noun	学生(がくせい)だ	学生(がくせい)じゃない	学生(がくせい)だった	学生(がくせい)じゃなかった

れんしゅう　Practice as in the example.

e.g. 

A：どうしましたか／どうしたんですか。
B：昨日(きのう)からあたまが痛(いた)いんです。

①

② 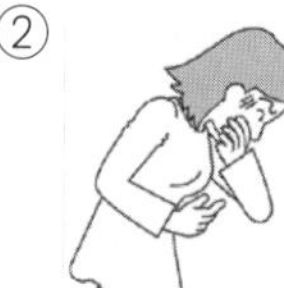

③ 

④ 

⑤ 

3. ～たことがあります

The た form is usually used when you talk about past events in your life. The expression of ～たことがある describes what you have experienced or done in the past.

① 私(わたし)はアルバイトをしたことがあります。　I have worked part-time before.

② 私(わたし)はインドへ行(い)ったことがありません。　I have never been to India.

れんしゅう 1　Practice as in the example.

e.g. 

私(わたし)は富士山(ふじさん)にのぼったことがあります。

① 

② 

③ 

④ 

れんしゅう 2 Talk about your experience using the pictures above as in the example.

e.g. A：富士山(ふじさん)にのぼったことがありますか。

B：はい、あります。

A：どうでしたか。

B：つかれましたが、とても楽(たの)しかったです。(comment)

A：リーさんものぼったことがありますか。(continue to talk)

4. Verb (た form／ない form) ほうがいいです

The expression ほうがいい is used to give advice or make suggestions to the listener and means "you should". To make a negative suggestion, use the ない-form instead of the た-form. ほうがいい expresses the feeling that if one does not follow the advice, there might be a problem. When you advise your superior, you might use "ほうがいいとおもいます" to make your advice softer.

A：どうしましたか。	What happened to you?
B：気分(きぶん)がわるいんです。	I don't feel good.
A：帰(かえ)って休(やす)んだほうがいいですよ。	You should go home and take a rest.

れんしゅう 1 Practice as in the example using the pictures on the previous page.

e.g. A：どうしましたか。　B：おなかが痛(いた)いんです。

A：病院(びょういん)へ行(い)ったほうがいいですよ。

れんしゅう 2 Ask your classmates about their worries. Give your advice to them.

5. ～てみる

Verb (て-form)＋みる is to express doing something in order to see how it is or what it is like.

1) ねつをはかってみてください。	Please take your temperature.
2) ケーキを作(つく)ったんです。食(た)べてみてください。	I made a cake. Please try it.

れんしゅう 1　Practice as in the example.

e.g.　ズボンをはいてみます。

①

②

③
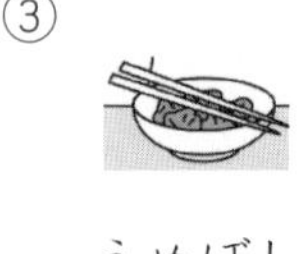
うめぼし

④

れんしゅう 2　Talk about your experiences and what you would like to try in the future.

e.g.　日本(にほん)で何(なに)をしてみましたか。何(なに)をしてみたいですか。

6. 〜ましょう

〜ましょう is used when a person offers to do something.

1) かんごし：ちゅうしゃをしましょう。　I will give you injection.

2) A：あついですねえ。　It's hot, is't it?

　B：じゃ、エアコンをつけましょう。　I'll turn on the air conditioner then.

　A：おねがいします。　Thank you.

れんしゅう　Practice as in the example.

e.g.
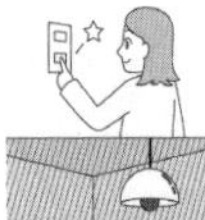
電気(でんき)をけしましょう。

①

②

③

④

⑤

7. Adverbial use of adjectives

Adjectives can modify nouns in Japanese as well as verbs. When an adjective is used to modify a verb, the い is dropped in an い adjective and replaced with く. In a な-adjective, the な is dropped and replaced with に. These words are called adverbs. Look at the following examples.

1) はやく帰(かえ)って休(やす)んだほうがいいですよ。　You should go home soon and take a rest.

2) 静(しず)かにあるいてください。　Please walk quietly.

	Modify a noun	Modify a verb
い-Adjective	大(おお)きい＋教室(きょうしつ)→大(おお)きい教室(きょうしつ)	大(おお)きい＋書(か)く→大(おお)きく書(か)く
な-Adjective	静(しず)かな＋部屋(へや)→静(しず)かな部屋(へや)	静(しず)かな＋話(はな)す→静(しず)かに話(はな)す

れんしゅう　Choose the correct answer as in the example.

e.g. トマトを（小(ちい)さい／**小(ちい)さく**）きってください。

　（**小(ちい)さい**／小(ちい)さく）トマトをください。

① 口(くち)を（大(おお)きい／大(おお)きく）あけてください。

② （大(おお)きい／大(おお)きく）車(くるま)がほしいです。

③ ホーさんは（まじめな／まじめに）学生(がくせい)です。

④ （まじめな／まじめに）聞(き)いてください。

⑤ 昨日(きのう)、テストのべんきょうをしましたから、（おそい／おそく）ねました。

⑥ 昨日(きのう)、（おそい／おそく）時間(じかん)に友達(ともだち)が部屋(へや)へ来(き)ました。

8. ～ています

① ～ています：て-form verbs together with います create the meaning that an action is in progress.

1) アートさんは今(いま)べんきょうしています。　Art is studying now.

2) ゆりさんは今音楽(いまおんがく)を聞(き)いています。　Yuri is listening to music now.

れんしゅう 1　Write what the people in the picture are doing.

①＿＿＿＿＿＿＿＿　②＿＿＿＿＿＿＿＿

③＿＿＿＿＿＿＿＿　④＿＿＿＿＿＿＿＿

⑤＿＿＿＿＿＿＿＿　⑥＿＿＿＿＿＿＿＿

②～ています：て -form verbs can be used to describe one's habits.

1) 私(わたし)は毎日(まいにち)４時間(じかん)べんきょうしています。　I study for four hours everyday.

2) 毎朝(まいあさ)、薬(くすり)を飲(の)んでいます。　I take medicine every morning

れんしゅう２ Describe each picture as in the example using the words in ☐.

e.g.

私(わたし)は毎晩(まいばん)５時間(じかん)ぐらい日本語(にほんご)をべんきょうしています。

①

②

③

④

⑤

毎日(まいにち)　毎朝(まいあさ)　毎晩(まいばん)　毎週(まいしゅう)＿＿＿曜日(ようび)に

れんしゅう３ Ask your classmates.

① いつも何時間(なんじかん)ぐらいねていますか。

② うんどうをしていますか。どんなうんどうをしていますか。

③ Own question

9. Sentence 1 ＋ので＋ Sentence 2（reason）

ので is used when describing a reason or a cause. The plain form should be used before ので. Both ので and から mean "because" but ので sounds a little softer than から.

1) Plain form Verb ＋ので　けがをしたので、病院(びょういん)へ行きます。
Because I am injured, I will go to the hospital.

2) い -adjective ＋ので　目(め)が痛(いた)いので、目医者(めいしゃ)に行(い)ってきます。
Because I have an eye ache, I will go to the eye doctor.

3) な -adjective ＋ので　ひまなので、さんぽしてきます。
Because I have free time, I will take a walk.

4) Noun- な＋ので	ミンさんは病気(びょうき)なので、1週間(いっしゅうかん)じゅぎょうを休(やす)みます。 Because Min-san is sick, she won't come to school for one week.

れんしゅう 1　Choose the best answer as in the example.

e.g. むしばがあるので（f）

① あついので(　)

② せきが出(で)るので(　)

③ アレルギーなので(　)

④ わからなかったので(　)

⑤ のどが痛(いた)いので(　)

a. セーターをぬぎます。

b. もう一度説明(いちどせつめい)してください。

c. うがいをします。

d. 薬(くすり)を飲(の)むことができません。

e. マスクをします。

~~f.~~ 歯医者(はいしゃ)へ行(い)ってきます。

れんしゅう 2　Make a sentence as in the example.

e.g. 食欲(しょくよく)がないので、今朝(けさ)ジュースしか飲(の)みませんでした。

① すこしふとったので、＿＿＿＿＿＿＿＿＿＿＿＿＿＿。

② かぜをひいたので、＿＿＿＿＿＿＿＿＿＿＿＿＿＿＿。

③ 漢字(かんじ)の読(よ)み方(かた)がわからないので、＿＿＿＿＿＿＿＿＿＿。

④ ＿＿＿＿＿＿＿＿＿＿＿＿＿＿＿ので、つかれました。

⑤ 友達(ともだち)は＿＿＿＿＿＿＿＿＿＿＿ので、日本語(にほんご)が上手(じょうず)です。

⑥ ＿＿＿＿＿＿＿＿＿＿＿＿ので、じゅぎょうにおくれました。

話します　Speaking

Check the following points:

1. Adding ねえ at the end of the sentence is used to explain from observation.

   のどがあかいですねえ。　　Your throat is red, isn't it?

2. Adding ね at the end of the sentence is used to request confirmation.

   休んでくださいね。　　Please rest , will you?

3. Adding よ at the end of the sentence is used for giving advice to the listener.

　休んだほうがいいですよ。　　You should take a rest.

4. お大事(だいじ)に means “take care”.

れんしゅう 1　Practice the conversation using the listening material.

れんしゅう 2　〈Role play〉 Practice the conversation with your partner. You take role A and your partner takes role B.

Situation: You have had a high fever since last night. See the nurse at the clinic and tell her/him your symptoms.

A (patient)
- Explain that you have had a high fever, sore throat, no appetite and a sneezing fit since last night.

B (nurse)
- Ask A about his/her symptoms.
- Give advice to take fluids and rest well.
- End the consultation.

れんしゅう 3　Ask your classmates how to relieve stress, as in the example. Give your own solutions.

e.g. リー：トムさんは、どうやってストレスをかいしょうしますか。

　トム：ぼくは、ジムに行ったり、友達(ともだち)と話したりします。

【話したあとで】After speaking 〈Self-check〉 Evaluate your speaking.

I was able to:

explain my symptoms.	☺	😐	☹
explain how to relieve stress.	☺	😐	☹

読みます　Reading

【読むまえに】Before reading

1. 今あなたはけんこうですか。　　（　）はい　（　）いいえ
2. 「けんこうチェック」のしつもんにこたえなさい。

新しいことば　学年(がくねん) school year　うんどう exercise

けんこうチェック

名前（なまえ）＿＿＿＿＿＿＿＿＿＿＿＿　性別（せいべつ）：男／女　　学年：＿＿＿年生

1. 朝食を食べますか。

① 毎日食べる　② ときどき食べる　③ 食べない

①・②→何を食べますか。（　　　　　　　　　　）

③→どうして食べませんか。（　　　　　　　　　　）

2. うんどうをしていますか。

① 毎日している　② ときどきしている　③ していない

①・②　→どんなうんどうをしていますか。（　　　　）

3. 毎日何時間ぐらいねますか。　① ３時間　② ４～６時間　③ ７～８時間

【読みましょう】Let's read

新しいことば

図（ず） chart　よい good　バランス balance　～かい a time　ひつような necessary
エネルギー energy　キロカロリー kcal　食生活（しょくせいかつ） eating habits　毎食（まいしょく） every meal
大切（たいせつ）な important　かんがえる consider

Read the paragraph and answer the questions.

しつもん

1. What is the chart about? Choose the best answer below.

a. 病気の人の食事（しょくじ）　b. いい食事（しょくじ）のバランス
c. 日本料理（にほんりょうり）の食べ方　d. よくない食べ物

2. If the statement is correct, write a ○ . If the statement is wrong, write an × .

① 朝ご飯、昼ご飯、晩ご飯を食べましょう。（　）

② ご飯やパンはあまり食べないほうがいいです。（　）

③ やさいもくだものもたくさん食べたほうがいいです。（　）

④ お水やお茶をあまり飲まないほうがいいです。（　）

⑤ あるいたり、はしったりしてうんどうをしたほうがいいです。（　）

⑥ １週間に３～４かい、６～７時間ぐらいねたほうがいいです。（　）

Reading tip

Pictures help you understand the contents of reading passage.

本文

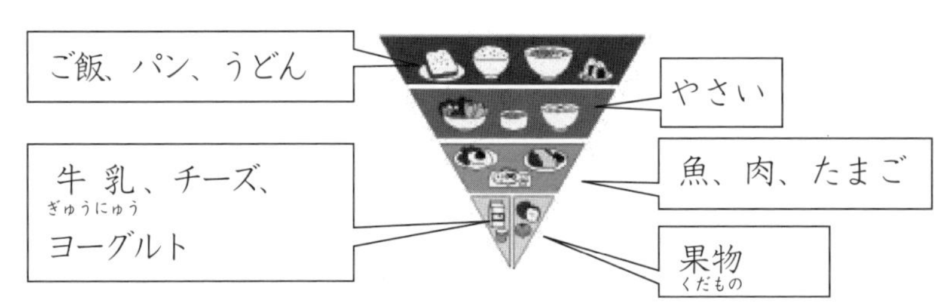

みなさんは毎日どんな食事(しょくじ)をしますか。好きな物しか食べなかったり、お酒をたくさん飲んだりしますか。ダイエットをして、あまり食べなかったりしますか。食事(しょくじ)はバランスが大切(たいせつ)です。上の図(ず)を見てあなたの食生活(しょくせいかつ)をかんがえてみてください。１日３かい、朝、昼、晩、食事(しょくじ)をしましょう。私たちはエネルギーが１日に2,200キロカロリーひつようです。ご飯やパンはエネルギーを作りますから毎食(まいしょく)食べましょう。やさいもたくさん食べてください。果物(くだもの)やチーズ、ヨーグルトや牛乳(ぎゅうにゅう)も食べたり飲んだりしたほうがいいですが、あまりたくさん食べないほうがいいです。水やお茶もいっしょに飲みましょう。けんこうにはうんどうも大切(たいせつ)です。１週間に３～４かい、25分ぐらいあるいたり、ジョギングをしたりしましょう。そして、毎晩６～７時間ぐらいねてください。

書きます　Writing － Advice －

【書くまえに】Before writing

Read the following explanation by Yan and write your advice.

ヤン

私は朝ごはんを食べません。やさいがきらいです。うんどうも好きじゃないです。１日に５時間ぐらいパソコンでゲームをします。毎晩３時ごろねます。５時間しかねません。

ヤンさんは、何をしたほうがいいですか。何をしないほうがいいですか。

① ＿＿＿＿＿＿　② ＿＿＿＿＿＿　③ ＿＿＿＿＿＿　④ ＿＿＿＿＿＿

【書きましょう】Let's write

Write your advice to Yan-san using the comments above.

【書いたあとで】After writing

〈For your partner's writing〉 Read your partner's writing out loud. Tell your partner if something is not clear.

〈For your writing〉 Improve your writing by including your partner's questions and comments.

〈Self-check〉 Evaluate your writing.

I can write my advice about other's health.	☺	😐	☹

Cultural Challenge

> I go to the fitness room on campus twice a week and chat with Japanese students in Japanese.

Your challenge: Stay fit! How do you keep fit? How do you stay in shape?

Additional information

1. Look at the signs outside. Check the following kanji.

薬局（やっきょく） pharmacy	内科（ないか） internal medicine	外科（げか） surgery
歯科（しか） dentist	整形外科（せいけいげか） orthopedics	産婦人科（さんふじんか） obstetrics
眼科（がんか） ophthalmology	耳鼻科（じびか） otolaryngology（ear, nose, throat）	

2. Useful words used at the hospital

受付（うけつけ） reception	問診票（もんしんひょう） questionnaire	診察券（しんさつけん） registration card
処方箋（しょほうせん） prescription	薬局（やっきょく） pharmacy, dispensary	保険証（ほけんしょう） health insurance card
尿（にょう） urine	便（べん） feces	便秘（べんぴ） constipation
血圧（けつあつ） blood pressure	体温計（たいおんけい）（clinical） thermometer	

3. 薬（くすり）の飲み方

のみぐすり 山田花子様	
1日　3回　7日分	→ 1日3回（かい）飲みます。
【内服】1日3回毎食後	→ 食事（しょくじ）のあとで飲みます。
1回　錠剤　　2個 お飲みください	→ 1回2つ飲んでください。

Kanji and Vocabulary

漢字・語彙練習

かんじ・ごいれんしゅう

Introduction to Kanji

1. About the Japanese Characters

In Japanese, three kinds of characters are used; Hiragana, Katakana and Kanji. Kanji is an ideographic script where each character has a meaning. Hiragana follows the Kanji and provides an infectional ending. It is also used for particles and some of the words in which Kanji are not used. Katakana is used mainly for writing foreign loan words.

e.g. 私 は パン を 食べます。(I eat bread.)
① ② ③ ④ ⑤

	①	②	③	④	⑤
Kind of character	Kanji	Hiragana	Katakana	Hiragana	Kanji+Hiragana
Part of speech	personal pronoun	particle	noun (loan words)	particle	verb
Meaning of vocabulary	I		bread		eat

2. History and Usage of Japanese Characters

There were no characters in Japan until Kanji was introduced. Kanji came to Japan from China in the 5th century. Since then, until today, Kanji characters have been used in the Japanese language. The Japanese language can be divided into "Wa-go", which uses the Kanji characters to represent the ancient Japanese language; and "Kan-go", which is Japanese language represented by the Chinese characters but with Chinese pronunciation. In addition, in the 9th century Hiragana and Katakana were also developed from Kanji in order to write original Japanese.

(1) Kanji

The reading of Kanji that indicates words of Japanese origin is called Kun-yomi: Japanese reading. The reading of Kanji that indicates words of Chinese origin is called On-yomi: Chinese reading. For many Kanji there are two or more pronunciations or readings.

In Kun-yomi, it is easy to understand the meaning of the Kanji through its reading;

but in the case of On-yomi, it is not so easy to understand the meaning of Kanji through its reading and thus often a combination of Kanji having On-yomi is used to make the meaning clear.

e.g. From Topic3

	Reading		Vocabulary
月	Kun	つき /tsuki/	月（つき） (moon)
	On	ゲツ /getsu/	月曜日（げつようび） (Monday)
水	Kun	みず /mizu/	水（みず） (water)
	On	スイ /sui/	水曜日（すいようび） (Wednesday)

(2) Hiragana

Hiragana is a character made by breaking Kanji apart. In total, there are 48 Hiragana characters.

例）安→あ　以→い　宇→う　衣→え　於→お

The hiragana characters represent sounds, not meaning. An individual character represents one syllable, and is known as a syllabic character.

【Writing of particle】

① 「は」「へ」 when used as particles、「は」 will be pronounced as /wa/、「へ」 will be pronounced as /e/.

e.g. 私は学校へ行きます。(I go to the school.)
　　は /wa/　へ /e/

② 「を」is pronounced like「お」or /o/、 and is also used as a particle.

e.g. お茶を飲みます。(I drink a cup of tea.)
　　お /o/　を /o/

(3) About Katakana

There are 48 characters in Katakana. Each character is made from a part of a Kanji. In addition, the sign "ー" is also used.

e.g. 阿→「ア」、伊→「イ」、宇→「ウ」、江→「エ」、於→「オ」

Just as in Hiragana, individual Katakana characters have no meaning. It is said the syllabic character, and an individual character shows one syllable. See above.

The symbol「ー」means a long extended sound of the vowel before this symbol.

e.g. ケーキ（cake）、コーヒー（coffee）
/keeki/ /koohii/

3. Four kinds of Kanji

Kanji is divided into four kinds which are roughly separated according to their structure.

① Some characters like → →「山」, → →「木」, → →「日」, can be illustrated in this manner. They developed into Kanji from pictures, and they are said to be the oldest of the characters. Moreover, they are also used as the parts of other kinds of Kanji.

② Some characters are made by using the point and the line. For instance, there is Kanji such as "上" and "一". These characters symbolize abstract concept such as numbers or positions.

③ Kanji made from the combination of two characters or more, creating a new meaning. For example,「日」+「月」→「明」、「木」+「木」→「林」.

④ Some Kanji are also made from the combination of two characters or more. One side of the combination shows a meaning and the other part shows a Chinese reading. 80% - 90% of Kanji has the combination. For example,「日」+「寺」→「時（ジ）」、「化」+「艹」→「花」.

Introduction for Kanji and Vocabulary

This part is for students who have no prior knowledge of Japanese language.

The objectives of this part are to study Kanji vocabulary and Katakana words.

Since Kanji vocabulary and Katakana words are related to each topic, the vocabulary learned in this part will be helpful when reviewing each topic in the textbook.

1. Contents

There are 10 topics. You will learn 148 Kanji, 390 Kanji vocabulary and 30 Katakana words. The following exercises are available from APU's website:

http://www.apu.ac.jp/language/

【Hiragana Practice】 Shape of Hiragana and Hiragana words

【Katakana Practice】 Shape of Katakana and Katakana words

【Kanji vocabulary Review】 Topic 1 - 10 Kanji vocabulary review

Each topic includes the following sections:

① Kanji reading and writing

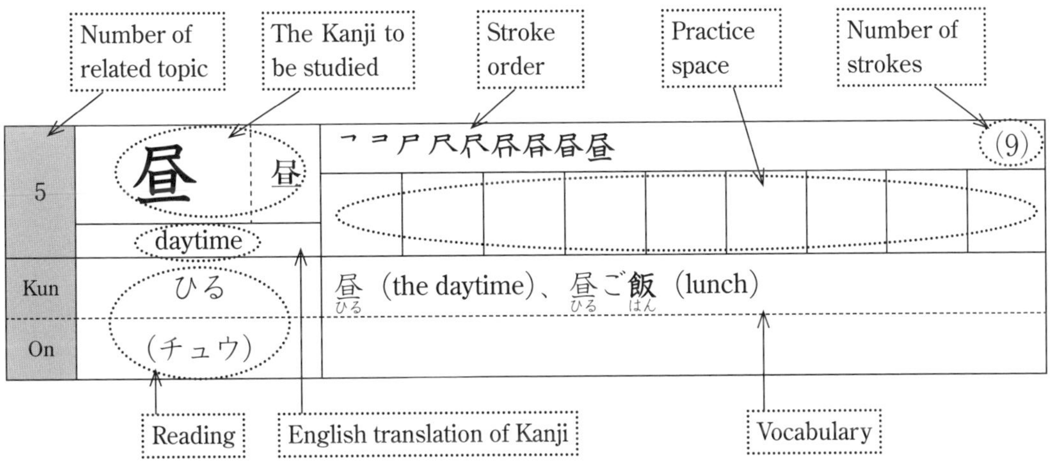

Notes:

- If a word has *, it means that the reading is an exception.
- The reading in (　) means that it will be introduced later.
- Kanji in bold font means that it hasn't been learned yet.

② Katakana words

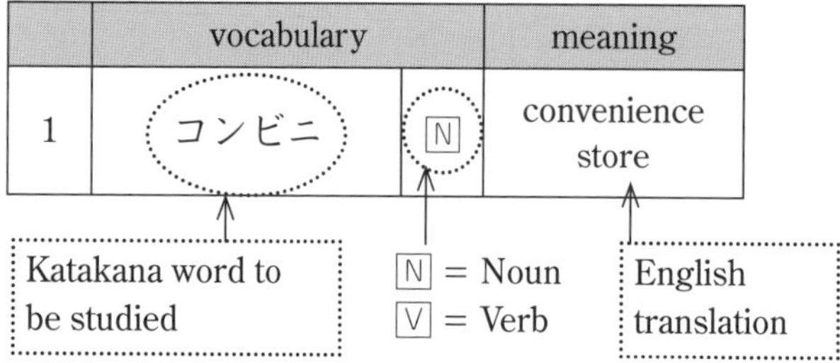

vocabulary
meaning
1
コンビニ
N
convenience store
Katakana word to be studied
N = Noun
V = Verb
English translation

③ Kanji vocabulary exercises

Memorizing the Kanji as an image

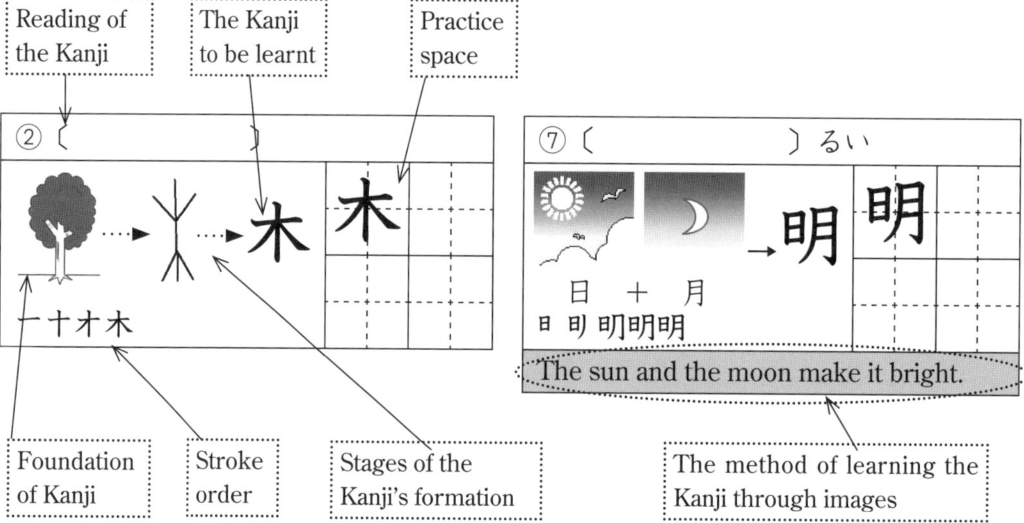

④ Practicing Kanji vocabulary in context and comprehending a short paragraph

⑤ Comprehending the real life Kanji

2. Characteristics of this part:

In order to make it easier for students to learn Kanji, this section contains the following ideas:

① Using illustrations and examples

② Making connections to the meaning of Kanji shapes using mental images

③ Using bold font and writing Hiragana below the Kanji that haven't been learned yet.

④ Learning how to read and write the Kanji in context.

⑤ Using the idea of lexical networks as follows:

Phonemic	· Vocabulary that share the same sound are collected in one section
Shape	· Words that contain the same shape or structure have been put together
Semantic	· Antonyms, synonyms (Japanese words · Kanji, etc.) and hyponyms have been collected together
Syntactic	· Categorizing by nouns, verbs, adjectives, and etc

⑥ Interacting with other students using what you have learnt and engaging in activities such as making questionnaires

⑦ Using real-life resources outside of class

Basic rules of stroke order

1	① ② ③ 一 二 三 ① Write from left to right. ②③ Then go down, and write from left to right.
2	① ② ③ 丿 川 川 (Start from the leftmost line and continue right words.) ① Write from top to bottom. ②③ Then go right, and write from top to bottom.
3	① ② 一 十 (Start from the horizontal line before the vertical line.) ① Write from left to right. ② Write from top to bottom.
4	① ② ③ ④ 一 十 才 木 (Write the center horizontal line before the outside "wings".) ① Write from left to right. ② Write from top to bottom. ③ Write from vertical cross point to lower left. ④ Write from vertical cross point to lower right.
5	① ② ③ 丨 冂 口 (Start from the upper left point to down in enclosing style Kanji.) ① Write from top to bottom. ② Write from left to right and down with one stroke. ③ Write from the bottom-left corner to right to complete the enclosure.
6	① ② ③ ④ ⑤ ⑥ 丨 冂 冂 冋 回 回 (Start from the outside of the Kanji.) ① Write from upper left point to bottom. ② Write from left to right and down with one stroke. ③ Write from the inside upper left point to bottom, before enclosing the outside. ④ Write from left to right and down with one stroke. ⑤ Write from the bottom-left corner to right to complete the inner enclosure. ⑥ Write from the bottom-left corner to right to complete the outer enclosure.
7	① ② 丿 人 (Start from top right point to bottom left in cross style Kanji.) ① Write from top right to bottom left. ② Write from upper left of cross point to the bottom right.

漢字・語彙練習

目　次

<table>
<tr><th colspan="11">Topic6　どこでかいますか</th></tr>
<tr><td colspan="10">勉強する漢字／カタカナ語</td><td rowspan="4">212</td></tr>
<tr><td>上</td><td>下</td><td>右</td><td>左</td><td>前</td><td>後</td><td>中</td><td>外</td><td>男</td><td>女</td></tr>
<tr><td>子</td><td>若</td><td>物</td><td>花</td><td>絵</td><td>細</td><td></td><td></td><td></td><td></td></tr>
<tr><td colspan="10">ボールペン　ホチキス　シャープペンシル</td></tr>
<tr><th colspan="11">Topic7　何が好きですか</th></tr>
<tr><td colspan="10">勉強する漢字／カタカナ語</td><td rowspan="4">220</td></tr>
<tr><td>茶</td><td>酒</td><td>飯</td><td>魚</td><td>鳥</td><td>牛</td><td>肉</td><td>米</td><td>食</td><td>飲</td></tr>
<tr><td>作</td><td>好</td><td>味</td><td>方</td><td></td><td></td><td></td><td></td><td></td><td></td></tr>
<tr><td colspan="10">チョコレート　コーヒー　ジュース　カレーライス</td></tr>
<tr><th colspan="11">Topic8　本をかりることができますか</th></tr>
<tr><td colspan="10">勉強する漢字／カタカナ語</td><td rowspan="4">227</td></tr>
<tr><td>行</td><td>来</td><td>帰</td><td>国</td><td>所</td><td>校</td><td>室</td><td>図</td><td>銀</td><td>家</td></tr>
<tr><td>部</td><td>泳</td><td>歌</td><td>会</td><td>話</td><td>買</td><td></td><td></td><td></td><td></td></tr>
<tr><td colspan="10">ビデオ　キャンパス</td></tr>
<tr><th colspan="11">Topic9　かしてください（りょうで）</th></tr>
<tr><td colspan="10">勉強する漢字／カタカナ語</td><td rowspan="4">235</td></tr>
<tr><td>場</td><td>紙</td><td>油</td><td>入</td><td>出</td><td>洗</td><td>料</td><td>便</td><td>利</td><td>不</td></tr>
<tr><td>明</td><td>暗</td><td>静</td><td>新</td><td>古</td><td></td><td></td><td></td><td></td><td></td></tr>
<tr><td colspan="10">アイロン　ランドリー　キッチン</td></tr>
<tr><th colspan="11">Topic10　どうしましたか</th></tr>
<tr><td colspan="10">勉強する漢字／カタカナ語</td><td rowspan="4">243</td></tr>
<tr><td>目</td><td>口</td><td>耳</td><td>手</td><td>足</td><td>体</td><td>薬</td><td>病</td><td>院</td><td>医</td></tr>
<tr><td>者</td><td>力</td><td>痛</td><td>元</td><td>気</td><td></td><td></td><td></td><td></td><td></td></tr>
<tr><td colspan="10">クリニック　アレルギー　ストレス</td></tr>
</table>

Topic 1　はじめまして

Ⅰ. Kanji Reading and Writing

◇ mark means that this Kanji is in Ⅱ-1.

1	山 (山) mountain	丨 山 山 ◇ (3)
Kun	やま	山(やま) (mountain)、山本(やまもと) (Japanese surname)
On	サン	富士山(ふじさん) (Mt.Fuji)

2	川 (川) river	丿 川 川 ◇ (3)
Kun	かわ、(がわ)	川(かわ) (river)
On	(セン)	

3	木 (木) tree/wood	一 十 才 木 ◇ (4)
Kun	き	木(き) (tree)、鈴木(すずき) (Japanese surname)
On	(モク)	

4	林 (林) grove	一 十 オ 木 木一 村 材 林 ◇ (8)
Kun	はやし	林(はやし) (grove/Japanese surname)、小林(こばやし) (Japanese surname)
On	(リン)	

5	森 (森) thick woods	一 十 オ 木 本 夲 夲 夲 森 森 森 森 ◇ (12)
Kun	もり	森(もり) (forest/Japanese surname)
On	(シン)	

6	田	田	丨 冂 冂 田 田 ◇I (5)
	rice field		
Kun	た、だ		田（た）(rice field)、田中（たなか）(Japanese surname)、山田（やまだ）(Japanese surname)
On	（デン）		

7	石	石	一 ア 不 石 石 ◇I (5)
	stone		
Kun	いし		石（いし）(stone)、石井（いしい）(Japanese surname)
On	（セキ）		

8	竹	竹	ノ ト 𠂉 竹 竹 竹 ◇I (6)
	bamboo		
Kun	たけ		竹（たけ）(bamboo)、竹内（たけうち）(Japanese surname)
On	（チク）		

9	人	人	ノ 人 ◇I (2)
	human being		
Kun	ひと		人（ひと）(person)
On	ジン、ニン		5人（ごにん）(five people)、〜人（じん）[suffix; nationality] …日本人（にほんじん）(Japanese)

10	私	私	ノ 二 千 禾 禾 私 私 (7)
	I/private		
Kun	わたし		私（わたし）(I)
On	シ		私立大学（しりつだいがく）(private university)

11	先	先	ノ ⺧ 牛 生 失 先 (6)
	ahead		
Kun	(さき)		
On	セン		先生（せんせい）(teacher)、先輩（せんぱい）(one's senior)

12	生	生	ノ ⺧ 牛 牛 生 (5)
	student/life/be born		
Kun	(い - きる)		
On	セイ		学生（がくせい）(student)

13	学	学	丶 丷 ⺍ ⺍ 𰀪 ⺍ 学 学 (8)
	study		
Kun	(まな - ぶ)		
On	ガク		大学（だいがく）(university)、大学生（だいがくせい）(university student)、学部（がくぶ）(college)

14	友	友	一 ナ 方 友 (4)
	friend		
Kun	とも		友達（ともだち）(friend)
On	(ユウ)		

15	門	門	丨 𠃌 ⼫ 戸 𠃍 門 門 門 ① (8)
	gate		
Kun			
On	モン		門（もん）(gate)、専門（せんもん）(specialty)

Ⅱ. Kanji and Vocabulary Exercises

Ⅱ - 1.　Memorize the Kanji as an image

Write the reading and Kanji seeing each picture as shown in the example.

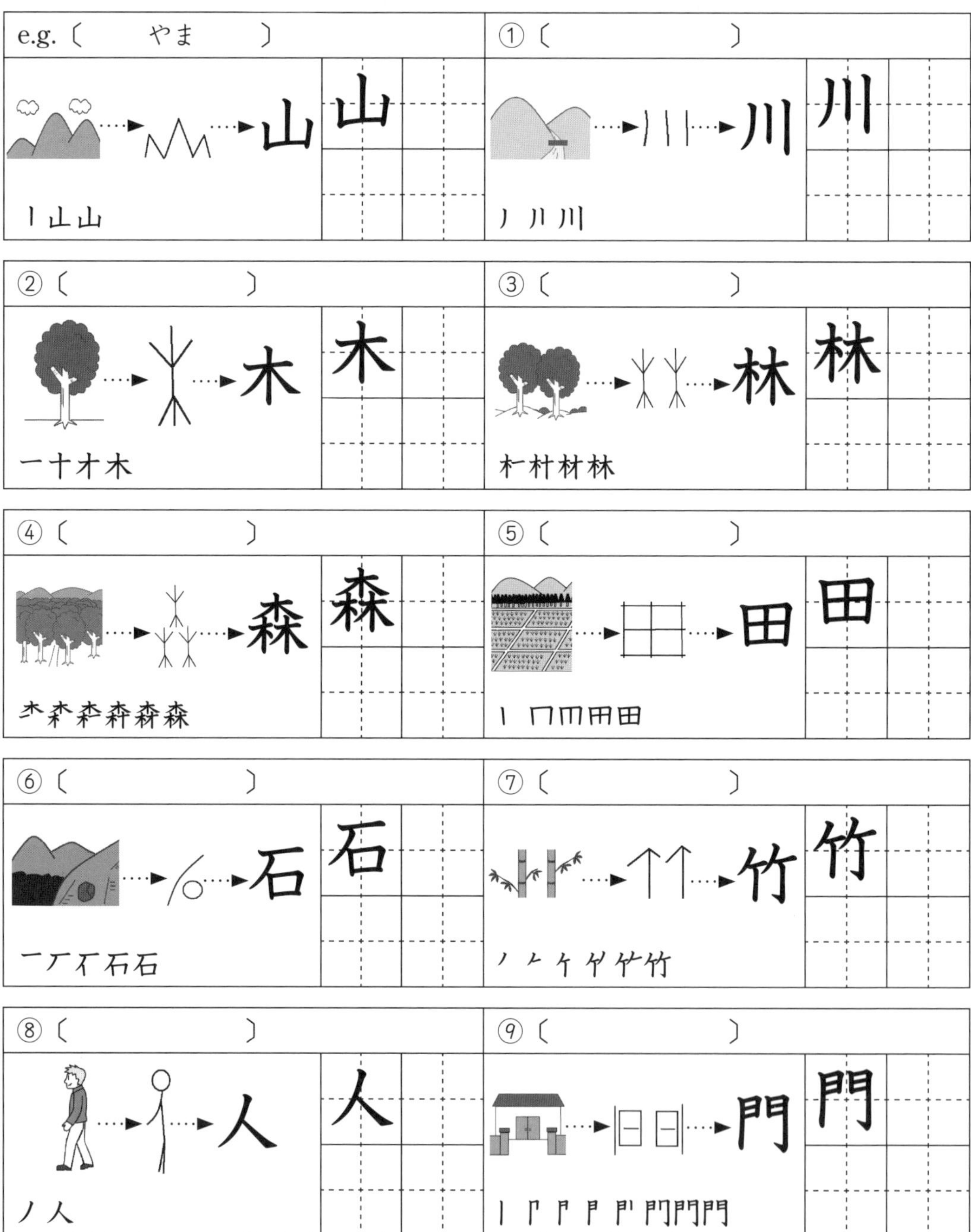

Ⅱ - 2. Writing Exercises

Choose the vocabulary from a to j below and put its Kanji on the ___ as shown in the example.

a. き	b. やま	c. もり	d. ひと
e. た	f. かわ	g. いし	h. たけ
i. はやし	j. もん		

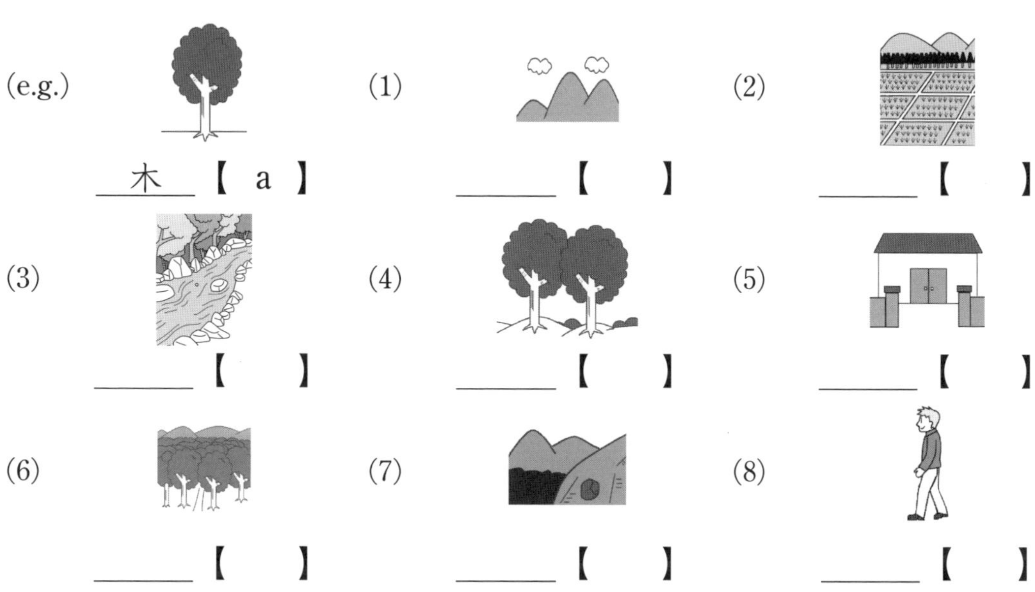

(e.g.) 木 【 a 】

(1) ______【　　】

(2) ______【　　】

(3) ______【　　】

(4) ______【　　】

(5) ______【　　】

(6) ______【　　】

(7) ______【　　】

(8) ______【　　】

(9)

______【　　】

Ⅲ. Exercises in context

Exercise A

Read the following sentences and choose the appropriate word.

はじまして。私は {友達(だち)・大学(だい)・山田} です。
りつめいかんアジアたいへいよう {先生・学生・大学(だい)} の
{友達(だち)・学生・大学(だい)} です。
よろしくおねがいします。

はじまして。ヤンです。

私のにほんごの｛先生・学生・山田｝は竹内（うち）先生です。

リーさんは　私の｛先生・学生・友達（だち）｝です。

どうぞよろしく。

Exercise B

Complete the following sentences about yourself using the Kanji that you learned.

＿＿＿＿＿は＿＿＿＿＿＿＿＿＿＿＿＿＿です。
（わたし）

＿＿＿＿＿＿＿＿＿＿＿から きました。
(your country)

りつめいかんアジアたいへいよう大（だい）＿＿＿＿＿の＿＿＿＿＿です。
（がく）　（がくせい）

せん＿＿＿＿は＿＿＿＿＿＿＿＿です。
（もん）

にほんごの＿＿＿＿＿は＿＿＿＿＿＿＿＿＿です。どうぞよろしく。
（せんせい）　your teacher's name　（せんせい）

Ⅳ. Challenge: Real Life Kanji

➢ Kanji in town

Look at the pictures below and circle the Kanji that you learned. And then choose the meaning of the picture from a-f below.

(1)

(2)

(3)

(4)

a.	Sign for shop	b.	Billboard	c.	Nameplate
d.	Sign for direction	e.	Nameplate of university	f.	Sign for river

Topic 2　きょうしつはどこですか

Ⅰ. Kanji Reading and Writing

1	一 (一) one	一 (1)
Kun	ひと-つ	一つ(ひと) (one thing)、*一人(ひとり) (one person)
On	イチ、(イッ)	一(いち) (one)

2	二 (二) two	一二 (2)
Kun	ふた-つ	二つ(ふた) (two things)、*二人(ふたり) (two people)
On	ニ	二(に) (two)

3	三 (三) three	一二三 (3)
Kun	みっ-つ	三つ(みっ) (three things)
On	サン	三(さん) (three)、三人(さんにん) (three people)

4	四 (四) four	丨 冂 冂 四 四 (5)
Kun	よん、よ、よっ-つ	四(よん) (four)、四人(よにん) (four people)、四つ(よっ) (four things)
On	シ	四(し) (four)

5	五	五	一 丅 五 五	(4)
	five			
Kun	いつ-つ		五つ(いつ) (five things)	
On	ゴ		五(ご) (five)、五人(ごにん) (five people)	

6	六	六	' 亠 六 六	(4)
	six			
Kun	むっ-つ、(むい)		六つ(むっ) (six things)	
On	ロク、ロッ		六(ろく) (six)、六人(ろくにん) (six people)	

7	七	七	一 七	(2)
	seven			
Kun	なな、(なの)		七(なな) (seven)、七つ(なな) (seven things)、七人(ななにん) (seven people)	
On	シチ		七(しち) (seven)、七人(しちにん) (seven people)	

8	八	八	ノ 八	(2)
	eight			
Kun	やっ-つ、(よう)		八つ(やっ) (eight things)	
On	ハチ、(ハッ)		八(はち) (eight)、八人(はちにん) (eight people)	

9	九	九	ノ 九	(2)
	nine			
Kun	ここの-つ		九つ(ここの) (nine things)	
On	キュウ、(ク)		九(きゅう) (nine)、九人(きゅうにん) (nine people)	

10	十	十	一十 (2)
	ten		
Kun	とお		十(とお) (ten things)
On	ジュウ、(ジッ／ジュッ)		十(じゅう) (ten)、十人(じゅうにん) (ten people)

11	百	百	一丆丆百百百 (6)
	hundred		
Kun			
On	ヒャク、ビャク ピャク		百(ひゃく) (one hundred)、二百(にひゃく) (two hundred)、三百(さんびゃく) (three hundred)、六百(ろっぴゃく) (six hundred)

12	千	千	ノ二千 (3)
	thousand		
Kun			
On	セン、ゼン		千(せん) (one thousand)、二千(にせん) (two thousand)、三千(さんぜん) (three thousand)

13	万	万	一万万 (3)
	ten thousand		
Kun			
On	マン		一万(いちまん) (ten thousand)、二万(にまん) (twenty thousand)

Ⅱ. Katakana Words

	vocabulary		meaning		vocabulary		meaning
1	コンビニ／コンビニエンスストア	N	convenience store	2	スーパー／スーパーマーケット	N	supermarket
3	レストラン	N	restaurant				

Summary of Reading Kanji

numbers		numbers (person) number＋人	numbers (things) number＋つ
1	一（いち）	一人（ひと・り）	一（ひと）つ
2	二（に）	二人（ふた・り）	二（ふた）つ
3	三（さん）	三人（さん・にん）	三（みっ）つ
4	四（よん／し）	四人（よ・にん）	四（よっ）つ
5	五（ご）	五人（ご・にん）	五（いつ）つ
6	六（ろく）	六人（ろく・にん）	六（むっ）つ
7	七（なな／しち）	七人（なな／しち・にん）	七（なな）つ
8	八（はち）	八人（はち・にん）	八（やっ）つ
9	九（きゅう／く）	九人（きゅう・にん）	九（ここの）つ
10	十（じゅう）	十人（じゅう・にん）	十（とお）
《Question word》		何人（なん・にん）	いくつ

Ⅲ. Kanji and Vocabulary Exercises

Ⅲ - 1.　Practice of Numbers

Write the reading of the following numbers in Hiragana and match the Hiragana with the Kanji as shown in the example.

e.g.	1	い ち	・	・ 四
(1)	2	□	・	・ 一
(2)	3	□□	・	・ 五
(3)	4	□□	・	・ 二
(4)	5	□	・	・ 十
(5)	6	□□	・	・ 三
(6)	7	□□	・	・ 六
(7)	8	□□	・	・ 八
(8)	9	□□□	・	・ 九
(9)	10	□□□	・	・ 七

Ⅲ - 2. Money

Choose the reading of the following currency in Hiragana.

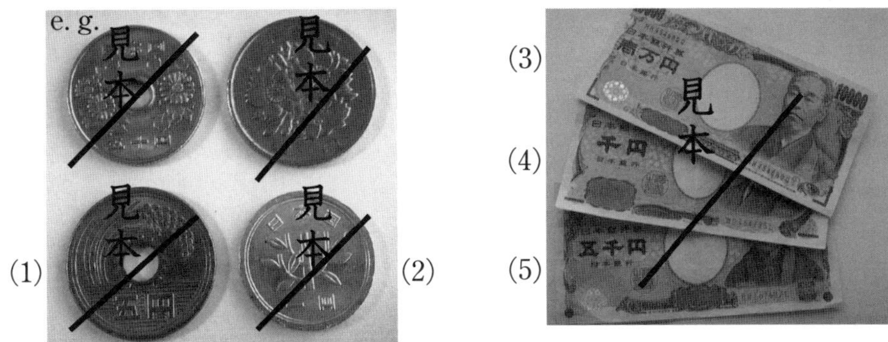

e.g. ごじゅう えん　　(1) ＿＿＿＿えん　　(2) ＿＿＿＿えん

(3) いち＿＿＿えん　　(4) ＿＿＿＿えん　　(5) ＿＿＿＿えん

Ⅲ - 3. Numbers

Practice as in the example.

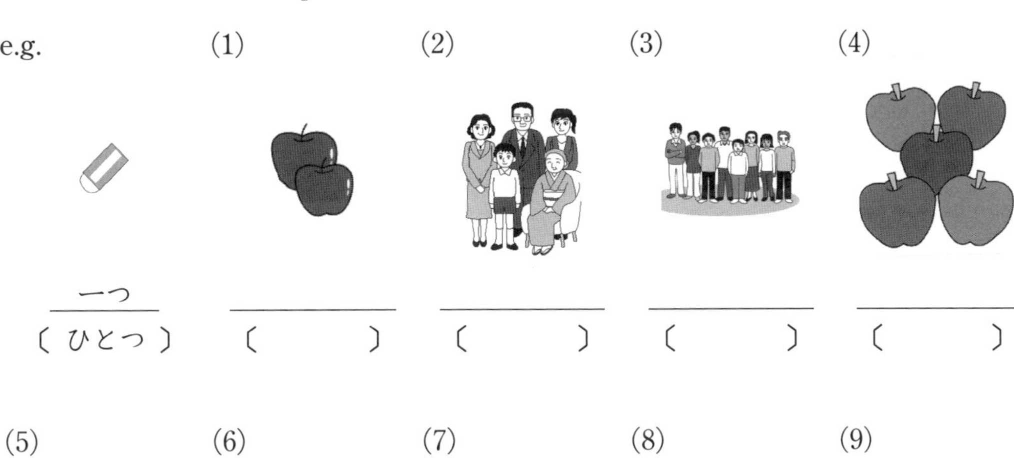

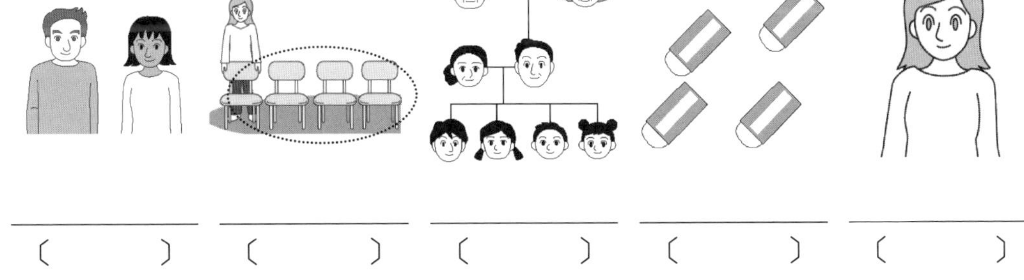

Ⅳ. Exercises in context

Ⅳ - 1.　Letter

Lee writes a letter to Yamada who is living in Kyoto. Read the address on the envelope. Write the reading of the following Kanji numbers.

① the front of an envelope

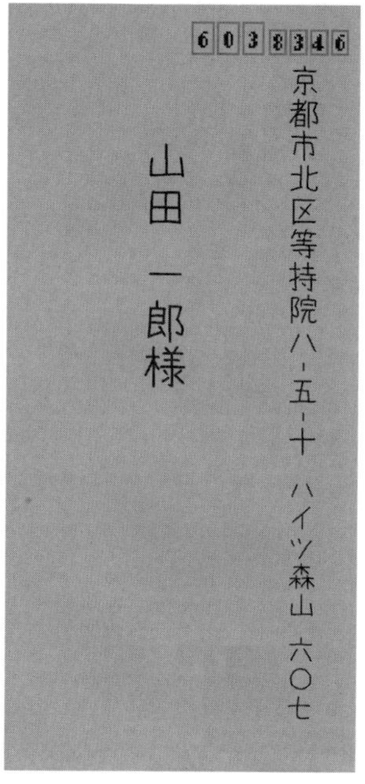

② the back of an envelope

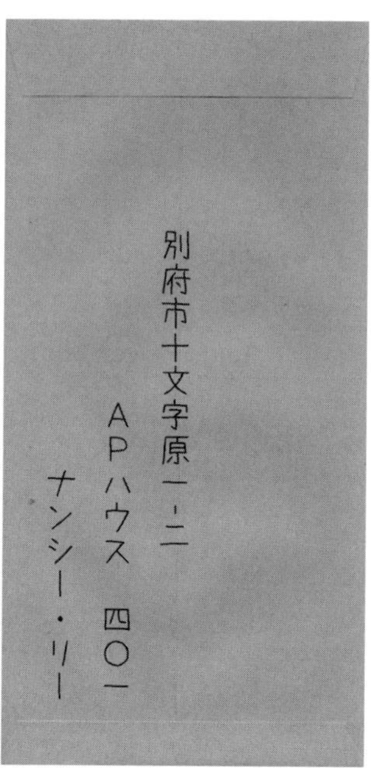

① Destination

なまえ（Name）　　　：山田一郎(ろう)

※～様(さま) is used after the name of the adressee when writing an adress on an envelope.

じゅうしょ（Address）：京都市北区等持院(きょうとしきたくとうじいん) ____ - ____ - ____ ハイツ森山 ______

② Sender

なまえ（Name）　　　：ナンシー・リー

じゅうしょ（Address）：別府市十文字原(べっぷしじゅうもんじばる) ______ - ______ APハウス ______

IV - 2. Map

Look at the picture below and write the appropriate word.

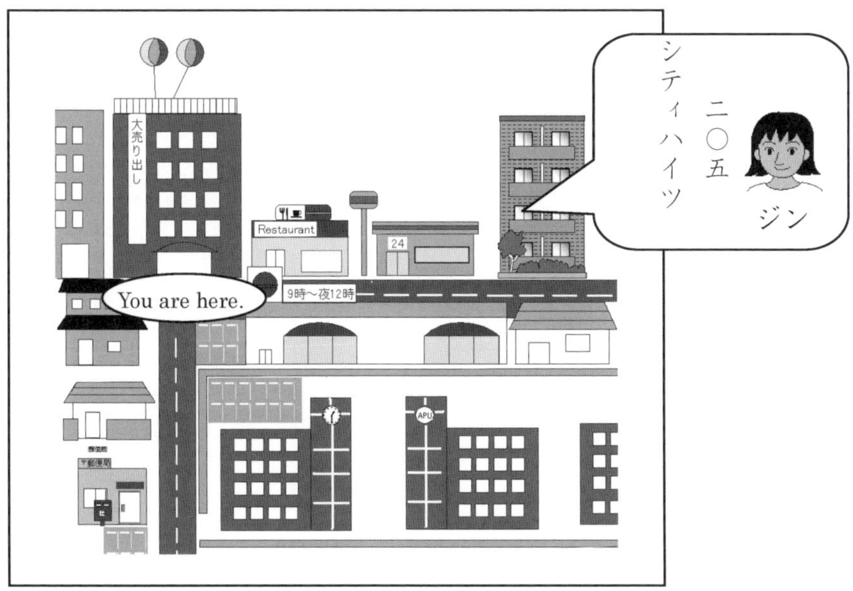

(1) ジンさんのへやはどこですか。　シティハイツの ＿＿＿＿＿＿ です。

(2) レストランはどこですか。　＿＿＿＿＿＿＿＿＿＿ のひだりです。

(3) デパートはどこですか。　＿＿＿＿＿＿＿＿＿＿ のひだりです。

(4) ゆうびんきょくはどこですか。　＿＿＿＿＿＿＿＿＿＿ のちかくです。

V. Challenge: Real life Kanji

➢ Menu（Meal Prices）

Look at the picture of a menu below and read the price in Kanji.

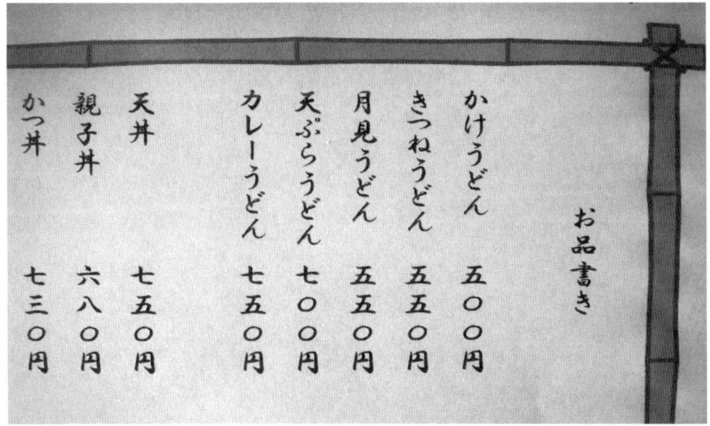

Topic 3　今何時ですか

Ⅰ. Kanji Reading and Writing

◇ mark means that this Kanji is in Ⅲ-1.

1	月 / 月	ノ 刀 月 月 ◇	(4)
	moon/month		
Kun	つき	月（moon/month）	
On	ゲツ、ガツ	月曜日（Monday）、1月（January）、1か月（one month）	

2	火 / 火	丶 丷 ⺌ 火 ◇	(4)
	fire		
Kun	ひ	火（fire）	
On	カ	火曜日（Tuesday）	

3	水 / 水	亅 才 才 水 ◇	(4)
	water		
Kun	みず	水（water）	
On	スイ	水曜日（Wednesday）、水泳（swimming）	

4	金 / 金	ノ 八 亼 亼 今 今 佘 金 ◇	(8)
	money/gold		
Kun	かね	お金（money）	
On	キン	金曜日（Friday）	

5	土 / 土	一 十 土 ◇	(3)
	soil		
Kun	つち	土（ground）	
On	ド	土曜日（Saturday）	

6	日	日	丨 冂 月 日 ① (4)
	sun/day		
Kun	ひ、び、(か)		日(ひ) (sun/day)
On	ニチ、ニ、ニッ		一日(いちにち) (one day)、日曜日(にちようび) (Sunday)、 日本(にほん)／日本(にっぽん) (Japan)、*一日(ついたち) (1st day of a month)

7	時	時	丨 冂 月 日 日一 日十 日土 日土 時 時 (10)
	time		
Kun	(とき)		
On	ジ		1時(いちじ) (one o'clock)

8	分	分	ノ 八 分 分 ① (4)
	minute/divide		
Kun	わ-かる		分(わ)かります (to understand)
On	フン、プン、 ブン		1時5分(いちじごふん) (one five)、10分(じっぷん) (ten minutes)

9	半	半	丶 丷 䒑 兰 半 (5)
	half		
Kun			
On	ハン		1時半(いちじはん) (half past one)、半分(はんぶん) (half)

10	間	間	丨 卩 尸 尸 尸' 門 門 門 門 門 間 間 ① (12)
	between/interval		
Kun	あいだ、(ま)		間(あいだ) (between)
On	カン		時間(じかん) (time)、1時間(いちじかん) (one hour)

11	何	何	ノ イ 仁 仃 伒 佢 何 ◇I (7)
	what		
Kun	なに、なん		何(なに) (what)、何時(なんじ) (what time)、何曜日(なんようび) (what day of the week)、何日(なんにち) (what day of the month/how long)
On			

12	今	今	ノ 人 亼 今 (4)
	present/this		
Kun	いま		今(いま) (now)
On	コン		今月(こんげつ) (this month)、*今日(きょう) (today)

13	休	休	ノ イ 仁 什 休 休 ◇I (6)
	rest		
Kun	やす - む		休(やす)みます (to take a rest)、休(やす)み (rest)
On	キュウ		休日(きゅうじつ) (holiday)

II. Katakana Words

	vocabulary		meaning		vocabulary		meaning
1	クイズ	N	quiz	2	テスト	N V	examination
3	ワークショップ	N	workshop	4	スケジュール	N	schedule

Ⅲ. Kanji and Vocabulary Exercises

Ⅲ - 1. Memorize the Kanji as an image

Write the reading and Kanji seeing each picture as shown in the example.

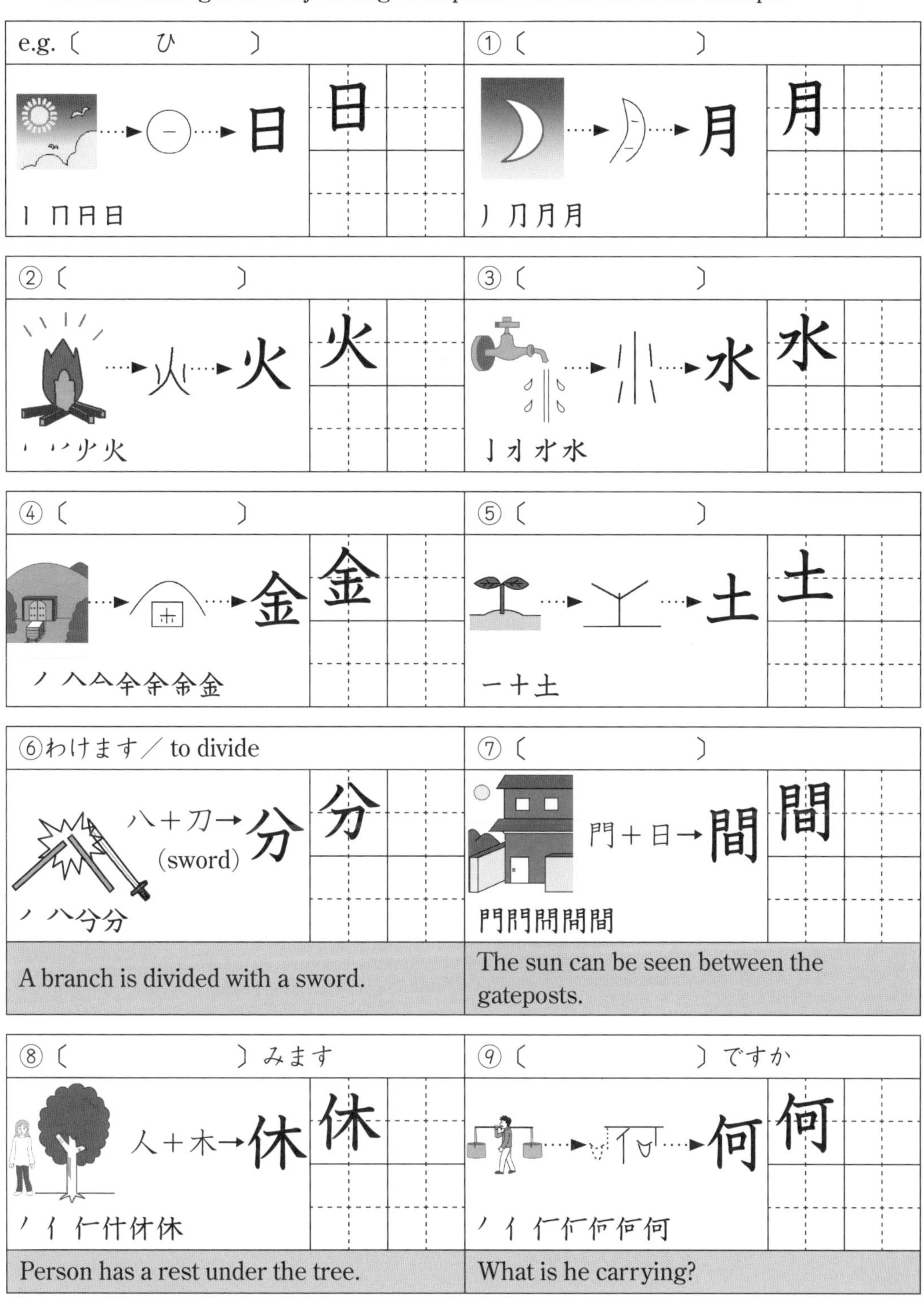

III - 2. Day of the week

Match a word with the appropriate day of the week. Also write the reading of the vocabulary in Hiragana.

(1)　Sun.　・　　・　火曜日（よう）〔　　　〕
(2)　Mon.　・　　・　日曜日（よう）〔　　　〕
(3)　Tue.　・　　・　月曜日（よう）〔　　　〕
(4)　Wed.　・　　・　水曜日（よう）〔　　　〕
(5)　Thu.　・　　・　金曜日（よう）〔　　　〕
(6)　Fri.　・　　・　土曜日（よう）〔　　　〕
(7)　Sat.　・　　・　木曜日（よう）〔　　　〕

IV. Exercises in context

IV - 1. Time expressions

Look at the following times and write the sentences as in the example.

(e.g.)

12時15分　です。
〔じゅうにじじゅうごふん〕

(1)

＿＿＿＿＿＿　です。
〔　　　〕

(2)

＿＿＿＿＿＿　です。
〔　　　〕

(3) September 1st

＿＿＿＿＿＿　です。
〔　　　〕

(4) May 2nd

＿＿＿＿＿＿　です。
〔　　　〕

(5) November 6th

＿＿＿＿＿＿　です。
〔　　　〕

IV - 2. Time schedule

Exercise A

Look at the following schedule and fill in the blanks with the appropriate word.

おととい (Tue.)	昨日（きのう） (Wed.)	今日 (Thu.)	明日（あした） (Fri.)	あさって (Sat.)
10：35 – 12：10 日本語（にほんご）	12：25 – 2：00 ワークショップ テスト	8：45 – 10：20 日本語（にほんご）	10：35 – 12：10 日本語（にほんご） かんじクイズ	休み

(1) 今日は何曜(よう)日ですか。　　　________曜(よう)日です。

(2) おとといは何曜(よう)日でしたか。　　　________曜(よう)日でした。

(3) 土曜(よう)日は__________ですか。　　　はい、そうです。

(4) いつ、かんじクイズがありますか。　　　________曜(よう)日です。

(5) ________曜(よう)日はテストがありましたか。　　　はい、ありました。

Exercise B

Complete the following sentences about your class schedule for yesterday and tomorrow with the appropriate Kanji vocabulary that you learned.

今日は__________月__________日です。__________曜(よう)日です。
昨日(きのう)、______________________のじゅぎょうがありました。
__________のじゅぎょうは__________から______________までです。
明日(あした)、______________________のじゅぎょうがあります。
__________のじゅぎょうは____________から____________までです。

V. Challenge: Real life Kanji

➢ Business hours

Look at the picture below and circle the Kanji that you learned. And explain about the information on the board using the expression pattern in the [ ] with your partner.

(1) びょういん

______曜(よう)日と______曜(よう)日は
______から______までです。
______曜(よう)日は休みです。

(2) みせ

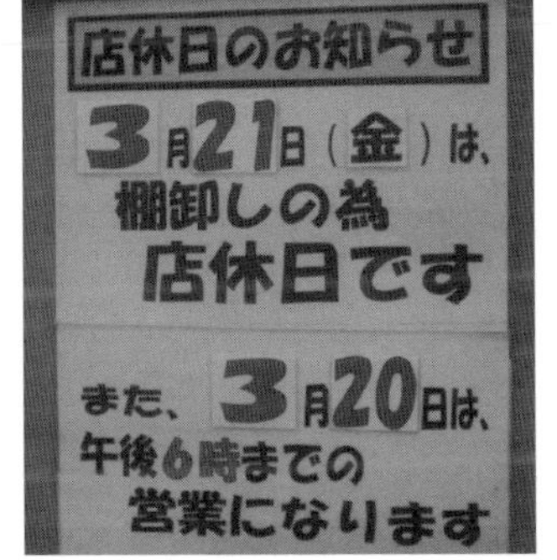

______月______日、______曜(よう)日は
______です。
______月______日は______までです。

Topic 4　どのぐらいかかりますか

Ⅰ. Kanji Reading and Writing

◇ mark means that this Kanji is in Ⅲ-1.

1	車	車	一 厂 戸 百 亘 亘 車 ◇ (7)
	vehicle		
Kun	くるま		車(くるま) (car)
On	シャ		自動車(じどうしゃ) (automobile)、自転車(じてんしゃ) (bicycle)

2	電	電	一 厂 戸 币 雨 雨 雨 雨 雪 雪 雪 雪 電 ◇ (13)
	electricity		
Kun			
On	デン		電車(でんしゃ) (train)、電話(でんわ) (telephone)、電気(でんき) (electricity)

3	円	円	丨 冂 冂 円 (4)
	yen/circle		
Kun	エン		五千円(ごせんえん) (5000yen)、五百円(ごひゃくえん) (500yen)、百円(ひゃくえん) (100yen)
On			

4	朝	朝	一 十 𠂇 古 古 吉 直 卓 卓 朝 朝 朝 ◇ (12)
	morning		
Kun	あさ		朝(あさ) (morning)、朝ご飯(あさごはん) (breakfast)、*今朝(けさ) (this morning)
On	(チョウ)		

5	昼	昼	一 コ 尸 尺 尺 尽 昼 昼 昼 (9)
	daytime		
Kun	ひる		昼(ひる) (the daytime)、昼ご飯(ひるごはん) (lunch)
On	(チュウ)		

6	夕 / 夕 evening	ノクタ ◇I (3)
Kun	ゆう	夕方 (evening)、夕べ (last night)
On		

7	晩 / 晩 night	丨 冂 日 日 日' 日" 日ᐟ 晗 晗 晗 晩 晩 (12)
Kun		
On	バン	晩 (night)、今晩 (tonight)、晩ご飯 (supper)

8	夜 / 夜 night	' 亠 广 疒 夜 夜 夜 夜 ◇I (8)
Kun	よる、(よ)	夜 (night)
On	ヤ	今夜 (tonight)

9	正 / 正 right	一 丅 下 正 正 ◇I (5)
Kun	ただ-しい	正しい (right/correct)
On	ショウ、(セイ)	正午 (noon)

10	午 / 午 noon	ノ 𠂉 𠂉 午 (4)
Kun		
On	ゴ	午前 (forenoon)、午後 (afternoon)

11	曜	曜	丨 日 日 日 日 日 日 日 日 日 日 日 日 日 日 曜 曜 曜 (18)
	day of the week		
Kun			
On	ヨウ		～曜日(ようび)［suffix; day of the week］…月曜日(げつようび)（Monday）

12	週	週	丿 冂 月 月 用 用 周 周 周 调 週 ◇I (11)
	week		
Kun			
On	シュウ		先週(せんしゅう)(last week)、今週(こんしゅう)(this week)、来週(らいしゅう)(next week)、一週間(いっしゅうかん)（one week）、週末(しゅうまつ)（weekend）

13	年	年	丿 𠂉 ⺧ 左 乍 年 ◇I (6)
	year		
Kun	とし		今年(ことし)（this year）、年(とし)（year/age）
On	ネン		2009年(ねん)(year of 2009)、来年(らいねん)(next year)、一年(いちねん)(one year)

14	去	去	一 十 土 去 去 (5)
	past		
Kun	（さ-る）		
On	キョ、（コ）		去年(きょねん)（last year）

15	毎	毎	丿 𠂉 𠂉 每 每 毎 (6)
	every		
Kun			
On	マイ		毎日(まいにち)（every day）、毎週(まいしゅう)（ever week）、毎月(まいつき)（every month）、毎年(まいとし)（every year）

Ⅱ. Katakana Words

	vocabulary		meaning		vocabulary		meaning
1	バス	N	bus	2	タクシー	N	taxi
3	フェリー	N	ferry	4	バイク	N	motorbike

Radical of Kanji

Most of Kanji are made from several parts. One of the most important parts is the "Radical" (ぶしゅ). Every radical has each meaning and style. When you learn Kanji, you may pay attention to the radical.

1	へん (left part of the radical)	亻	→	休
2	つくり (right part of the radical)	月	→	朝
3	かんむり (upper part of the radical)	亠	→	夜
4	あし (bottom part of the radical)	儿	→	先
5	たれ (upper left part of the radical)	广	→	広
6	にょう (lower left part of the radical)	辶	→	週
7	かまえ (enclosure part of the radical)	門	→	間
		口	→	国

Ⅲ. Kanji and Vocabulary Exercises

Ⅲ - 1. Memorize the Kanji as an image

Write the reading and Kanji seeing each picture as shown in the example.

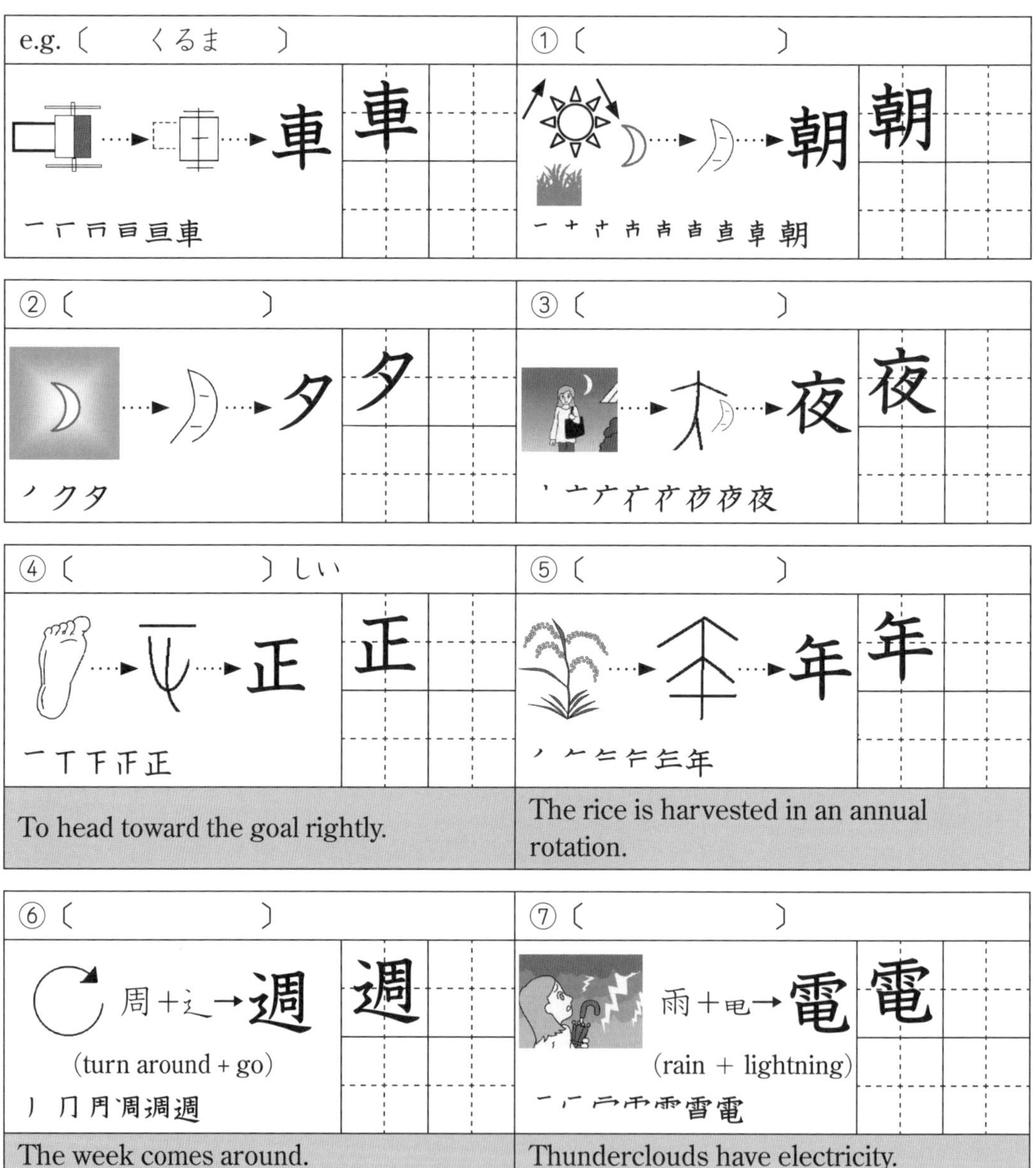

Ⅲ - 2. The meaning of Kanji parts and their combination

Match the Kanji Part A and Part B. Then write Kanji by combining them.

	(Part A)				(Part B)	
(1)	雨	(rain)	▀	·	· 卓	＿＿＿＿
(2)	月	(moon)	▐	·	· 翟	＿＿＿＿
(3)	辶	(go)	▙	·	· 电	＿＿＿＿
(4)	日	(sun)	▌	·	· 周	＿＿＿＿

Ⅲ - 3. Time word 1

Choose the appropriate Kanji from the ☐, put it on the＿＿. And write the reading of the Kanji in Hiragana in the〔　　〕.

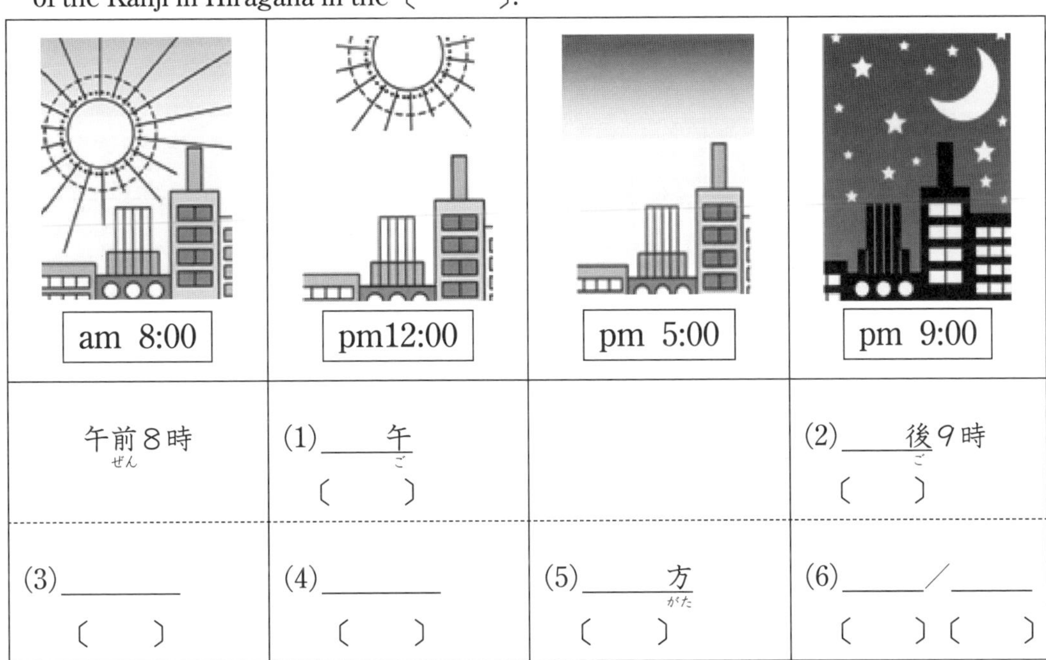

am 8:00	pm12:00	pm 5:00	pm 9:00
午前(ぜん)8時	(1)＿＿午(ご) 〔　　〕		(2)＿＿後(ご)9時 〔　　〕
(3)＿＿＿＿ 〔　　〕	(4)＿＿＿＿ 〔　　〕	(5)＿＿方(がた) 〔　　〕	(6)＿＿／＿＿ 〔　　〕〔　　〕

夕・晩・正・朝・昼・夜・午

Ⅲ - 4. Time word 2

Look at the calendar below and write the appropriate time word. Put its Kanji on the ＿＿, and the reading of the Kanji in Hiragana in the〔　　　〕.

(きょう → 11)

2017年10月						
Sun.	Mon.	Tue.	Wed.	Thu.	Fri.	Sat.
1	2	3	4	5	6	7
8	9	10	(11)	12	13	14
15	16	17	18	19	20	21
22	23	24	25	26	27	28
29	30	31				

Year			Month		
2016年	＿＿	〔　　　〕	9月	先月	せんげつ
2017年	＿＿	〔　　　〕	10月	今月	こんげつ
2018年	来(らい)年	〔　　　〕	11月	来(らい)月	〔　　　〕
Week			**The day of the week**		
10／5	＿＿	〔　　　〕	きのう	＿＿	〔　　　〕
10／12	＿＿	〔　　　〕	きょう	水曜日	〔　　　〕
10／19	来(らい)週	〔　　　〕	あした	＿＿	〔　　　〕

Ⅲ - 5. Vehicle

Fill in the blanks with the appropriate word. Put Kanji on the＿＿ and Hiragana in the〔　　〕.

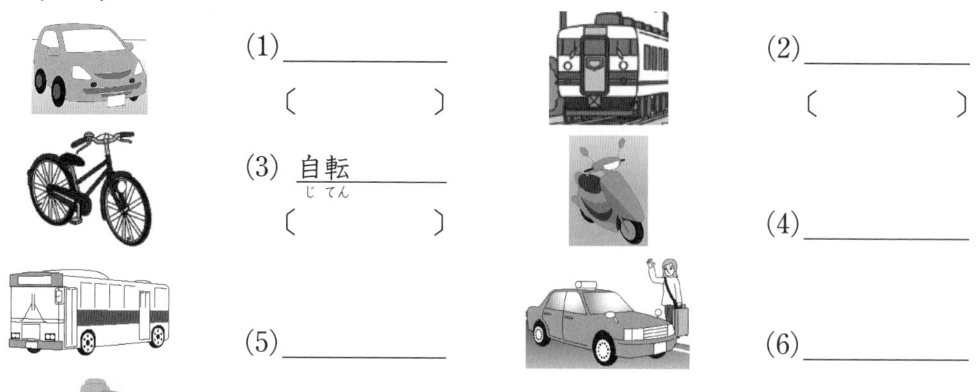

(1) ＿＿＿＿〔　　　〕

(2) ＿＿＿＿〔　　　〕

(3) 自転(じてん)＿＿〔　　　〕

(4) ＿＿＿＿

(5) ＿＿＿＿

(6) ＿＿＿＿

(7) ＿＿＿＿

Ⅳ. Exercises in context

Choose the appropriate word from the [ ], and put its Kanji on the____.

(1)

《私の日曜日》

日曜日、①__________で森山えきまでいきます。森山えきまで400②__________です。

(2)

《ジンさんの毎日》

私は③__________8時におきます。午前(ぜん)10時35分から12時10分までべんきょうします。

土曜日と日曜日は休みです。

④__________、⑤__________に友達(だち)の⑥__________でスーパーへいきます。スーパーでかいものします。

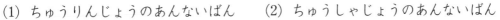

まいしゅう ・ まいにち ・ でんしゃ ・ くるま ・ どようび ・ えん

Ⅴ. Challenge: Real life Kanji

➢ Parking

Look at the pictures below and circle the Kanji that you learned.

(1) ちゅうりんじょうのあんないばん

(2) ちゅうしゃじょうのあんないばん

Topic 5　じゅぎょうはどうですか

Ⅰ. Kanji Reading and Writing

◇① mark means that this Kanji is in Ⅲ-1.

1	本	本	一十才木本 (5)
	book		
Kun	もと		山本(やまもと) (Japanese surname)
On	ホン		本(ほん) (book)、日本(にほん) (Japan)、日本語(にほんご) (Japanese language)、日本人(にほんじん) (Japanese people)

2	英	英	一十廾艹艹芇苎英英 (8)
	england		
Kun			
On	エイ		英語(えいご) (English language)

3	語	語	丶亠亠亠言言言訁訂訂語語語語 (14)
	language/word		
Kun	(かた - る)		
On	ゴ		～語(ご) [suffix; language] … 中国語(ちゅうごくご) (Chinese language)

4	文	文	丶亠ナ文 ◇① (4)
	letter/writings		
Kun			
On	ブン、(モン)		文(ぶん) (sentence)、文化(ぶんか) (culture)、文法(ぶんぽう) (grammar)

5	漢	漢	漢 (13)
	chinese		
Kun			
On	カン		漢字（かんじ）（Kanji）

6	字	字	字 ◇I (6)
	character		
Kun			
On	ジ		字（じ）（letter）、文字（もじ）（character）、数字（すうじ）（number/figure）

7	見	見	見 ◇I (7)
	see		
Kun	み - る		見（み）ます（to see/to look/to watch）
On	（ケン）		

8	聞	聞	聞 ◇I (14)
	hear		
Kun	き - く		聞（き）きます（to listen/to hear/to ask）
On	ブン		新聞（しんぶん）（newspaper）

9	読	読	読 (14)
	read		
Kun	よ - む		読（よ）みます（to read）
On	ドク		読書（どくしょ）（reading）、読書（どくしょ）します（to read a book）

10	書	書	書 (10)
	write/book		
Kun	か - く		書(か)きます (to write)
On	ショ		辞書(じしょ) (dictionary)、教科書(きょうかしょ) (textbook)

11	使	使	ノ イ 亻 亻 使 使 使 使 (8)
	use		
Kun	つか - う		使(つか)います (to use)
On	(シ)		

12	大	大	一 ナ 大 ◇1 (3)
	big		
Kun	おお - きい		大(おお)きい (big/large)、*大人(おとな) (adult)
On	ダイ、(タイ)		大学(だいがく) (university)、大学院(だいがくいん) (graduate school)

13	小	小	亅 小 小 ◇1 (3)
	small		
Kun	ちい - さい		小(ちい)さい (small)
On	ショウ		小学校(しょうがっこう) (elementary school)

14	忙	忙	丶 丷 忄 忄 忙 忙 (6)
	busy		
Kun	いそが - しい		忙(いそが)しい (busy)
On	(ボウ)		

15	広	広	' 亠广広広 (5)
	wide		
Kun	ひろ - い		広い (spacious/wide) ひろ
On	(コウ)		

16	楽	楽	' 亻 白 白 白 泊 泊 泊' 泊 泊 楽 楽 楽 (13)
	pleasure/music		
Kun	たの - しい		楽しい (enjoyable/delightful/pleasant) たの
On	ガク、(ラク)		音楽 (music) おんがく

II. Katakana Words

	vocabulary		meaning		vocabulary		meaning
1	コンピューター	N	computer	2	ノート	N	notebook
3	ペン	N	pen/marker	4	テレビ	N	television

III. Kanji and Vocabulary Exercises

III - 1. Remember the Kanji as an image

Write the reading and Kanji seeing each picture as shown in the example.

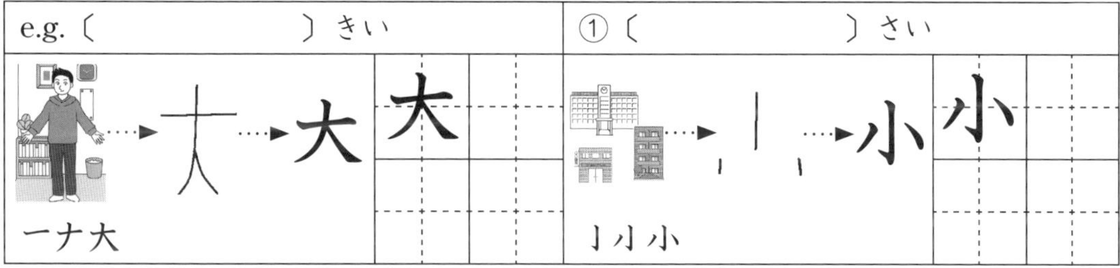

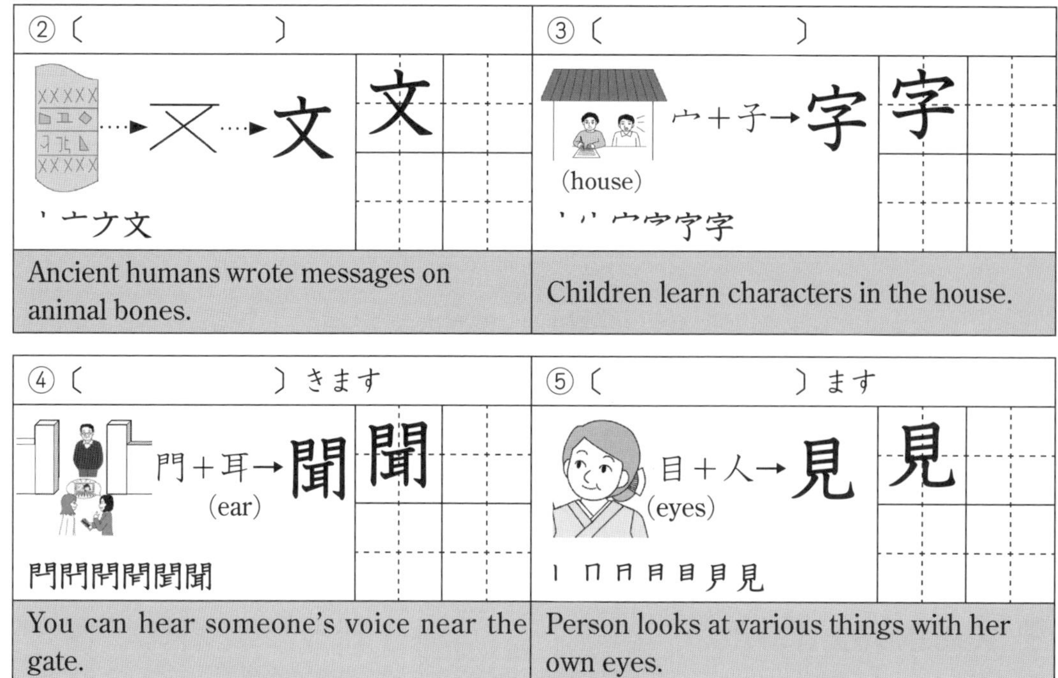

②〔　　　　　　〕
文
丶亠ナ文
③〔　　　　　　〕
宀＋子→字
字
(house)
丶丶宀宁字字
Ancient humans wrote messages on animal bones.
Children learn characters in the house.

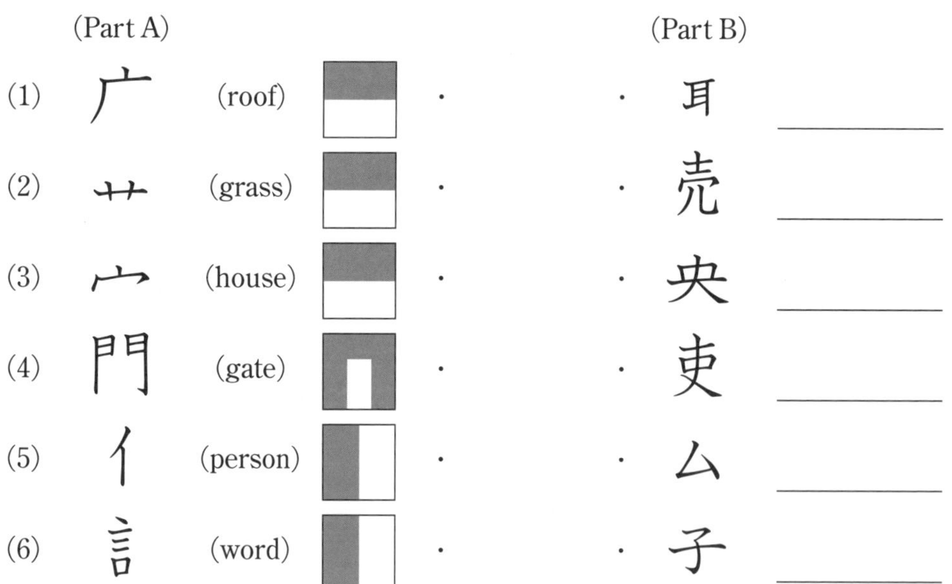

④〔　　　　　　〕きます
門＋耳→聞
聞
(ear)
門門門門聞聞
⑤〔　　　　　　〕ます
目＋人→見
見
(eyes)
丨冂月月目貝見
You can hear someone's voice near the gate.
Person looks at various things with her own eyes.

Ⅲ - 2.　The meaning of Kanji parts and their combination

Match the Kanji Part A and Part B. Then write Kanji by combining them.

	(Part A)				(Part B)	
(1)	广	(roof)	・	・	耳	________
(2)	艹	(grass)	・	・	売	________
(3)	宀	(house)	・	・	央	________
(4)	門	(gate)	・	・	吏	________
(5)	亻	(person)	・	・	ム	________
(6)	言	(word)	・	・	子	________

Ⅲ - 3. Kanji Exercises

Look at the pictures and choose the appropriate Kanji from the [ ]. Then write the word by using Kanji and Hiragana as in the example.

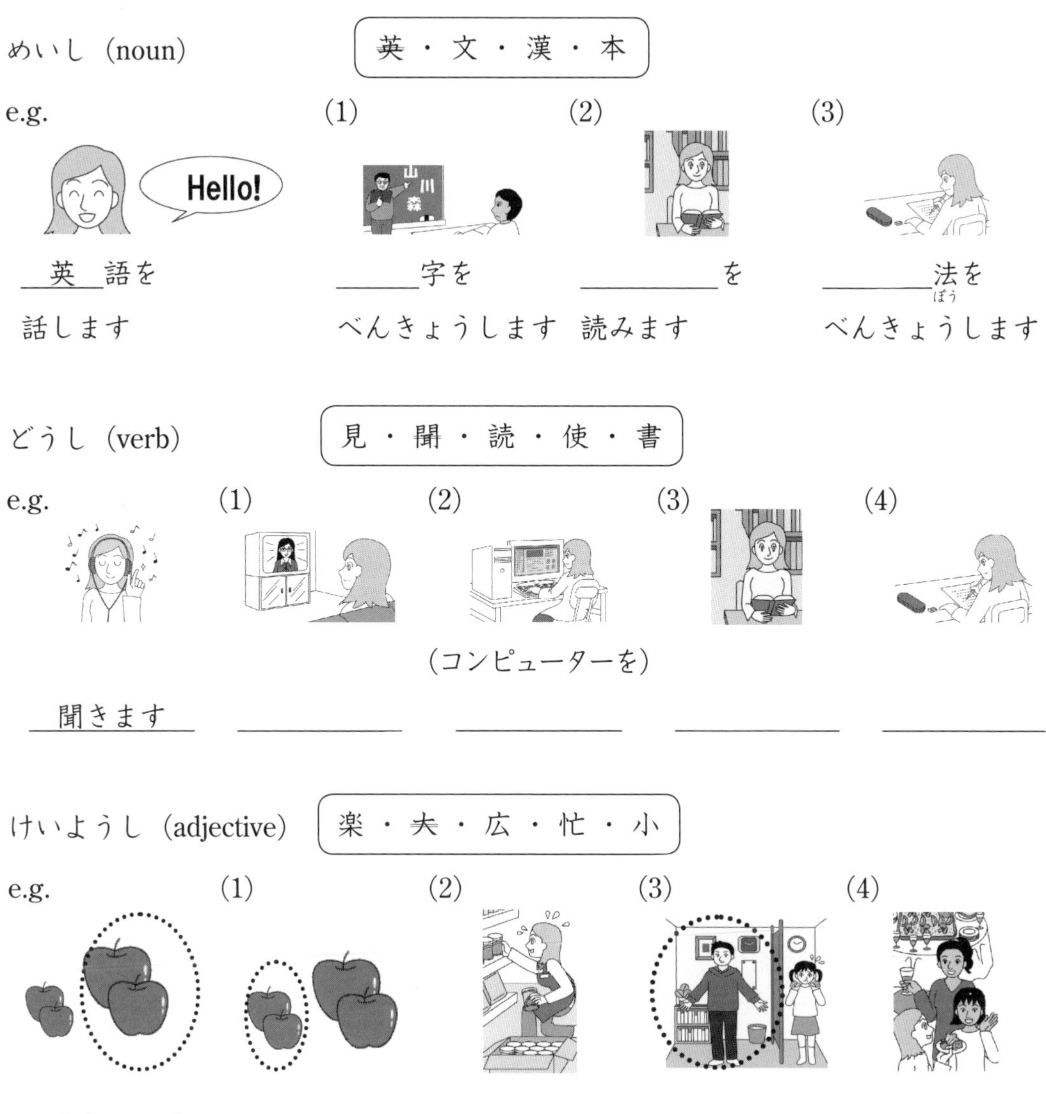

Ⅳ. Exercises in context

Exercise A

Choose the appropriate word from the [ ], and put its Kanji on the____. You may use each word only once.

(1)

《大学のべんきょう》

私は大学で①__________をべんきょうします。

②________はむずかしいです。

明日(あした)、クイズがあります。今日はとても③__________です。

(2)

《土曜日》

今日、友達(だち)のへやで音(おん)楽を④____________。

それから、⑤_______の本も⑥_____________。

明日(あした)は、友達(だち)とえいがを⑦____________。

えいご・ききました・よみました・みます・かんじ・いそがしい・にほんご

Exercise B

Write about your Japanese study with the appropriate vocabulary that you learned. Use Kanji as much as possible.

私は毎日__________で____________をべんきょうします。

今週の____________に____________のクイズがあります。

日本語のべんきょうは______________ですが、__________です。

V. Challenge: Real life Kanji

➢ The goods used by students

Look at the pictures below and circle the Kanji that you learned.

(1) 電子辞書

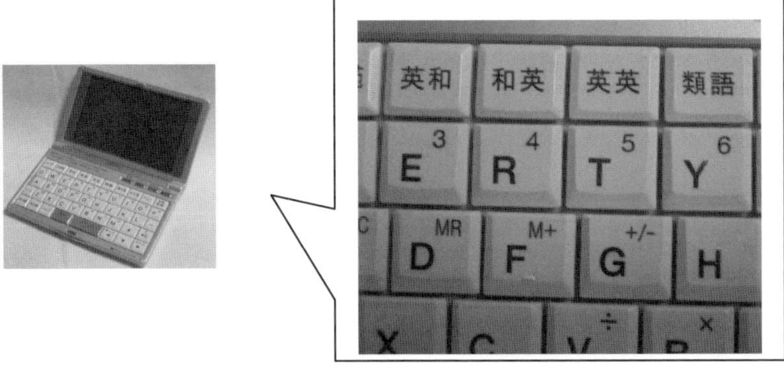

(2) 教科書

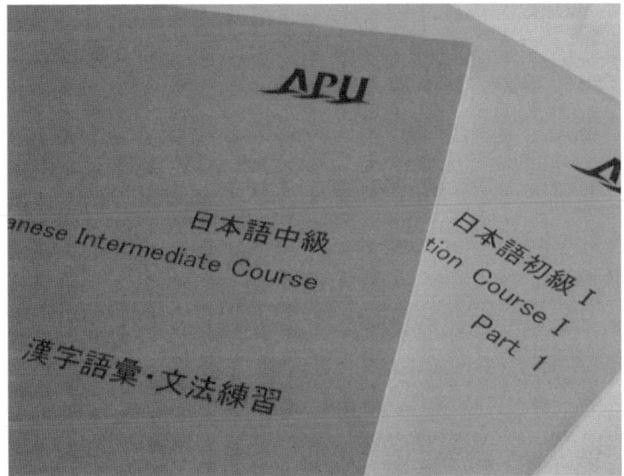

Topic 6　どこでかいますか

Ⅰ. Kanji Reading and Writing

◇ mark means that this Kanji is in Ⅲ-1.

1	上	上	ｌ ト 上 ◇ (3)
	up		
Kun	うえ、(あ-がる、の-ぼる)		上（うえ）(up)、年上（としうえ）(elder)
On	ジョウ		上手な（じょうず）(skillfull/be good at)

2	下	下	一 丅 下 ◇ (3)
	down		
Kun	した、(さ-がる、お-りる)		下（した）(down)、年下（としした）(younger)
On	(カ、ゲ)		*下手な（へた）(unskillfull)

3	右	右	ノ ナ ナ 右 右 ◇ (5)
	right		
Kun	みぎ		右（みぎ）(right)、右側（みぎがわ）(right side)
On	(ユウ、ウ)		

4	左	左	一 ナ ナ 左 左 ◇ (5)
	left		
Kun	ひだり		左（ひだり）(left)、左側（ひだりがわ）(left side)
On	(サ)		

5	前	前	丶 丷 䒑 产 前 前 前 前 前 (9)
	before		
Kun	まえ		前[まえ]（front）、３時間前[じかんまえ]（three hours ago）
On	ゼン		午前[ごぜん]（before noon）

6	後	後	ノ ク 彳 彳 𢓜 𢓜 徉 後 後 (9)
	after		
Kun	うし-ろ、あと		後[うし]ろ（back）、後[あと]で（after/later）
On	ゴ、コウ		午後[ごご]（afternoon）、３時間後[じかんご]（3 hours later）、後輩[こうはい]（junior）

7	中	中	丨 口 口 中 ◇I (4)
	middle/in		
Kun	なか		中[なか]（inside）
On	チュウ、ジュウ		中学校[ちゅうがっこう]（junior high school）、一日中[いちにちじゅう]（all day long）

8	外	外	ノ ク タ 外 外 (5)
	outside		
Kun	そと		外[そと]（outside）
On	ガイ、（ゲ）		外国[がいこく]（foreign country）、外国人[がいこくじん]（foreigner）

9	男	男	丨 口 日 田 田 男 男 ◇I (7)
	man		
Kun	おとこ		男[おとこ]の人[ひと]（man）、男[おとこ]の子[こ]（boy）
On	ダン、（ナン）		男性[だんせい]（male）

10	女	女	く 夂 女 ◇I (3)
	woman		
Kun	おんな		女(おんな)の人(ひと) (woman)、女(おんな)の子(こ) (girl)
On	ジョ		女性(じょせい) (female)、彼女(かのじょ) (she/girl friend)

11	子	子	㇇ 了 子 ◇I (3)
	child		
Kun	こ		子供(こども) (child)
On	(シ)		

12	若	若	一 十 艹 艹 芐 芐 若 若 (8)
	young		
Kun	わか-い		若(わか)い (young)、若者(わかもの) (young person)
On			

13	物	物	ノ 𠂉 牛 牛 牜 物 物 物 (8)
	thing		
Kun	もの		物(もの) (thing)、食(た)べ物(もの) (food)、飲(の)み物(もの) (beverage)
On	ブツ		動物(どうぶつ) (animal)

14	花	花	一 十 艹 艹 芢 芲 花 ◇I (7)
	flower		
Kun	はな		花(はな) (flower)、花火(はなび) (fireworks)
On	カ		花(か)びん (flower vase)

15	絵	絵	〈 幺 幺 糸 糸 糸 糸 紒 紒 絵 絵 絵 (12)
	picture		
Kun			
On	エ		絵(え) (drawing/painting)

16	細	細	〈 幺 幺 糸 糸 糸 糸 糿 紃 細 細 (11)
	slender		
Kun	ほそ-い		細(ほそ)い (slender/thin)
On	(サイ)		

Ⅱ. Katakana Words

	vocabulary		meaning		vocabulary		meaning
1	ボールペン	N	ball point pen	2	ホチキス	N	stapler
3	シャープペンシル	N	mechanical pencil				

Ⅲ. Kanji and Vocabulary Exercises

Ⅲ - 1. Memorize the Kanji as an image

Write the reading and Kanji seeing each picture as shown in the example.

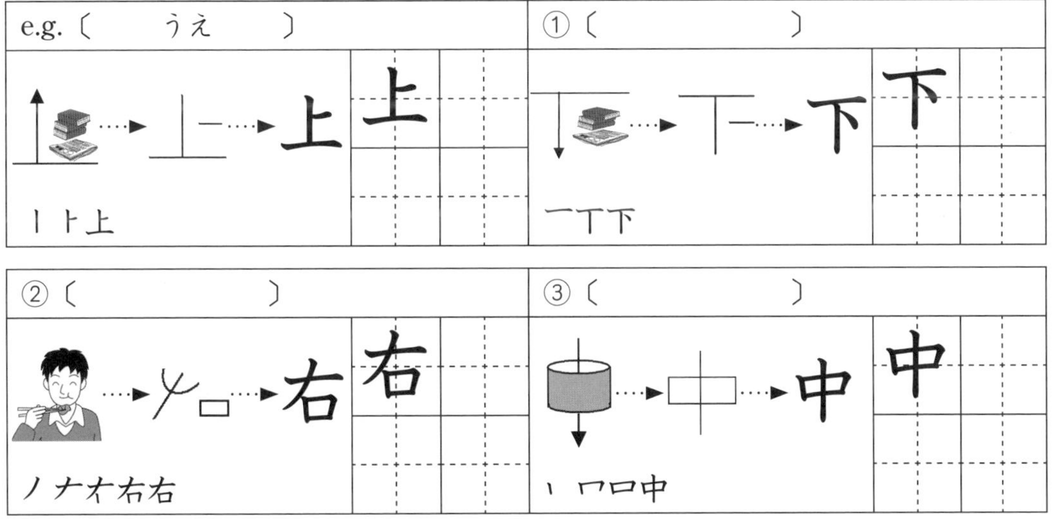

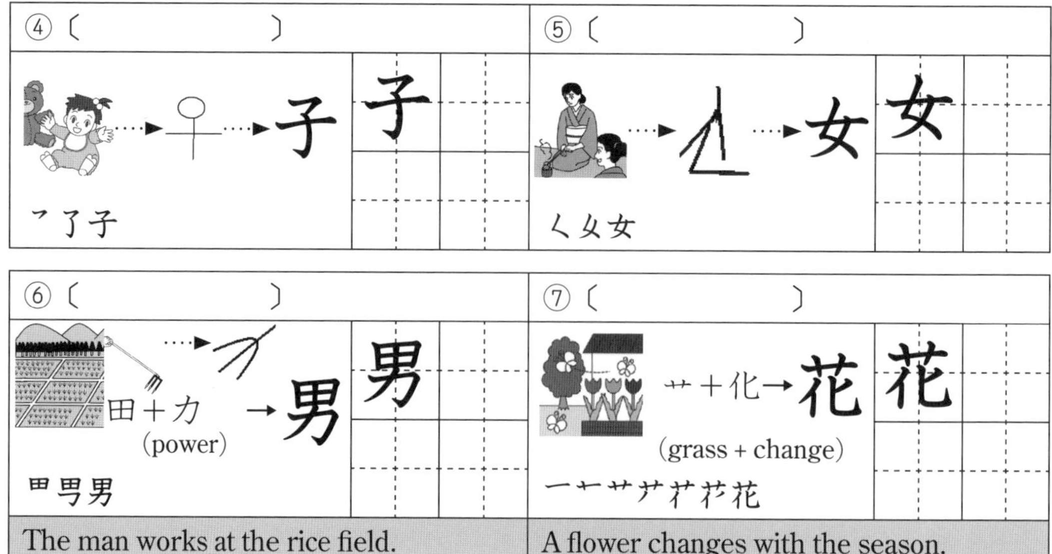

Ⅲ - 2.　Location word

Fill in the blanks with an appropriate Kanji as in the example.

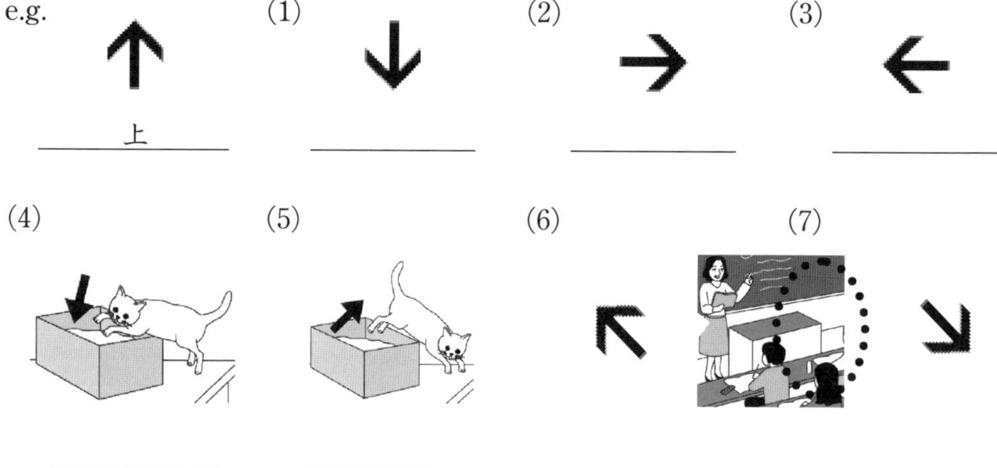

Ⅲ - 3. The meaning of Kanji parts and its combination

Match the Kanji Part A and Part B. Then write Kanji by combining them.

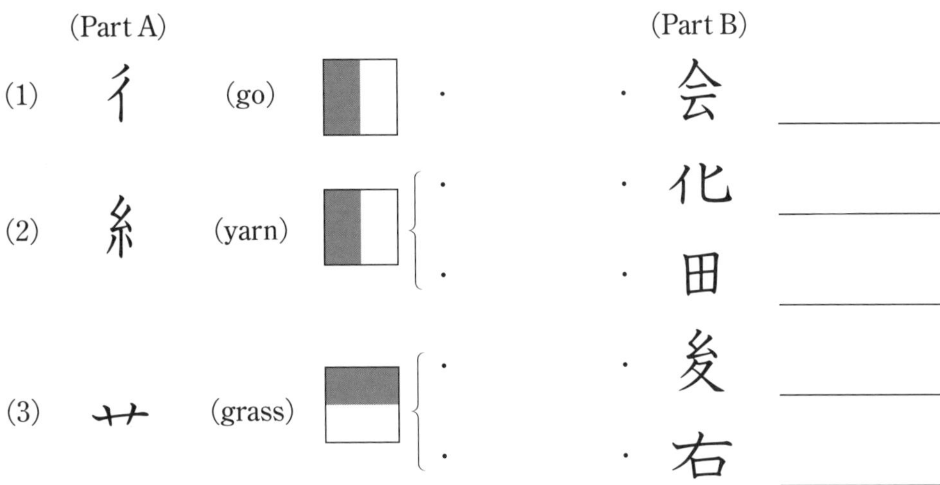

Ⅲ - 4. People

Look at the pictures and choose two appropriate Kanji from the ☐.

Then write their reading in Hiragana.

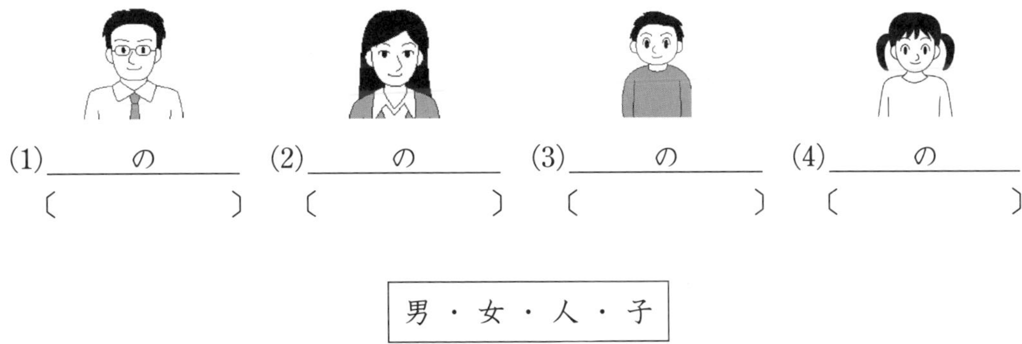

Ⅳ. Exercises in context

Ⅳ - 1. Location

Choose the appropriate word from the [　　], and put its Kanji on the ______.

(1)

ここはリーさんのへやです。今、テーブルの上にはナイフとフォークがあります。さら（plate）も２まいあります。食(た)べ①________はありません。

リーさんのへやには小さい本だなもあります。本だなの上に人形(にんぎょう)（doll）と②__________があります。人形(にんぎょう)（doll）の左に③________があります。

え・はな・もの

(2)

(You are explaining the picture to your family.)

パクさんは私の友達(だち)です。

パクさんは①________の人です。

パクさんはチョウさんの②________にいます。

チョウさんは③________男の人です。

シンさんは大きい男の人です。

シンさんの④________にプロイさんがいます。

プロイさんは細い⑤________の人です。

プロイさんはチョウさんの⑥________にいます。

おとこ・おんな・わかい・みぎ・ひだり・うしろ

IV - 2. In the store

Fill in the blanks using the picture below. Then ask your partner where the things are.

(1) ボールペンはどこにありますか。　　ノートの＿＿＿＿＿＿＿＿にあります。

(2) ノートはどこにありますか。　　ボールペンの＿＿＿＿＿＿にあります。

(3) 食べ物はどこにありますか。　　＿＿＿＿＿＿＿＿＿＿＿＿にあります。

(4) サンドイッチの右に何がありますか。　　＿＿＿＿＿＿＿＿＿＿＿＿があります。

V. Challenge: Real life Kanji

➢ Bulding and institution

Look at the pictures below and circle the Kanji that you learned. Then use a dictionary and check the meaning of each word.

(1) たてもののいち

(2) しょうひん

Topic 7　何が好きですか

Ⅰ. Kanji Reading and Writing

◇ mark means that this Kanji is in Ⅲ-1.

1	茶	茶	一 十 艹 艾 艾 苁 茶 茶 茶 (9)
	tea		
Kun			
On	チャ、(サ)		お茶(ちゃ) (tea)、紅茶(こうちゃ) (black tea)、日本茶(にほんちゃ) (Japanese green tea)

2	酒	酒	丶 丶 氵 汀 汀 沂 洏 洒 酒 酒 (10)
	alcoholic drink		
Kun	さけ、さか		お酒(さけ) (alcoholic drink/liquor)、酒屋(さかや) (liquor store)
On	シュ		日本酒(にほんしゅ) (sake)

3	飯	飯	ノ 𠆢 𠆢 今 今 今 皀 食 飠 飣 飯 飯 (12)
	meal/cooked rice		
Kun	(めし)		
On	ハン		ご飯(はん) (cooked rice/meal)、朝ご飯(あさごはん) (breakfast)、昼ご飯(ひるごはん) (lunch)、晩ご飯(ばんごはん) (dinner/supper)

4	魚	魚	ノ ク 𠂊 𠂊 各 角 角 鱼 鱼 魚 魚 ① (11)
	fish		
Kun	さかな		魚(さかな) (fish)、魚屋(さかなや) (fish shop)
On	(ギョ)		

5	鳥	鳥	′ ⺁ 𠂆 户 户 鸟 鳥 鳥 鳥 鳥 鳥 ◇I (11)
	bird		
Kun	とり		鳥(とり) (bird)、鳥肉(とりにく) (chicken)
On	(チョウ)		

6	牛	牛	ノ 𠂉 仁 牛 ◇I (4)
	cattle		
Kun	うし		牛(うし) (cow)
On	ギュウ		牛肉(ぎゅうにく) (beef)

7	肉	肉	丨 冂 内 内 肉 肉 ◇I (6)
	meat/fresh		
Kun			
On	ニク		肉(にく) (meat)、肉屋(にくや) (meat shop)

8	米	米	丶 丷 䒑 半 米 米 ◇I (6)
	rice		
Kun	こめ		米(こめ) (rice)
On	(ベイ、マイ)		

9	食	食	ノ 人 𠆢 今 今 今 食 食 食 ◇I (9)
	eat/food		
Kun	た-べる		食(た)べます (to eat)
On	ショク		食事(しょくじ) (meal)、朝食(ちょうしょく) (breakfast)、昼食(ちゅうしょく) (lunch)、夕食(ゆうしょく) (supper)

10	飲	飲	ノ 𠆢 𠆢 今 今 今 刍 食 食 飲 飲 飲 (12)
	drink		
Kun	の - む		飲みます (to drink)
On	(イン)		

11	作	作	ノ イ 亻 作 作 作 作 (7)
	make		
Kun	つく - る		作ります (to make)
On	サク		作文 (composition/writing)

12	好	好	く 女 女 好 好 好 (6)
	like/favorable		
Kun	す - き		好きな (like/favorite)
On	(コウ)		

13	味	味	丨 口 口 口 口 吽 味 味 (8)
	taste		
Kun	あじ		味 (taste)
On	ミ		意味 (meaning)、趣味 (hobby)

14	方	方	丶 亠 方 方 (4)
	direction/way		
Kun	かた		使い方 (how to use)
On	ホウ		方法 (method/how to)、方向 (direction)、方言 (dialect)

Ⅱ. Katakana Words

	vocabulary		meaning		vocabulary		meaning
1	チョコレート	N	chocolate	2	コーヒー	N	coffee
3	ジュース	N	juice	4	カレーライス	N	curry rice

Ⅲ. Kanji and Vocabulary Exercises

Ⅲ - 1. Memorize the Kanji as an image

Write the reading and Kanji seeing each picture as shown in the example.

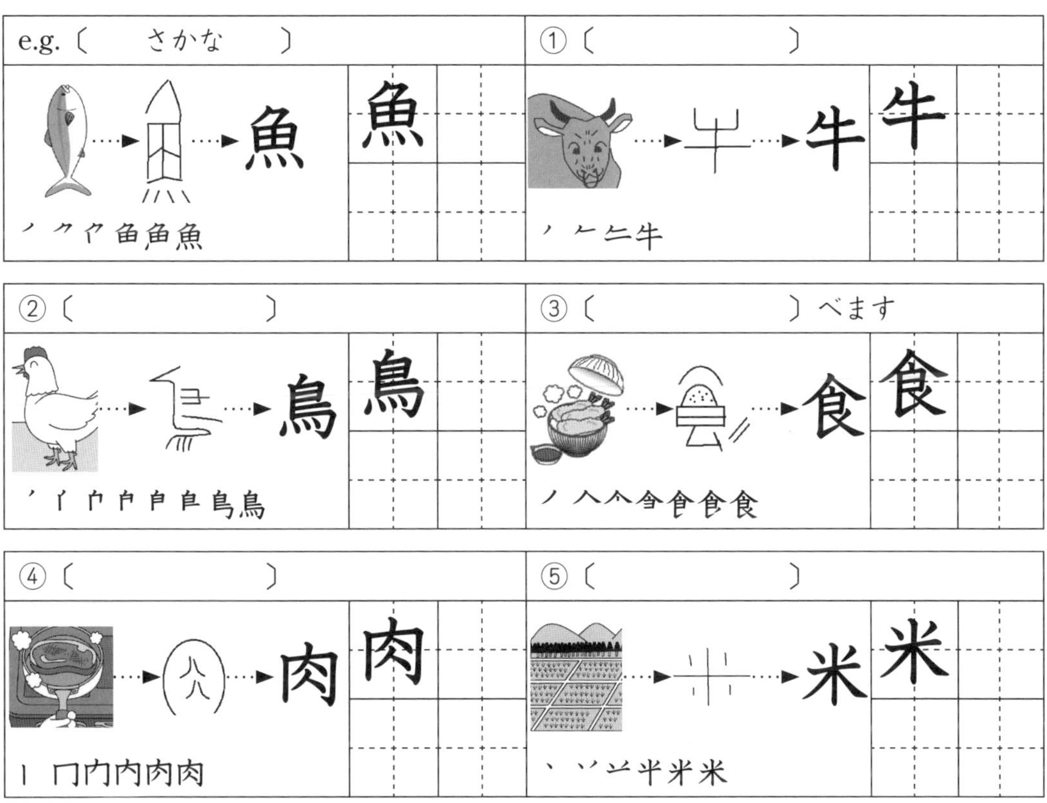

Ⅲ - 2. The meaning of Kanji parts and its combination

Match the Kanji Part A and Part B. Then write Kanji by combining them.

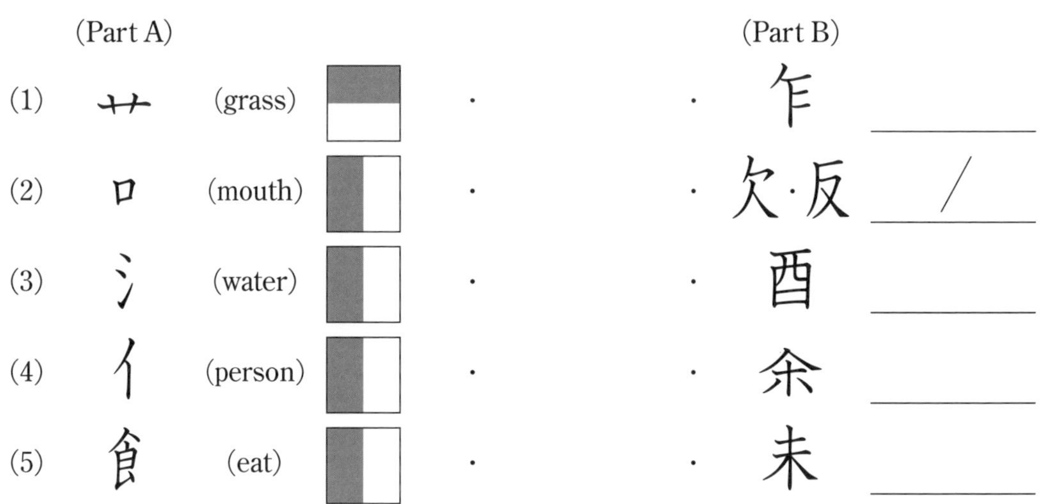

Ⅲ - 3. Kanji Exercises

Look at the pictures and choose the appropriate Kanji from the [box]. Then write the word by using Kanji and Hiragana as in the example.

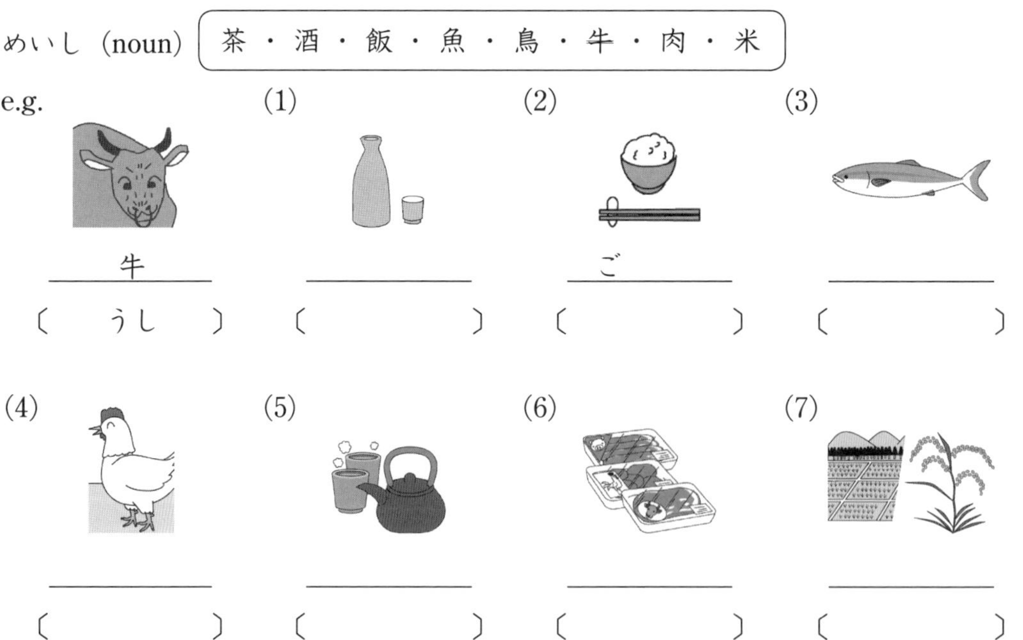

Ⅳ. Exercises in context

Ⅳ - 1. A meal

Choose the appropriate word from the ［　］ and put its Kanji on the___.

(1)

きのう、私は友達(だち)と①＿＿＿＿＿を②＿＿＿＿＿＿＿。
友達(だち)はお酒を飲みましたが、私はお茶を飲みました。
私は日本の③＿＿＿＿＿＿＿が④＿＿＿＿＿＿＿＿＿。

すきです・たべました・おちゃ・ばんごはん

(2)

日曜日、友達(だち)と⑤＿＿＿＿＿のりょうりを⑥＿＿＿＿＿＿。
私と友達(だち)は魚のりょうりが好きじゃありません。それから
⑦＿＿＿＿＿も⑧＿＿＿＿＿＿＿。とても楽しかったです。

おさけ・ぎゅうにく・たべました・のみました

IV - 2.　Questionnaire about food

Answer the following questionnaire and ask your partner.

(1)　あなたは牛肉が好きですか、鳥肉が好きですか。

□牛肉　□鳥肉　□食べません

(2)　あなたはどこで食べ物をかいますか。　＿＿＿＿＿＿＿＿

(3)　あなたは日本のお茶を飲みましたか。　□はい　□いいえ

「はい」→日本のお茶の味はどうですか。　＿＿＿＿＿＿＿＿

(4)　日本りょうりを食べましたか。　□はい　□いいえ

「はい」→どんな日本りょうりを食べましたか。　＿＿＿＿＿＿＿＿

(5)　あなたは日本りょうりの作り方がわかりますか。　□はい　□いいえ

V. Challenge: Real life Kanji

➢ Supermarkets

Look at the pictures below and circle the Kanji that you learned.

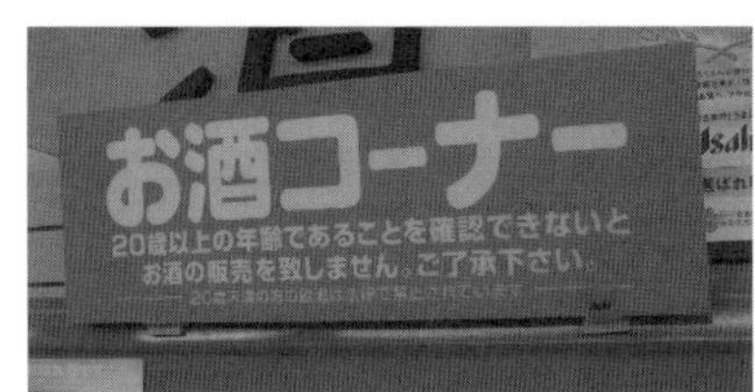

Topic 8　本をかりることができますか

Ⅰ. Kanji Reading and Writing

◇ mark means that this Kanji is in Ⅲ-1.

1	行 　行	ノ ク 彳 彳 行 行 ◇	(6)
	go/act/line		
Kun	い-く おこな-う	行きます(い) (to go)、～行き(い) (bound for ～)、 行います(おこな) (to carry out)	
On	コウ、(ギョウ)	旅行(りょこう) (travel)	

2	来 　来	一 ㇀ ㇇ 立 平 来 来	(7)
	come		
Kun	き-ます (く-る、こ-ない)	来ます(き) (to come)	
On	ライ	来週(らいしゅう) (next week)、来月(らいげつ) (next month)、来年(らいねん) (next year)	

3	帰 　帰	' リ リ フ リ ヨ リ ヨ リ 帰 帰 帰 帰	(10)
	return		
Kun	かえ-る	帰ります(かえ) (to go home/to return)	
On	キ	帰国(きこく) (homecoming)、帰国します(きこく) (to return one's country)	

4	国 　国	丨 冂 冂 冂 冂 国 国 国	(8)
	country		
Kun	くに	国(くに) (country)	
On	コク、ゴク	外国(がいこく) (foreign country)、中国(ちゅうごく) (China)、 外国人登録証明書(がいこくじんとうろくしょうめいしょ) (foreign resident's registration card)	

5	所 所 place	所 (8)
Kun	ところ	所(ところ) (place)、台所(だいどころ) (kitchen)
On	ショ、(ジョ)	場所(ばしょ) (place)、市役所(しやくしょ) (City Hall)、住所(じゅうしょ) (address)

6	校 校 school	校 (10)
Kun		
On	コウ	学校(がっこう) (school)、小学校(しょうがっこう) (elementary school)、中学校(ちゅうがっこう) (junior high school)、高校(こうこう) (senior high school)

7	室 室 room	室 (9)
Kun		
On	シツ	教室(きょうしつ) (classroom)、研究室(けんきゅうしつ) (faculty office/laboratory)

8	図 図 drawing	図 (7)
Kun		
On	ズ、ト	図書館(としょかん) (library)、地図(ちず) (map)

9	銀 銀 silver	銀 (14)
Kun		
On	ギン	銀行(ぎんこう) (bank)、銀行員(ぎんこういん) (bank clerk)

10	家	家	丶 丷 宀 宀 宀 宇 字 家 家 家 ◇I (10)
	house/family		
Kun	いえ、(や)		家(いえ) (house/home)
On	カ、(ケ)		家族(かぞく) (family)

11	部	部	丶 亠 亠 立 立 产 咅 咅 咅 咅 部 (11)
	section		
Kun			*部屋(へや) (room)
On	ブ		全部(ぜんぶ) (all)

12	泳	泳	丶 冫 氵 氵 汀 汸 泳 泳 ◇I (8)
	swim		
Kun	およ-ぐ		泳(およ)ぎます (to swim)
On	エイ		水泳(すいえい) (swimming)、水泳(すいえい)します (to swim)

13	歌	歌	一 ｢ 可 可 可 哥 哥 哥 哥 哥 哥 歌 歌 歌 (14)
	song		
Kun	うた、うた-う		歌(うた) (song)、歌(うた)います (to sing)
On	カ		歌手(かしゅ) (singer)

14	会	会	ノ 人 亼 会 会 会 (6)
	meet/society		
Kun	あ-う		会(あ)います (to meet)
On	カイ		会話(かいわ) (conversation)、会話(かいわ)します (to have a conversation)、会社(かいしゃ) (company)

15	話	話	丶 亠 亠 亠 言 言 言 言 訁 訐 訐 話 話 話 (13)
	speak		
Kun	はな - す、はなし		話(はな)します (to speak/to talk)、話(はなし) (talk/conversation)
On	ワ		電話(でんわ) (telephone)

16	買	買	丶 冖 冂 罒 罒 罒 冃 胃 胃 買 買 買 買 ① (12)
	buy		
Kun	か - う		買(か)います (to buy)、買(か)い物(もの) (shopping)、 買(か)い物(もの)します (to go shopping)
On	(バイ)		

Ⅱ. Katakana Words

	vocabulary		meaning		vocabulary		meaning
1	ビデオ	N	video tape	2	キャンパス	N	campus

Ⅲ. Kanji and Vocabulary Exercises

Ⅲ - 1.　Memorize the Kanji as an image

Write the reading and Kanji seeing each picture as shown in the example.

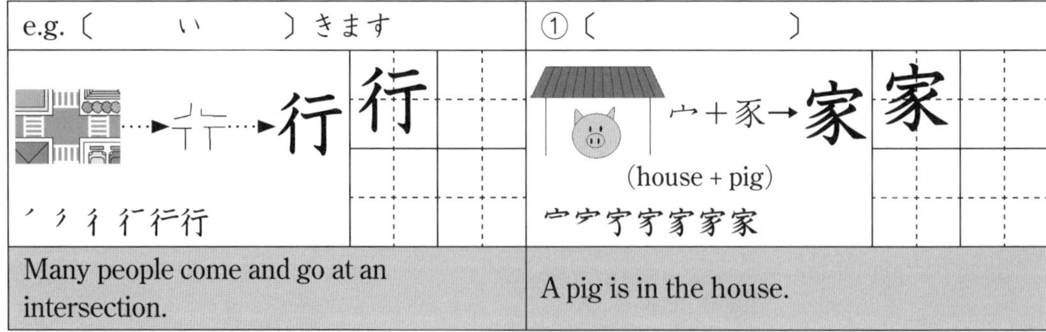

e.g.〔　い　〕きます
行
行
Many people come and go at an intersection.
①〔　　〕
宀＋豕→家
家
(house + pig)
A pig is in the house.

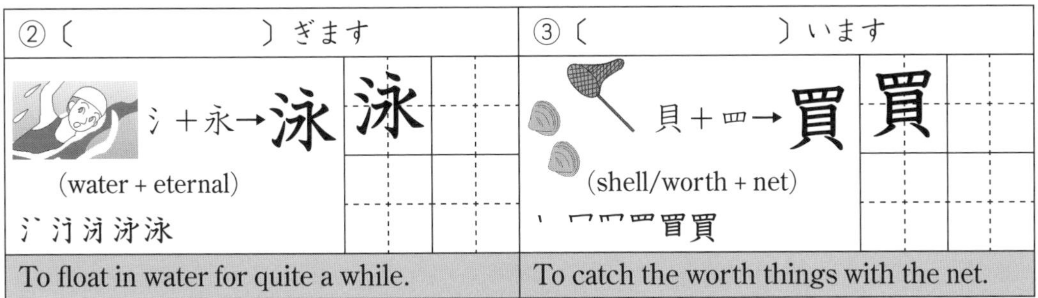

②〔　　　　　　　〕ぎます
氵＋永→泳
泳
(water + eternal)
To float in water for quite a while.
③〔　　　　　　　〕います
貝＋罒→買
買
(shell/worth + net)
To catch the worth things with the net.

Ⅲ - 2. The meaning of Kanji parts and its combination

Match the Kanji Part A with the meaning. Then write the Kanji by combining Part A and Part B.

	(Part A)		(meaning)		(Part B)		かんじ
e.g.	氵	・———・	(water)	+	永	→	泳
(1)	木	・　　・	(shell/worth)	+	罒	→	____
(2)	宀	・　　・	(tree)	+	交	→	____
(3)	貝	・　　・	(gold/metal)	+	艮	→	____
(4)	亻	・　　・	(word)	+	舌・吾	→	___/___
(5)	囗	・　　・	(house)	+	至・豕	→	___/___
(6)	阝	・　　・	(place)	+	音	→	____
(7)	言	・　　・	(enclosure)	+	玉・乂	→	___/___
(8)	金	・　　・	(go)	+	亍	→	____

Ⅲ - 3. Kanji Exercises

Look at the pictures and choose the appropriate Kanji from the ▭. Then write the word by using Kanji and Hiragana as in the example.

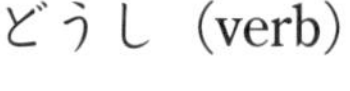

どうし (verb)　　来・行・帰・買・泳・歌・会・話

e.g.

(大学へ)
行きます

(1)

____

(2)
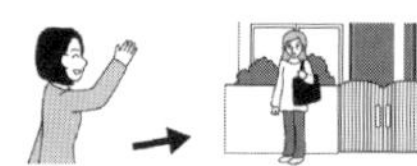
(友達が)
____

(3)

____

(4)

(友達に)
____

(5)

____

(6)

(友達と)
____

(7)

(家へ)
____

場所のことば (Place)　　国・部・家・銀・所・校・室・図

e.g.

市役(しやく)__所__

(1)
私の________

(2)

リーさんの______

(3)

学________

(4)

教(きょう)________

(5)
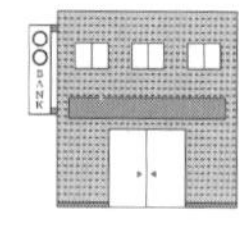
________行

(6)

________屋(や)

(7)

________書館(かん)

Ⅳ. Exercises in context

Exercise A

Choose the appropriate vocabulary from the [ ], and write the word using Kanji and Hiragana as in the example.

e.g. 研究室(けんきゅう)　へ　先生に＿会い＿に行きます。

(1) ＿＿＿＿＿＿　で　友達(だち)と＿＿＿＿＿＿ます。

(2) ＿＿＿＿＿＿　へ　帰りたいです。

(3) 図書館(かん)　へ　DVD を見に＿＿＿＿＿＿。

(4) プール　で　泳ぐことができます。

(5) 部屋(や)　で　歌を＿＿＿＿＿＿ます。

(6) ＿＿＿＿＿＿　へ　お金をおろしに行きます。

(7) スーパー　へ　食べ物を＿＿＿＿＿＿に行きます。

くに・~~あいます~~・がっこう・うたいます
はなします・かいます・いきます・ぎんこう

Exercise B

Fill in the blanks a-i with the appropriate Kanji. Then match the action with the location a-i.

a. ＿＿＿＿館(かん)〔としょかん〕　b. ＿＿＿＿〔ぎんこう〕
c. 教(きょう)＿＿＿＿〔きょうしつ〕　d. 市役(しやく)＿＿＿〔しやくしょ〕
e. ＿＿＿＿堂(どう)〔しょくどう〕　f. ＿＿＿〔いえ〕／＿＿＿屋(や)〔へや〕
g. カラオケ　h. デパート　i. プール

e.g. 飲みます〔 e 〕

(1) 本を読みます〔　〕　(2) お金をあずけます〔　〕

(3) 本をかります〔　〕　(4) コンピュータを使います〔　〕

(5) 先生と話します〔　〕　(6) DVD を見ます〔　〕

(7) 買い物します〔　〕　(8) 泳ぎます〔　〕

(9) お金をおろします〔　〕　(10) 歌を歌います〔　〕

(11) しゅくだいをします〔　〕　(12) 食べます〔　〕

(13) 友達(だち)と会います〔　〕　(14) 外国人登録証明書(とうろくしょうめい)をもらいます〔　〕

Exercise C

Ask your partner as in the example.

A：どこで＿＿＿＿＿＿ことができますか。

B：＿＿＿＿で＿＿＿＿＿ことができます。

e.g. A：どこでコーヒーを飲むことができますか。

B：食堂(どう)で飲むことができます。

Ⅴ. Challenge: Real life Kanji

➢ Building and institution（Name for an institution）

Look at the pictures below and circle the Kanji that you learned. Use a dictionary and check the meaning of ①－③ .

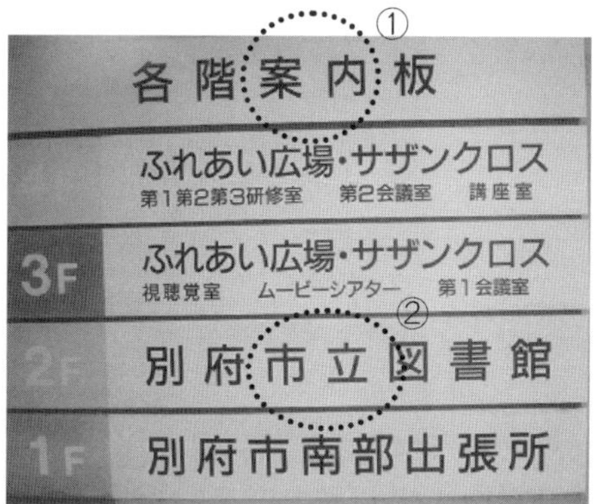

Topic 9　かしてください（りょうで）

Ⅰ. Kanji Reading and Writing

◇ mark means that this Kanji is in Ⅲ-1.

1	場 (場) place	一 十 ま ま 圹 圹 坦 坦 坦 場 場 場 (12)
Kun	ば	場所（place）、ごみ置き場（garbage dumping area）
On	ジョウ	駐車場（car parking）、駐輪場（bicycle parking spot）

2	紙 (紙) paper	く 幺 幺 糸 糸 糸 紅 紅 紙 紙 ◇ (10)
Kun	かみ	紙（paper）、手紙（letter）
On	（シ）	

3	油 (油) oil	丶 丶 氵 氵 汩 油 油 油 ◇ (8)
Kun	あぶら	油（oil）
On	ユ	石油（petroleum）

4	入 (入) enter/put in	ノ 入 ◇ (2)
Kun	はい－る、い－れる	入ります（to enter/to join）、入れます（to put in）
On	ニュウ	入学します（to enter a school）

5	出	出	丨 ㄐ 屮 出 出 ◇Ⅰ	(5)
	out			
Kun	で-る、だ-す		出(で)ます（to go out/to leave）、 出(だ)します（to send/to submit/to take out）	
On	シュッ（シュツ）		出発(しゅっぱつ)します（to depart）	

6	洗	洗	丶 冫 氵 氵 氵 汁 洪 涉 洗 ◇Ⅰ	(9)
	wash			
Kun	あら-う		洗(あら)います（to wash）、お手洗(てあら)い（toilet）	
On	セン		洗濯(せんたく)します（to do the laundry）、洗面台(せんめんだい)（washstand）、 洗面所(せんめん)（bathroom）	

7	料	料	丶 丷 䒑 半 米 米 米 米 料 料	(10)
	fee			
Kun				
On	リョウ		料理(りょうり)します（to cook）、料金(りょうきん)（fare/charge）、 無料(むりょう)（free of charge）	

8	便	便	ノ 亻 亻 亻 伒 伊 伊 便 便	(9)
	convenient/post			
Kun	（たよ-り）			
On	ベン、ビン		便利(べんり)な（convenient）、郵便局(ゆうびんきょく)（post office）	

9	利	利	ノ 二 千 千 禾 和 利 ◇Ⅰ	(7)
	advantage			
Kun	（き-く）			
On	リ		利用(りよう)します（to make use of something）	

10	不	不	一 ア 不 不 (4)
	not		
Kun			
On	フ、(ブ)		不便な（ふべん）(inconvenient)、不親切な（ふしんせつ）(unkind)、不安な（ふあん）(anxious)

11	明	明	丨 П 日 日 明 明 明 明 ⟨I⟩ (8)
	bright/clear		
Kun	あか-るい		明るい（あか）(light/cheerful)、*明日（あした）(tomorrow)
On	メイ		説明します（せつめい）(to explain)

12	暗	暗	丨 П 日 日 日' 日亠 日立 日立 暗 暗 暗 暗 暗 ⟨I⟩ (13)
	dark		
Kun	くら-い		暗い（くら）(dark/gloomy)
On	(アン)		

13	静	静	一 十 十 主 丰 青 青 青 青' 青ク 静 静 静 静 (14)
	quiet		
Kun	しず-か		静かな（しず）(quiet/silent)
On	(セイ)		

14	新	新	' 亠 亠 亡 立 立 辛 辛 亲 亲' 新 新 新 ⟨I⟩ (13)
	new		
Kun	あたら-しい		新しい（あたら）(new)
On	シン		新聞（しんぶん）(newspaper)、新車（しんしゃ）(new automobile)

15	古	古	一十ナ古古 ⓘ (5)
	old		
Kun	ふる-い		古い(ふるい) (old)、古本(ふるほん) (secondhand book)
On	コ		中古(ちゅうこ) (secondhand goods)

Ⅱ. Katakana Words

	vocabulary		meaning		vocabulary		meaning
1	アイロン	N	iron	2	ランドリー	N	laundry
3	キッチン	N	kitchen				

Ⅲ. Kanji and Vocabulary Exercises

Ⅲ - 1. Memorize the Kanji as an image

Write the reading and Kanji seeing each picture as shown in the example.

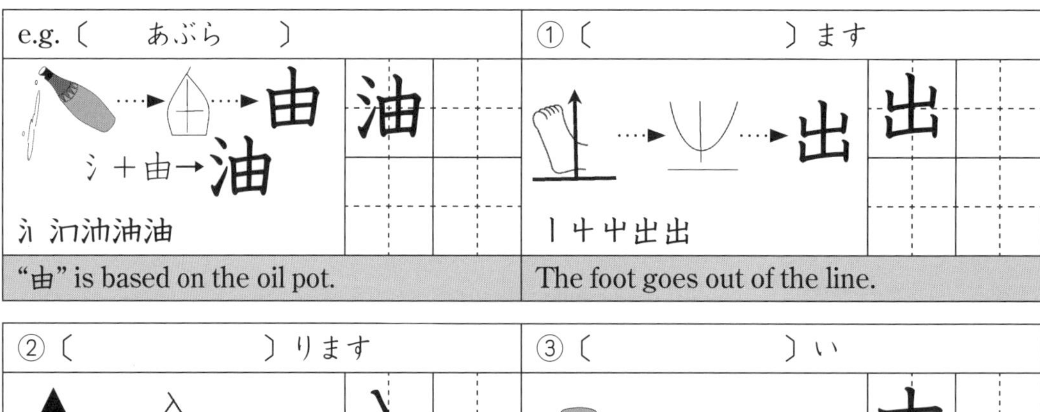

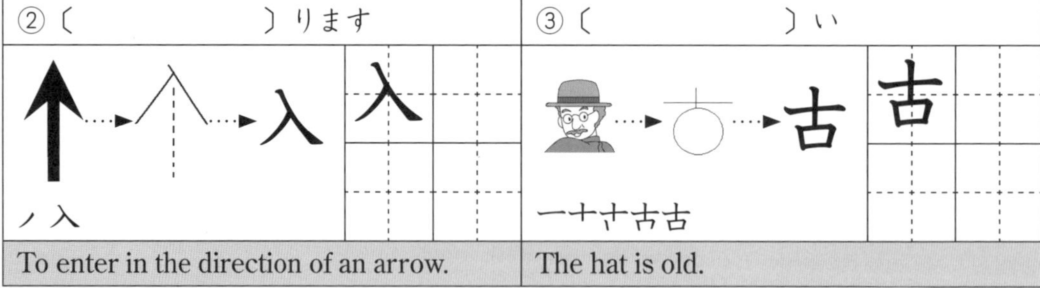

e.g.〔　あぶら　〕

"由" is based on the oil pot.

The foot goes out of the line.

②〔　　　〕ります
入
入
ノ 入
To enter in the direction of an arrow.
③〔　　　〕い
古
古
一十ナ古古
The hat is old.

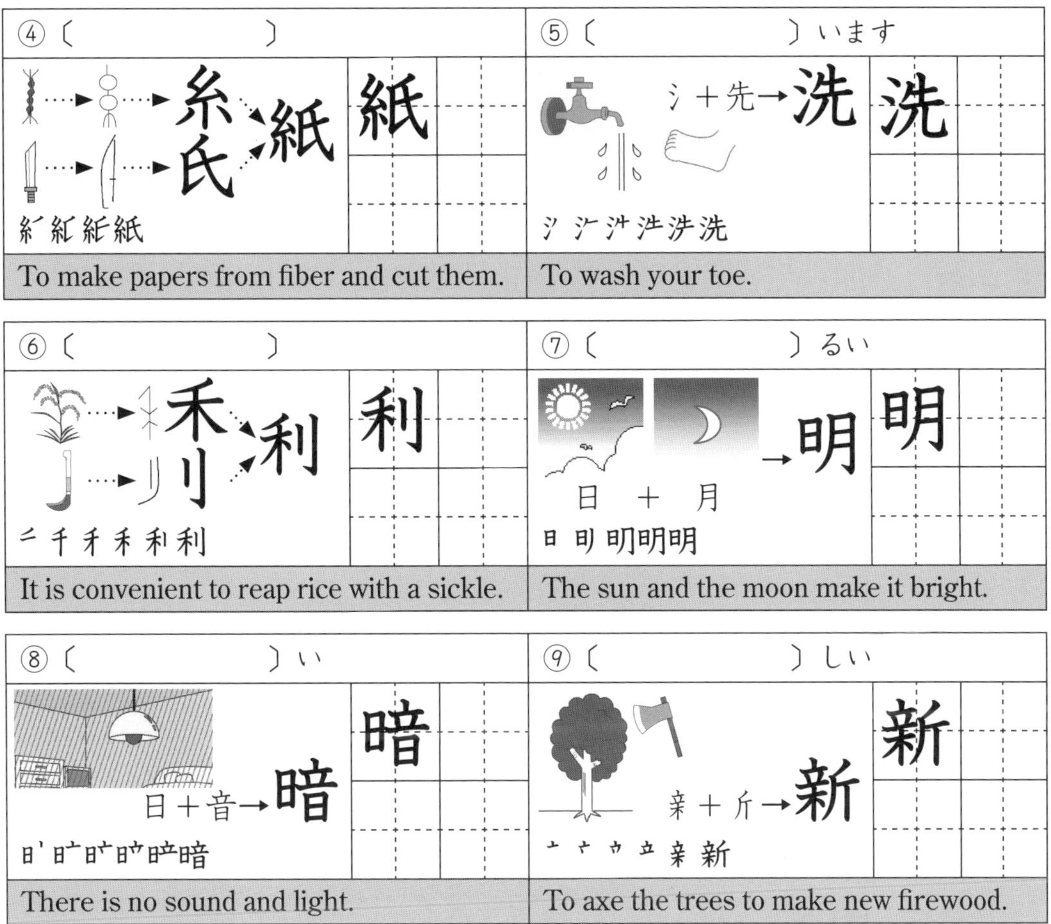

④〔　　　　　　〕
糸
氏
紙
To make papers from fiber and cut them.
⑤〔　　　　　　〕います
氵＋先→洗
To wash your toe.
⑥〔　　　　　　〕
禾
刂
利
It is convenient to reap rice with a sickle.
⑦〔　　　　　　〕るい
日　＋　月
明
The sun and the moon make it bright.
⑧〔　　　　　　〕い
日＋音→暗
There is no sound and light.
⑨〔　　　　　　〕しい
亲＋斤→新
To axe the trees to make new firewood.

III - 2.　Kanji parts and their combination

Choose the appropriate Kanji-part a or b, then write Kanji by combining them.

		a	b	読み方	漢字
e.g.	糸	氏	会	かみ	(a) 紙
(1)	亻	更	吏	べん利な	(　) ＿＿＿
(2)	氵	由	酉	あぶら	(　) ＿＿＿
(3)	日	音	音	くらい	(　) ＿＿＿

Ⅲ - 3. Paired words: adjective

Choose the appropriate Kanji from the ▭ and write it on the ＿＿＿. Then write its reading in Hiragana in the 〔　　〕 as in the example.

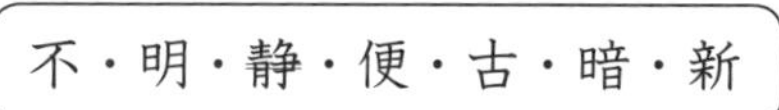

e.g.	(1)	(2)	(3)
	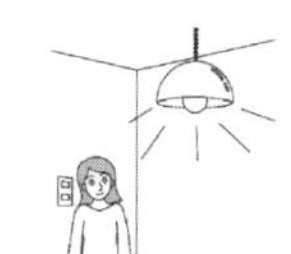	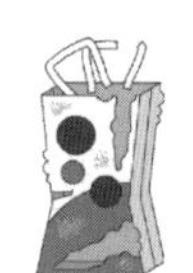	
静かです。	＿＿＿です。	＿＿＿です。	＿＿＿利です。
〔しずかです〕	〔　　　〕	〔　　　〕	〔　　　〕
↕	↕	↕	↕
うるさいです。	＿＿＿です。	＿＿＿です。	不＿＿です。
	〔　　　〕	〔　　　〕	〔　　　〕

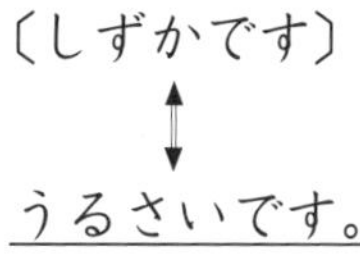
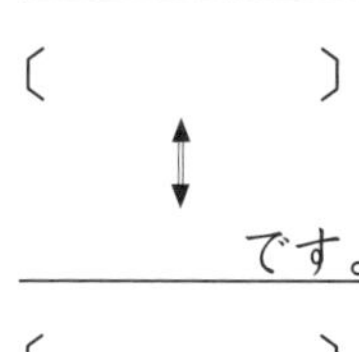

Ⅲ - 4. Verb

Choose the appropriate verb to make a sentence. Then write the reading of the underlined Kanji.

(1)		ご飯を食べて、さらを　・	・	洗います。〔　　　〕
(2)		ジュースをれいぞうこに　・	・	出します。〔　　　〕
(3)		朝、8時半までにごみを　・	・	料理（り）します。〔　　　〕
(4)	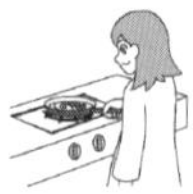	キッチンで　・	・	入れます。〔　　　〕

Ⅳ. Expression Exercises

Ⅳ - 1. Life at the dormitory

Complete the following sentences about one day in the dormitory. Fill in the all blanks with the appropriate word from the [N] and the [V] below.

※ Write the word using Kanji and Hiragana except for Katakana words.

[N]	ランドリー	キッチン	ごみ置(お)き場	駐輪(ちゅうりん)場
[V]	入れます	出します	洗います	
	洗濯(たく)します	料理(り)します	シャワーを浴(あ)びます	

今日の朝

(1) 朝9時におきて、かおを[V]＿＿＿＿て、はをみがきました。

(2) [N]＿＿＿＿で友達(だち)と[V]＿＿理(り)し＿て、朝ご飯を食べました。

(3) それから、さらを[V]＿＿＿＿て、キッチンのごみをごみばこにすてました。ごみは木曜日の朝に[N]＿＿＿＿＿＿に[V]＿＿＿＿ます。

(4) それから、管理(かんり)人室でそうじきをかりて、部屋(や)をそうじしました。その後で、[N]＿＿＿＿＿＿でシャツやズボンを[V]＿＿＿濯(たく)し＿ました。シャツとズボンはクローゼットの中に[V]＿＿＿＿ました。

Ⅳ - 2. Explain your room

Make some sentences about your room or kitchen in the dormitory using two adjectives from the [ ]. Use the Kanji that you learned in the sentence.

あかるい・あたらしい・ふべんな・ふるい・おおきい
しずかな・べんりな・ちいさい・くらい・ひろい

e.g. 1（－くて）：私の部屋(や)は古くて、きたないです。

e.g. 2（－で）　：私の部屋(や)はきれいで、明るいです。

e.g. 3（－が）　：私の部屋(や)は古いですが、きれいです。

(1) 私の部屋(や)は＿＿＿＿＿＿＿＿、＿＿＿＿＿＿＿＿です。

(2) キッチンは＿＿＿＿＿＿＿＿、＿＿＿＿＿＿＿＿です。

(3) 私の大学は＿＿＿＿＿＿＿＿、＿＿＿＿＿＿＿＿です。

V. Challenge: Real life Kanji

➢ Garbage collection day

Look at the picture below and circle the Kanji that you learned.

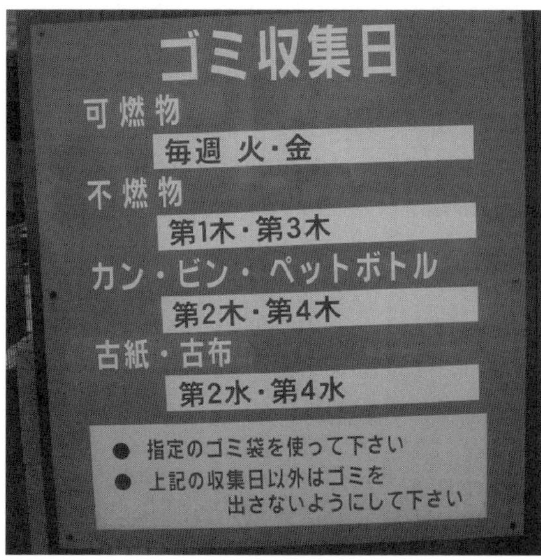

かんがえてみよう

(1) これは何を説明(せつ)していますか。一つえらびなさい。

① ごみの出し方　② キッチンの使い方　③ ランドリーの使い方

(2) 何曜日に出しますか。

① 食べ物のごみ　② ペットボトル　③ 紙

Topic 10　どうしましたか

Ⅰ. Kanji Reading and Writing

◇ mark means that this Kanji is in Ⅲ-1.

1	目	目	丨 冂 冃 冃 目 ◇Ⅰ (5)
	eye		
Kun	め		目(め)（eye）、目上(めうえ)の人(ひと)（one's superiors）、目下(めした)の人（one's inferiors）
On	（モク）		

2	口	口	丨 冂 口 ◇Ⅰ (3)
	mouth		
Kun	くち、ぐち		口(くち)（mouth）、出口(でぐち)（exit）、入口(いりぐち)（entrance）
On	コウ		人口(じんこう)（population）

3	耳	耳	一 丅 下 下 王 耳 ◇Ⅰ (6)
	ear		
Kun	みみ		耳(みみ)（ear）
On	（ジ）		

4	手	手	一 二 三 手 ◇Ⅰ (4)
	hand		
Kun	て		手(て)（hand）、右手(みぎて)（right hand）、左手(ひだりて)（left hand）、手紙(てがみ)（letter）、切手(きって)（stamp）
On	（シュ）		*上手(じょうず)な（skillful/be good at）、*下手(へた)な（unskillful）

5	足 / 足	丶 口 口 ⺊ 早 𧾷 足 ◇I	(7)
	foot/suffice		
Kun	あし、た-りる	足(あし) (foot/leg)、足(た)ります (to be enough)	
On	(ソク)		

6	体 / 体	ノ イ 仁 什 付 休 体	(7)
	body		
Kun	からだ	体(からだ) (body)	
On	タイ	体重(たいじゅう) (body weight)、体調(たいちょう) (one's health condition)	

7	薬 / 薬	一 艹 艹 艹 芇 苩 苩 荰 菹 菹 䓕 蕐 薬 薬 薬	(16)
	medicine		
Kun	くすり、ぐすり	薬(くすり) (medicine)、目薬(めぐすり) (eye drop)	
On	ヤッ、(ヤク)	薬局(やっきょく) (pharmacy)	

8	病 / 病	' 亠 广 广 疒 疒 疔 疠 病 病 ◇I	(10)
	illness		
Kun	(やまい)		
On	ビョウ	病気(びょうき) (illness)	

9	院 / 院	７ ３ 阝 阝' 阝' 阝' 阝' 陀 院 院 ◇I	(10)
	institution		
Kun			
On	イン	病院(びょういん) (hospital)、入院(にゅういん)します (to be hospitalized)、大学院(だいがくいん) (graduate school)	

10	医	医	一ㄱ𠂆𠂇矢医	(7)
	doctor			
Kun				
On	イ		医者（doctor）、歯医者（dentist）	

11	者	者	一十土耂耂者者者	(8)
	person			
Kun	もの		若者（young person）	
On	シャ			

12	力	力	フ力 ①	(2)
	power			
Kun	ちから		力（power）	
On	リョク		体力（force, stamina）	

13	痛	痛	丶一广广疒疒疒疔痟痟痛痛	(12)
	pain			
Kun	いた-い		痛い（painful）	
On	ツウ		頭痛（headache）	

14	元	元	一二テ元 ①	(4)
	origin			
Kun	（もと）			
On	ゲン、（ガン）		元気な（healthy/being well）	

15	気	気	ノ ㇒ ㇐ 气 気 気 ① (6)
	spirit/gas		
Kun			
On	キ		気持ち(きもち) (feeling/sensation)、気分(きぶん) (feeling/mood)、天気(てんき) (weather)、人気(にんき)があります (to be popular with)

Ⅱ. Katakana Words

	vocabulary		meaning		vocabulary		meaning
1	クリニック	N	clinic	2	アレルギー	N	allergy
3	ストレス	N	stress				

Ⅲ. Kanji and Vocabulary Exercises

Ⅲ - 1. Memorize the Kanji as an image

Write the reading and Kanji seeing each picture as shown in the example.

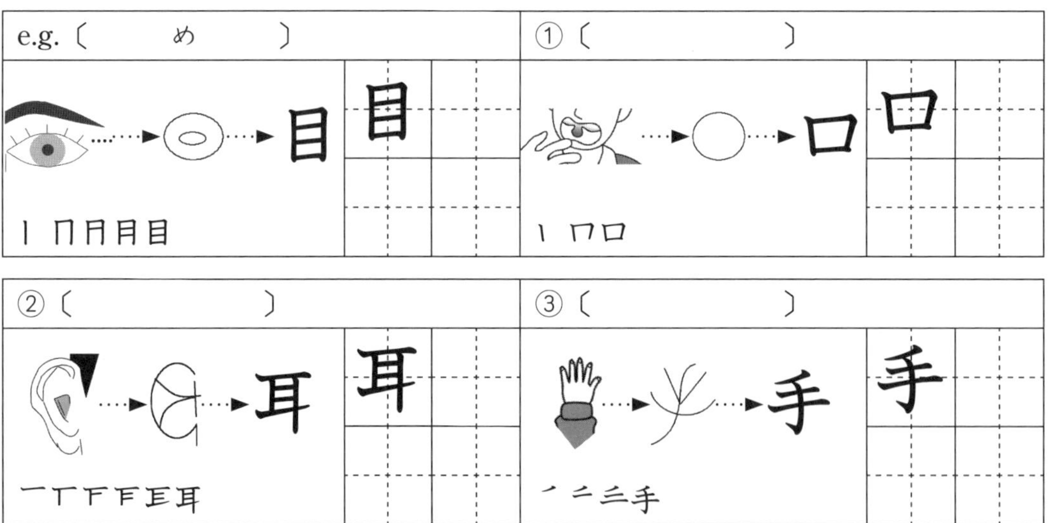

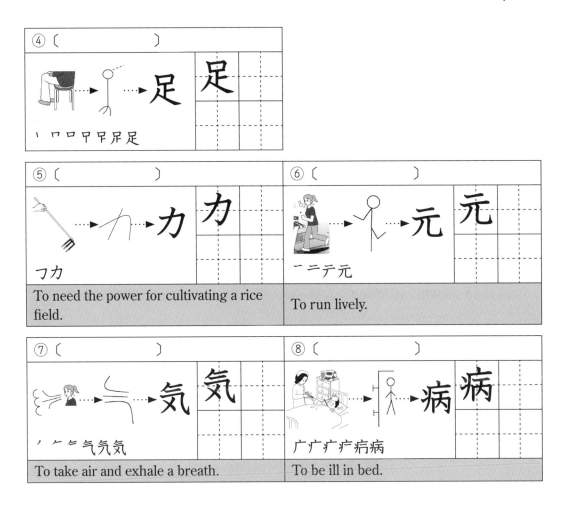

④〔　　　　　　　〕

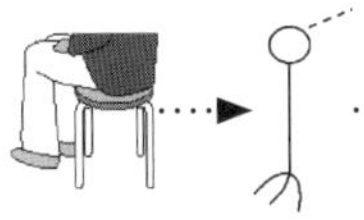

足

丶 口 口 ⻊ ⻊ 卫 足

⑤〔　　　　　　　〕

力

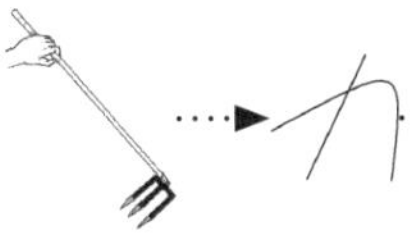

フカ

To need the power for cultivating a rice field.

⑥〔　　　　　　　〕

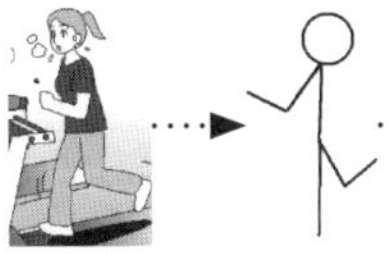

元

一 二 テ 元

To run lively.

⑦〔　　　　　　　〕

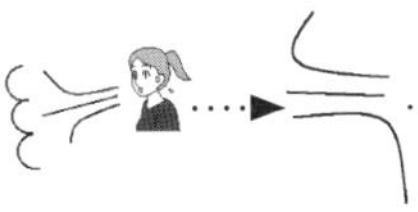

気

ノ 𠂉 ⺈ 气 気 気

To take air and exhale a breath.

⑧〔　　　　　　　〕

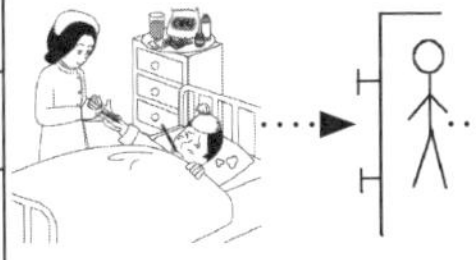

病

广 疒 疒 疔 病 病

To be ill in bed.

III - 2. The meaning of Kanji parts and their combination

Match the Kanji Part A and Part B. Then write Kanji by combining them.

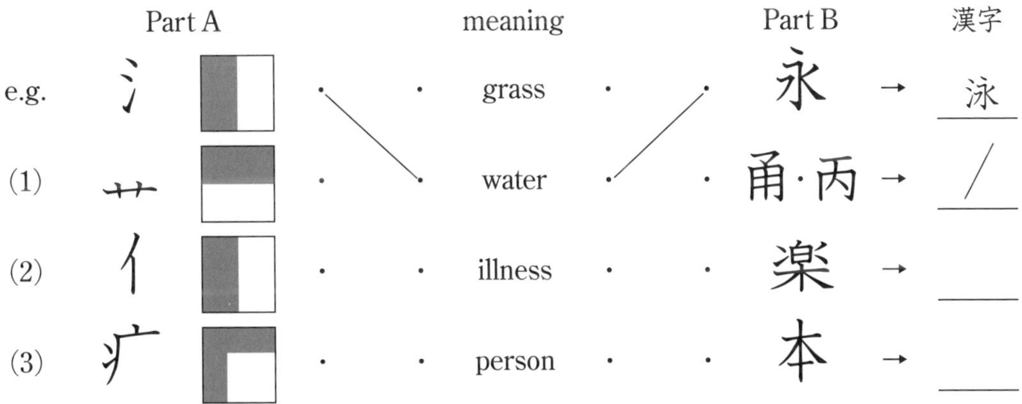

Ⅲ - 3. Kanji parts and their combination

Choose the appropriate Kanji-part a or b, and then write Kanji by combining them.

		a	b	読み方	漢字
e.g.	糸	氏	会	かみ	(a) 紙
(1)	阝	完	売	病いん	(　) ____
(2)	耂	日	目	わかもの	(　) ____

Ⅲ - 4. Body

Look at the picture and write the appropriate Kanji and the reading in Hiragana.

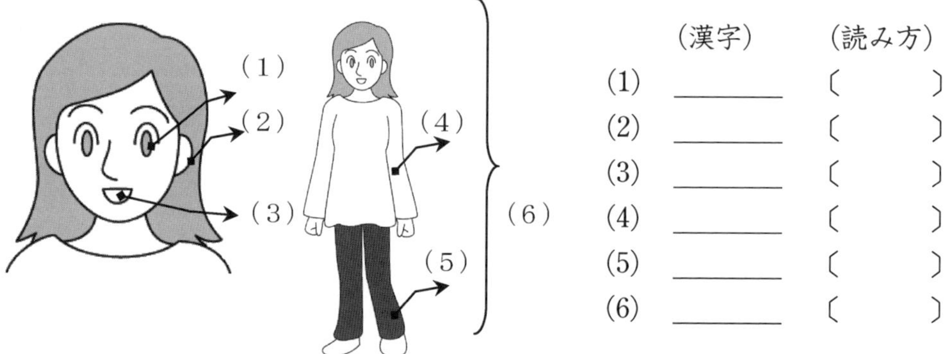

	(漢字)	(読み方)
(1)	____	〔　　〕
(2)	____	〔　　〕
(3)	____	〔　　〕
(4)	____	〔　　〕
(5)	____	〔　　〕
(6)	____	〔　　〕

Ⅲ - 5. Medical words

Look at the picture and choose the appropriate Kanji from the ▭ . Complete the word by using Kanji and Hiragana. Then write their reading in Hiragana.

医・薬・院・力・元・痛

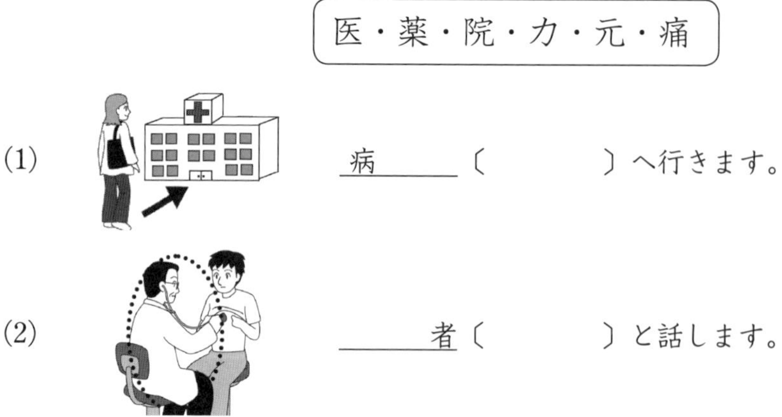

(1) 病____〔　　　〕へ行きます。

(2) ____者〔　　　〕と話します。

(3) ＿＿＿＿〔　　　　〕を飲みます。

(4) 私は足が＿＿＿＿いです。〔　　　　　　〕

(5) リーさんはいつも＿＿＿＿気です。〔　　　　　　〕

Ⅳ. Exercises in context

Exercise A

Give advice to Yoshida-san who has a sore throat. Change each Hiragana word in the 〔　〕 to Kanji and write it on the ＿＿＿ in each sentence. Then put the (a)-(g) in order in the ⬚.

(a) e.g. 大学 のクリニックに行きます。〔だいがく〕

(b) ＿＿＿＿＿に行きます。〔びょういん〕

(c) 病院で＿＿＿＿＿と話します。〔いしゃ〕

(d) ＿＿＿＿＿になります。〔げんき〕

(e) 病院の＿＿＿＿＿を聞きます。〔ばしょ〕

(f) 薬をもらって、その＿＿＿＿＿を飲みます。〔くすり〕

(g) のどが＿＿＿＿＿です。〔いたい〕

(g) →　　→　　→　　→　　→　　→ (d)

Exercise B

Someone catches a cold or has a sore throat. Give advice to him/her using the following patterns.

まず＿＿＿＿＿＿てください。
つぎに、＿＿＿＿＿て、＿＿＿＿＿てください。
病院で医者と＿＿＿＿＿て、＿＿＿＿＿てください。
そうすれば（then）、すぐに（immediately）元気になります。

V. Challenge: Real life Kanji

➢ At the hospital

First look at the picture below and circle the Kanji that you learned. Use a dictionary and check the meaning of the words (a) to (d) below.

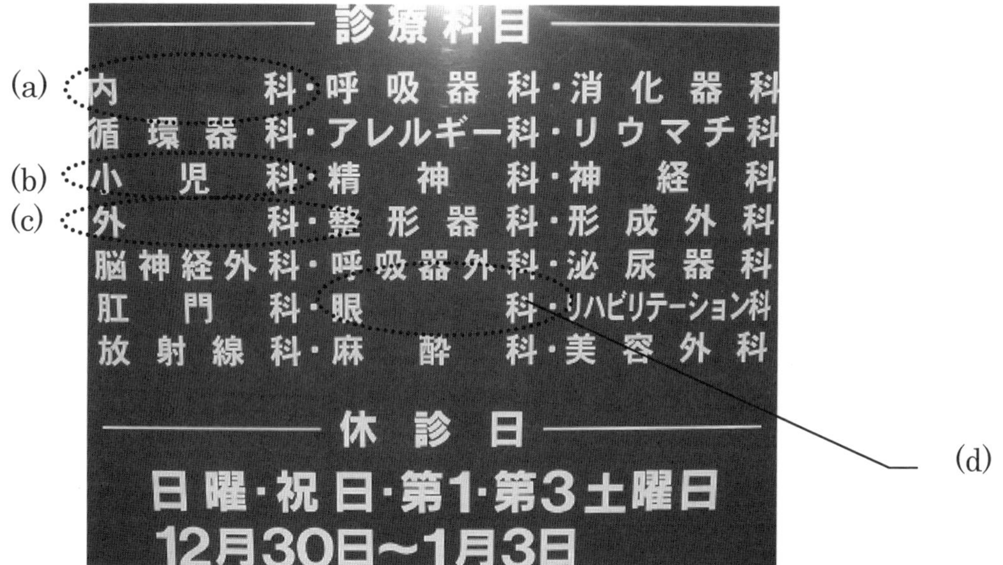

かんがえてみよう

(1) Aさんはかぜをひきました。どこに行きますか。

①内科（ないか）　②外科（げか）　③アレルギー科（か）

(2) Bさんは足をけがしました。どこに行きますか。

①内科（ないか）　②外科（げか）　③アレルギー科（か）

（※～科（か）…medical department）

漢字総画数索引（さくいん）

(Kanji Strokes INDEX)

[1画]

一	ひと-つ	イチ、(イッ)	2

[2画]

人	ひと	ジン、ニン	1
二	ふた-つ	ニ	2
七	なな、(なの)	シチ	2
八	やっ-つ、(よう)	ハチ、(ハッ)	2
九	ここの-つ	キュウ、(ク)	2
十	とお	ジュウ、(ジッ、ジュッ)	2
入	はい-る、いれ-る	ニュウ	9
力	ちから	リョク	10

[3画]

山	やま	サン	1
川	かわ、(がわ)	(セン)	1
三	みっ-つ	サン	2
千		セン、ゼン	2
万		マン	2
土	つち	ド	3
夕	ゆう		4
大	おお-きい	ダイ、(タイ)	5
小	ちい-さい	ショウ	5
上	うえ、(あ-がる、の-ぼる)	ジョウ	6
下	した、(さ-がる、お-りる)	(カ、ゲ)	6
女	おんな	ジョ	6
子	こ	(シ)	6
口	くち、ぐち	コウ	10

[4画]

木	き	(モク)	1
友	とも	(ユウ)	1
五	いつ-つ	ゴ	2
六	むっ-つ、(むい)	ロク、ロッ	2
月	つき	ゲツ、ガツ	3
火	ひ	カ	3
水	みず	スイ	3
日	ひ、び、(か)	ニチ、ニ、ニッ	3
分	わ-かる	フン、プン、ブン	3
今	いま	コン	3
円		エン	4
午		ゴ	4
文		ブン、(モン)	5
中	なか	チュウ、ジュウ	6
牛	うし	ギュウ	7
方	かた	ホウ	7
不		フ、(ブ)	9
手	て	(シュ)	10
元	(もと)	ゲン、(ガン)	10

[5画]

田	た、だ	(デン)	1
石	いし	(セキ)	1
生	(い-きる)	セイ	1
四	よん、よ、よっ-つ	シ	2
半		ハン	3
正	ただ-しい	ショウ、(セイ)	4
去	(さ-る)	キョ、(コ)	4
本	もと	ホン	5
広	ひろ-い	(コウ)	5
右	みぎ	(ユウ、ウ)	6
左	ひだり	(サ)	6
外	そと	ガイ、(ゲ)	6

漢字	訓読み	音読み	課
出	で-る、だ-す	シュッ、(シュツ)	9
古	ふる-い	コ	9
目	め	(モク)	10

[6画]

漢字	訓読み	音読み	課
竹	たけ	(チク)	1
先	(さき)	セン	1
百		ヒャク、ビャク、ピャク	2
休	やす-む	キュウ	3
年	とし	ネン	4
毎		マイ	4
字		ジ	5
忙	いそが-しい	(ボウ)	5
肉		ニク	7
米	こめ	(ベイ、マイ)	7
好	す-き	(コウ)	7
行	い-く、おこなう	コウ、(ギョウ)	8
会	あ-う	カイ	8
耳	みみ	(ジ)	10
気		キ	10

[7画]

漢字	訓読み	音読み	課
私	わたし	シ	1
何	なに、なん		3
車	くるま	シャ	4
見	み-る	(ケン)	5
男	おとこ	ダン、(ナン)	6
花	はな	カ	6
作	つく-る	サク	7
来	き-ます、(く-る、こ-ない)	ライ	8
図		ズ、ト	8
利	(き-く)	リ	9
足	あし、た-りる	(ソク)	10
体	からだ	タイ	10
医		イ	10

[8画]

漢字	訓読み	音読み	課
林	はやし	(リン)	1
学	(まな-ぶ)	ガク	1
門		モン	1
金	かね	キン	3
夜	よる、(よ)	ヤ	4
英		エイ	5
使	つか-う	(シ)	5
若	わか-い		6
物	もの	ブツ	6
味	あじ	ミ	7
国	くに	コク、ゴク	8
所	ところ	ショ、(ジョ)	8
泳	およ-ぐ	エイ	8
油	あぶら	ユ	9
明	あか-るい	メイ	9
者	もの	シャ	10

[9画]

漢字	訓読み	音読み	課
昼	ひる	(チュウ)	4
前	まえ	ゼン	6
後	うし-ろ、あと	ゴ、コウ	6
茶		チャ、(サ)	7
食	た-べる	ショク	7
室		シツ	8
洗	あら-う	セン	9
便	(たよ-り)	ベン、ビン	9

[10画]

漢字	訓読み	音読み	課
時	(とき)	ジ	3

書	か-く	ショ	5
酒	さけ、さか	シュ	7
帰	かえ-る	キ	8
校		コウ	8
家	いえ、(や)	カ、(ケ)	8
紙	かみ	(シ)	9
料		リョウ	9
病	(やまい)	ビョウ	10
院		イン	10

[11画]

週		シュウ	4
細	ほそ-い	(サイ)	6
魚	さかな	(ギョ)	7
鳥	とり	(チョウ)	7
部		ブ	8

[12画]

森	もり	(シン)	1
間	あいだ、(ま)	カン	3
朝	あさ	(チョウ)	4
晩		バン	4
絵		エ	6
飯	(めし)	ハン	7
飲	の-む	(イン)	7
買	か-う	(バイ)	8
場	ば	ジョウ	9
痛	いた-い	ツウ	10

[13画]

電		デン	4
漢		カン	5
楽	たの-しい	ガク、(ラク)	5
話	はな-す、はなし	ワ	8
暗	くら-い	(アン)	9
新	あたら-しい	シン	9

[14画]

語	(かた-る)	ゴ	5
聞	き-く	ブン	5
読	よ-む	ドク	5
銀		ギン	8
歌	うた、うた-う	カ	8
静	しず-か	(セイ)	9

[16画]

薬	くすり、ぐすり	ヤッ、(ヤク)	10

[18画]

曜		ヨウ	4

日本語語彙索引
にほんごごいさくいん

(Vocabulary INDEX)

G is Grammar section. / K is Kanji and Vocaburaly section.

[あ]

アイスクリーム		ice cream	G7
あいだ	［間］	between	G2/K3
あいます	［会います］	to meet	K8
アイロン		iron	G9/K9
アイロンだい	［アイロン台］	ironing board	G9
あおい	［青い］	blue	G6
あかい	［赤い］	red	G6
アカデミックオフィス		academic office	G2
あかるい	［明るい］	bright	G5/K9
あけます	［開けます］	to open	G9
あげます		to give	G6
あさ	［朝］	morning	G3/K4
あさごはん	［朝ご飯］	breakfast	G5/K4,K7
あさって		the day after tomorrow	G3
あし	［足］	leg/foot	G10/K10
あじ	［味］	taste	K7
アシスタント		assitant	G9
あした	［明日］	tomorrow	G3/K9
あずかります	［預かります］	to keep	G9
あずけます	［預けます］	to leave things/ to deposit	G8
あそこ		over there	G2
あそびます	［遊びます］	to play	G8
あたま	［頭］	head	G10
あたらしい	［新しい］	new	G5/K9
あつい	［厚い］	thick	G6
あつい	［暑い／熱い］	hot	G7
あとで	［後で］	after/later	K6
アニメ		animation	G5
あの		that (noun/over there)	G2
アパート		apartment house	G2
［シャワーを］あびます	［浴びます］	to take a shower	G9
あぶら	［油］	oil	K9
あまい		sweet	G7
あまり		not so much/often	G5
あらいます	［洗います］	to wash	G7/K9
あります		to have	G3
あるきます	［歩きます］	to walk	G4
アルバイト		part time job	G7
あれ		that one (over there)	G2
アレルギー		allergy	K10
アレルギーがあります		to be allergic to…	G10
アンケート		questionnaire	G5

[い]

いい		good	G5
いえ	［家］	house/home	G4/K8
～いき	［～行き］	bound for	G4/K8
いきます	［行きます］	to go	G4/K8
いくら		how much	G4
いざかや	［居酒屋］	pub	G7
いし	［石］	stone	K1
いしい	［石井］	Ishii (japanese surname)	K1
いしゃ	［医者］	doctor	G10/K10
いす		chair	G6
いそがしい	［忙しい］	busy	G5/K5
いたい	［痛い］	ache/sore/painful	G10/K10
いち	［１／一］	one	G1/K2
いちがつ	［１月／一月］	January	G3/K3
いちじ	［１時］	one o'clock	G3/K3
いちじかん	［１時間］	one hour	K3
いちじごふん	［１時５分］	one five	K3
いちじはん	［１時半］	half past one	K3
いちにち	［１日］	one day	K3
いちにちじゅう	［一日中］	all day long	K6
いちねん	［１年］	one year	K4
いちまん	［一万］	ten thousand	K2
いつ		when	G3
いつか	［５日／五日］	5th (day of the month)	G3
いっかげつ	［１か月］	one month	K3

いっしゅうかん	[1週間]	one week	K4
いっしょ[に]		together	G7
いつつ	[五つ]	five things	K2
いっぷん	[1分]	one minute	G3
いぬ	[犬]	dog	G9
いま	[今]	now	G3/K3
いみ	[意味]	meaning	K7
いりぐち	[入口]	entrance	G6/K10
いれます	[入れます]	to put in	G8/K9
いろ	[色]	color	G6
インテリア		interior	G6
インド		India	G1
インドネシア		Indonesia	G1

[う]

うえ	[上]	up	K6
うがいをします		to gargle	G10
うし	[牛]	cow	K7
うしろ	[後ろ]	back	G2/K6
うすい	[薄い]	thin	G6
うた	[歌]	song	G8/K8
うたいます	[歌います]	to sing	G8/K8
うち		home/house	G4
うどん		Japanese wheat-based noodle	G7
うりば	[売り場]	section/floor	G6
うるさい		noisy	G5
うんちん	[運賃]	fare	G4
うんてんします	[運転します]	to drive	G8
うんどうします	[運動します]	to do physical exercise	G10

[え]

え	[絵]	drawing/painting	G8/K6
エアコン		air conditioner	G10
えいが	[映画]	movie	G1
えいがかん	[映画館]	movie theater	G2
えいご	[英語]	English language	G1/K5
エーティーエム	[ATM]	Automatic Teller Machine	G2
えき	[駅]	station	G4
～えん	[円]	1 yen	K4
えんぴつ		pencil	G6

[お]

おいしい		delicious/tasty	G5
おおい	[多い]	many/a lot of	G6
おおきい	[大きい]	big/large	G5/K5
オーストラリア		Australia	G1
おかね	[お金]	money	G5/K3
おきます	[起きます]	to get up	G4
おきます	[置きます]	to place/to put down	G9
おくります		to send/to present	G6
おくれます	[遅れます]	to be late	G9
おこないます	[行います]	to carry out	K8
おこのみやき		Japanese pizza	G7
おさけ	[お酒]	alcoholic drink/liquor	K7
おしえます	[教えます]	to teach/to tell	G6
おそい	[遅い]	slow/late	G10
おだいじに	[お大事に]	take care	G10
おちゃ	[お茶]	tea	G5/K7
おてあらい	[お手洗い]	toilet	G2/K9
おとこ		man	G6
おとこのこ	[男の子]	boy	G6/K6
おとこのひと	[男の人]	man	G6/K6
おととい		the day before yesterday	G3
おとな	[大人]	adult	K5
おなか	[お腹]	stomach	G10
おなかがすきます	[お腹が空きます]	to get hungry	G8
おにぎり		rice ball	G7
オフィス		office	G2
おふろ	[お風呂]	bath	G9
おぼえます	[覚えます]	to memorize	G8
おもい	[重い]	heavy	G6
おもしろい		fun/interesting	G5
およぎます	[泳ぎます]	to swim	G8/K8
オリエンテーション		orientation	G2
[お金を]おろします	[下ろします]	to withdraw	G8

おんがく	[音楽]	music	G1/K5
おんせん	[温泉]	hot spring	G10
おんな	[女]	woman	G6
おんなのこ	[女の子]	girl	K6
おんなのひと	[女の人]	woman	G6/K6

[か]

～かい／がい	[～階]	counter for floors (of a building)	G2
がいこく	[外国]	foreign country	K6,K8
がいこくじん	[外国人]	foreigner	K6
がいこくじんとうろくしょうめいしょ	[外国人登録証明書]	foreign resident's registration card	K8
かいしゃ	[会社]	company	K8
[ストレスを] かいしょうします	[解消します]	to get rid of stress	G10
かいてんずし	[回転寿司]	fast-food sushi	G7
かいます	[飼います]	to keep a pet	G9
かいます	[買います]	to buy	G5/K8
かいもの	[買い物]	shopping	K8
かいものします	[買い物します]	to go shopping	G5/K8
かいわ	[会話]	conversation	K8
かいわします	[会話します]	to have a conversation	K8
カウンター		counter	G6
かえします	[返します]	to return	G8
かえます	[変えます]	to change	G9
かえります	[帰ります]	to go home/ to return	G4/K8
かかります		to take (time duration)	G4
かぎ		key	G9
かきます	[書きます]	to write	G5/K5
かきます	[描きます]	to draw	G8
かぐ	[家具]	furniture	G6
がくせい	[学生]	student	G1/K1
がくせいか	[学生課]	student office	G2
がくせいしょう	[学生証]	student ID card	G8
がくぶ	[学部]	college	G1/K1
～かげつ [～か月]		month(duration)	G4
[めがねを] かけます		to wear (glasses)	G10
[かぎを] かけます		to lock	G9
[でんわ] かけます		to make a phone call	G9
かさ		umbrella	G6
かしだします	[貸し出します]	to loan	G8
かします	[貸します]	to lend	G6
かしゅ	[歌手]	singer	K8
かぜをひきます	[風邪を引きます]	to catch a cold	G10
かぞく	[家族]	family	G9/K8
かた	[肩]	shoulder	G10
～がつ	[～月]	counter for months	G3
がっか	[学科]	department	G1
がっこう	[学校]	school	G4/K8
カップ		cup	G6
かのじょ	[彼女]	she/girl friend	K6
かばん／バッグ		bag	G6
かびん	[花びん]	flower vase	K6
[ぼうしを] かぶります		to put on (a cap/hat)	G10
かべ		wall	G9
かみ	[紙]	paper	K9
カメラ		camera	G6
かようび	[火曜日]	Tuesday	G3/K3
からあげ		fried chicken	G7
からい		hot	G7
カラオケ		karaoke/ karaoke studio	G1
からだ	[体]	body	G10/K10
かります	[借ります]	to borrow	G5
かるい	[軽い]	light	G6
カレー（ライス）		curry rice	G7/K7
カレンダー		calendar	G3
かわ	[川]	river	K1
かん	[缶]	can	G9
かんこく	[韓国]	Korea	G1
かんごし	[看護師]	nurse	G10
かんじ	[漢字]	Kanji	G5/K5
かんたん [な]	[簡単 [な]]	easy/simple	G5
かんりにん	[管理人]	caretaker	G9

[き]

き	[木]	tree	K1

ききます	[聞きます]	to listen/to hear/ to ask	G5, G8/ K5
きこく	[帰国]	home coming	K8
きこくします	[帰国します]	to return one's country	K8
きたない	[汚い]	dirty	G5
キッチン		kitchen	G9/K9
きって	[切手]	stamp	K10
きっぷ	[切符]	ticket	G5
きのう		yesterday	G3
きびしい		strict/hard	G5
きぶん	[気分]	feeling/mood	K10
きぶんがわるいです	[気分が悪いです]	to feel ill	G10
[ふくを] きます	[着ます]	to get dressed	G10
きます	[来ます]	to come	G4/K8
きもち	[気持ち]	feeling/sensation	K10
キャンディー		candy	G7
キャンパス		campus	G2/K8
きゅう／く	[9／九]	nine	G1/K2
きゅうじつ	[休日]	holiday	K3
ぎゅうにく	[牛肉]	beef	G7/K7
きょう	[今日]	today	G3/K3
きょうかしょ	[教科書]	textbook	G6/K5
きょうしつ	[教室]	classroom	G2/K8
きょうむか	[教務課]	academic office	G2
きょねん	[去年]	last year	G3/K4
きらい [な]	[嫌い [な]]	dislike	G7
きります	[切ります]	to cut	G7
きれい [な]		clean/beautiful	G5
[でんきゅうが] きれます		The electric bulb burns out	G9
きをつけます		to be careful	G9
ぎんこう	[銀行]	bank	G2/K8
ぎんこういん	[銀行員]	bank clerk	K8
きんようび	[金曜日]	Friday	G3/K3

[く]

クイズ		quiz	G3/K3
くうこう	[空港]	airport	G4
くがつ	[9月／九月]	September	G3
くすり	[薬]	medicine	K10
くすりをのみます	[薬を飲みます]	to take medicine	G10
くだもの	[果物]	fruit	G7
くち	[口]	mouth	G10/K10
くつ	[靴]	shoes/boots	G6
くつした	[靴下]	socks/stockings	G6
くつや	[靴屋]	shoe shop	G2
くに	[国]	country	G1/K8
くらい	[暗い]	dark	G5/K9
クラス		class	G5
クラスメート		classmate	G5
クリニック		clinic	G2/K10
くるま	[車]	car	G4/K4
くろい	[黒い]	black	G6

[け]

けいえい	[経営]	management	G1
けいざい	[経済]	economics	G1
けいたいでんわ	[携帯電話]	cellular phone	G6
ケーキ		cake	G6
けがをします	[怪我をします]	to be injured	G10
けさ	[今朝]	this morning	G4/K4
けしゴム		eraser	G6
けします		to turn off	G9
けしょうひん		cosmetics	G6
けっこう [な]		fine/excellent	G9
げつようび	[月曜日]	Monday	G3/K3
げんき [な]	[元気 [な]]	healthy/being well	G10/K10
けんきゅう	[研究]	research	G2
けんきゅうしつ	[研究室]	faculty office/ laboratory	K8
けんきゅうとう	[研究棟]	faculty building	G2
けんこう	[健康]	health	G10
けんさくします		to search	G8

[こ]

こ	[子]	child/boy/girl	G6
ご	[5／五]	five	G1/K2
～ご	[～語]	～language	G1/K5

こうえん	[公園]	park	G2
～ごうかん		counter for buildings	G2
こうぎ		lecture	G5
こうこう	[高校]	senior high school	K8
～ごうしつ	[～号室]	counter for rooms (room number)	G2
こうちゃ	[紅茶]	black tea	G7/K7
こうどう		lecture hall	G2
こうはい	[後輩]	junior	K6
コート		coat	G10
コーヒー		coffee	G5/K7
コーヒーショップ		coffee shop	G6
コピーき	[コピー機]	copy machine	G8
コープ		CO-OP shop	G2
ごがつ	[5月／五月]	May	G3
こくさいかんけい	[国際関係]	international relations	G1
こくさいでんわ	[国際電話]	international phone call	G9
ここ		here	G2
ごご	[午後]	afternoon/p.m.	G3/K4,K6
ここのか	[9日／九日]	9th (day of the month)	G3
ここのつ	[九つ]	nine things	K2
こし	[腰]	waist/hip	G10
こしょう		pepper	G7
ごぜん	[午前]	forenoon/a.m.	G3/K4,K6
こたえます	[答えます]	to answer	G8
こちら		this way/this place	G6
ことし	[今年]	this year	G3/K4
こども	[子供]	child/boy/girl	G6/K6
この		this(noun)	G2
こばやし	[小林]	Kobayashi (Japanese surname)	K1
ごはん	[ご飯]	cooked rice/meal	G7/K7
ごはんをたきます		to cook rice	G7
ごみ		garbage	G9
ごみおきば	[ごみ置き場]	garbage dumping area	G9/K9
ごみばこ		trashcan	G9
こめ	[米]	rice	K7
これ		this one	G2
コーラ		coke	G7
ころびます	[転びます]	to fall down	G10
こんげつ	[今月]	this month	G3/K3
こんしゅう	[今週]	this week	G3/K4
こんばん	[今晩]	tonight	G4/K4
コンビニ／コンビニエンスストア		convenience store	G2/K2
コンピューター		computer	G5/K5
コンピュータールーム		computer room	G5
こんや	[今夜]	tonight	K4

[さ]

サークルかつどう	[サークル活動]	circle activity	G5
さいきん	[最近]	recently	G10
ざいりょう		ingredients	G7
さがします	[探します]	to look for	G8
さかな	[魚]	fish	G7/K7
さかなや	[魚屋]	fish shop	K7
さかや	[酒屋]	liquor store	K7
さくぶん	[作文]	composition/writing	G9/K7
～さつ		counter for books	G2
サッカー		soccer	G1
ざっし	[雑誌]	magazine	G5
さとう	[砂糖]	sugar	G7
さむい	[寒い]	cold (weather)	G7
さら		plate/dish	G7
サラダ		salad	G7
さん	[3／三]	three	G1/K2
～さん	[～さん]	term used when addressing people	G1
さんがつ	[3月／三月]	March	G3
さんじかんご	[3時間後]	three hours later	K6
さんじかんまえ	[3時間前]	three hours ago	K6
さんじっぷん／さんじゅっぷん	[30分]	twenty minutes	G3
サンドイッチ		sandwitch	G7
さんにん	[三人]	three people	K2
さんぽする		to take a walk	G10

[し]

し	[4／四]	four	G1/K2

じ	［字］	character	K5
～じ	［～時］	o'clock	G3
シーツ		sheets	G9
シーディー	［CD］	CD	G5
しお	［塩］	salt	G7
しおからい	［塩辛い］	salty	G7
しがつ	［４月／四月］	April	G3
じかん	［時間］	time	K3
～じかん	［～時間］	hour(duration)	G4
じこくひょう	［時刻表］	time table	G4
じこしょうかい		self-introduction	G8
じしょ	［辞書］	dictionary	G2/K5
しずか［な］		quiet/silent	G5/K9
した	［下］	under	K6
しち／なな	［７／七］	seven	G1/K2
じてんしゃ	［自転車］	bicycle	G4/K4
じどうしゃ	［自動車］	automobile	K4
じどうはんばいき	［自動販売機］	vending machine	G2
しにます	［死にます］	to die/to pass away	G9
じぶん	［自分］	oneself	G9
します		to do	G5
ジム		gymnasium	G2
しめきり	［締切］	deadline	G9
しめます	［閉めます］	to close	G9
シャープペンシル		mechanical pencil	G6/K6
しゃかいがくぶ	［社会学部］	college of sociology	G1
しやくしょ	［市役所］	City Hall	G4/K8
しゃしんを［写真］をとります		to take a picture	G8
シャツ		shirt	G6
シャンプー		shampoo	G6
しゅう	［週］	week	G3/K4
じゅう	［10／十］	ten	G1/K2
じゅういちがつ	［11月／十一月］	November	G3
じゅういちにち	［11日］	11th (day of the month)	G3
じゅうがつ	［10月／十月］	October	G3
～しゅうかん	［～週間］	week	G4

じゅうしょ	［住所］	address	K8
ジュース		juice	G5/K7
じゅうにがつ	［12月／十二月］	December	G3
しゅうまつ	［週末］	weekend	K4
じゅぎょう	［授業］	class	G3
しゅくじつ		national holiday	G3
しゅくだい	［宿題］	homework	G3
しゅっぱつします	［出発します］	to depart	K9
しゅみ	［趣味］	hobby	G1/K7
しょうがっこう	［小学校］	elementary school	K5,K8
しょうご	［正午］	noon	K4
［の］しょうじょうがあります	［［の］症状があります］	to have symptom of …	G10
じょうず［な］	［上手［な］］	skillful/be good at	K6,K10
しょうせつ		novel	G8
しょうゆ		soy sauce	G7
しょくじ	［食事］	meal	K7
しょくじします	［食事します］	to have a meal	G4
しょくどう	［食堂］	cafeteria	G2
しょくよくがありません	［食欲がありません］	to have poor appetite	G10
しょくりょうひん	［食料品］	food	G6
じょせい	［女性］	female	K6
ショッピングセンター		shopping center	G6
しらべます	［調べます］	to research/ to investigate	G8
しりつだいがく	［私立大学］	private university	K1
しりょう		material	G8
しろい	［白い］	white	G6
じろじろ見ます	［じろじろ見ます］	to stare at	G9
～じん	［～人］	～people (sufiix attached to a country)	G1/K1
しんかんせん	［新幹線］	Shinkansen	G4
じんこう	［人口］	population	K10
しんしゃ	［新車］	new automobile	K9
しんせつ［な］	［親切［な］］	kind	G6
しんぶん	［新聞］	newspaper	G5/ K5,K9

［す］

すいえい	［水泳］	swimming	G1/ K3,K8
すいえいします	［水泳します］	to swim	K8

すいぶんを とります	[水分を 取ります]	to drink fluids	G10
すいます	[吸います]	to smoke	G9
すいようび	[水曜日]	Wednesday	G3/K3
すうじ	[数字]	number/figure	K5
スーツ		suit	G6
スーパー／スー パーマーケット		supermarket	G2/K2
スカート		skirt	G10
すき［な］	[好き［な］]	like/favorite	G7/K7
スキー		skiing	G8
すくない	[少ない]	a few/a little	G6
スケジュール		schedule	K3
すこし	[少し]	a little/a few	G6
すし		sushi	G7
すずき	[鈴木]	Suzuki(Japanese surname)	K1
スチューデント オフィス		student office	G2
ずつう	[頭痛]	headache	K10
すっぱい		sour	G7
すてます	[捨てます]	to dump/ to throw away	G9
ストレス		stress	K10
ストレスが たまります		to be under stress	G10
スプーン		spoon	G6
スポーツ		sport	G1
ズボン		trousers	G6
すわります		to sit down	G9

[せ]

せいかつ	[生活]	life	G5
せいきょう	[生協]	CO-OP shop	G2
セーター		sweater	G6
セール		sale	G6
せきがでます	[咳が出ます]	to cough	G10
せきゆ	[石油]	petroleum	K9
せっけん		soap	G6
せつめいします	[説明します]	to explain	G8/K9
せなか	[背中]	back	G10
せまい	[狭い]	narrow/ small(space)	G5
セミナー		seminar	G3
ゼロ		zero	G1
せん	[千]	one thousand	K2
せんげつ	[先月]	last mouth	G3
せんざい	[洗剤]	detergent	G6
せんしゅう	[先週]	last week	G3/K4
せんせい	[先生]	teacher/professor	G1/K1
ぜんぜん		not at all	G5
せんたくします	[洗濯します]	to do the laundry	G9/K9
せんぱい	[先輩]	senior	G8/K1
ぜんぶ	[全部]	all	G7/K8
せんめんじょ	[洗面所]	bathroom	K9
せんめんだい	[洗面台]	washing stand	G9/K9
せんもん	[専門]	major/specialty	G1/K1

[そ]

そうこ		storage room	G9
そうじき	[掃除機]	vacuum cleaner	G9
そうじします	[掃除します]	to clean	G8
そこ		there	G2
そと	[外]	outside	G2/K6
その		that(noun)	G2
そば		buckwheet noodle	G7
それ		that one	G2

[た]

た	[田]	rice field	K1
タイ		Thailand	G1
たいいくかん	[体育館]	gymnasium	G2
だいがく	[大学]	university	G1/ K1,K5
だいがくいん	[大学院]	graduate school	G2/ K5,K10
だいがくせい	[大学生]	university student	K1
たいじゅう	[体重]	body weight	K10
たいちょう	[体調]	one's health condition	K10
だいどころ	[台所]	kitchen	G9/K8
だいどころ ようひん	[台所用品]	kitchen goods	G6
たいりょく	[体力]	force/stamina	K10
たかい	[高い]	expensive	G5
たくさん		many/a lot	G5

タクシー		taxi	G4/K4
たけ	[竹]	bamboo	K1
たけうち	[竹内]	Takeuchi (japanese surname)	K1
だします	[出します]	to take out	G9/K9
だします	[出します]	to submit/to hand in an assignment	G8/K9
だします	[出します]	to send	G6/K9
ただしい	[正しい]	right/correct	K4
たちます	[立ちます]	to stand up	G9
たっきゅう		pingpong	G1
たてもの	[建物]	building	G2
たなか	[田中]	Tanaka (japanese surname)	K1
たのしい	[楽しい]	enjoyable/ delightful/pleasant	G5/K5
たばこ		cigarett	G9
たべます	[食べます]	to eat	G5/K7
たべもの	[食べ物]	food	G5/K6
たまご	[卵]	egg	G7
たりません	[足りません]	not enough	K10
だれ		who	G1
たんじょうび	[誕生日]	birthday	G3
ダンス		dance	G8
だんせい	[男性]	male	K6

[ち]

ちいさい	[小さい]	small	G5/K5
ちか	[地下]	basement	G6
ちかく	[近く]	near	G2/K8
ちから	[力]	power	K10
ちず	[地図]	map	G2/K8
ちゅうがっこう	[中学校]	junior high school	K6,K8
ちゅうこ	[中古]	secondhand goods	K9
ちゅうごく	[中国]	China	G1/K8
ちゅうごくご	[中国語]	Chinese language	K5
ちゅうしゃじょう	[駐車場]	car parking	G9/K9
ちゅうしゃをします	[注射をします]	to inject	G10
ちゅうしょく	[昼食]	lunch	K7
ちゅうもんします	[注文します]	to order	G7
ちゅうりんじょう	[駐輪場]	bicycle parking spot	G9/K9
ちょうしょく	[朝食]	breakfast	K7
ちょうみりょう	[調味料]	seasoning	G7
チョコレート		chocolate	G7/K7
ちょっと		for a moment/ a little	G9

[つ]

ついたち	[１日／一日]	1st (day of the month)	G3/K3
つかいかた	[使い方]	how to use	K7
つかいます	[使います]	to use	G5/K5
つかれます	[疲れます]	to get tired	G10
つき	[月]	moon/month	K3
つくえ	[机]	desk	G6
つくります	[作ります]	to make	G7/K7
つけます		to turn on a light	G9
つけもの		pickles	G7
つち	[土]	ground	K3
つまらない		boring	G5
つめたい	[冷たい]	cold (to the touch)	G7

[て]

て	[手]	hand	G9/K10
ティーシャツ	[Tシャツ]	T-shirt	G6
ディーブイディー	[DVD]	DVD	G8
ティッシュペーパー		tissue	G6
ていしょく	[定食]	set menu	G7
テーブル		table	G6
てがみ	[手紙]	letter	G6/ K9,K10
できます		to be able to	G8
でぐち	[出口]	exit	K10
デザイン		design	G6
テスト		examination	G3/K3
テニス		tennis	G1
デパート		department store	G6
でます	[出ます]	to go out/to leave	K9
テレビ		television	G5/K5
テレビゲーム		video game	G7
てんいん	[店員]	shop clerk	G6
てんき	[天気]	weather	K10

でんき	［電気］	electricity	G9/K4
でんきせいひん	［電気製品］	electric applience	G6
でんきや	［電気屋］	electrical appliance shop	G2
でんきゅう	［電球］	light bulb	G9
でんしじしょ	［電子辞書］	electronic dictionary	G6
でんしゃ	［電車］	train	G4/K4
でんしレンジ	［電子レンジ］	microwave	G7
てんちょう	［店長］	manager	G6
てんぷら	［天ぷら］	tempura	G7
でんわ	［電話］	telephone	K4,K8
でんわばんごう	［電話番号］	telephone number	G1

[と]

ど	［度］	counter for temperature/ degree	G10
ドア		door	G9
トイレ		toilet	G2
～とう	［～棟］	counter for large buildings	G2
どうぶつ	［動物］	animal	K6
どうやって		how to (do something)	G4
とお	［十］	ten things	K2
とおか	［10日／十日］	10th (day of the month)	G3
どくしょ	［読書］	reading	G1/K5
どくしょします	［読書します］	to read a book	K5
とけい	［時計］	clock/watch	G6
どこ		where	G1
ところ	［所］	place	K8
とし	［年］	year/age	K4
としうえ	［年上］	elder	K6
としした	［年下］	younger	K6
としょかん	［図書館］	library	G2/K8
どちら		where	G1
とても		very	G5
どなた		who	G1
となり	［隣］	next to	G2
どの		which one	G2
どのぐらい		how long/many/ much	G4
トマト		tomato	G10
とめます	［停めます］	to park (a car)	G9
とめます	［泊めます］	to take a person in	G9
ともだち	［友達］	friend	G1/K1
どようび	［土曜日］	Saturday	G3/K3
ドラッグストア		drugstore	G2
とり	［鳥］	bird	K7
とりかえます		to change	G9
とりにく	［鳥肉］	chicken	G7/K7
［めがねを］とります	［取ります］	to take off (one's glasses)	G10
とります	［取ります］	to take	G8
とります	［撮ります］	to take (a picture)	G8
ドル		dollar	G9
どれ		which one	G2
どんな		what kind of things	G6

[な]

なか	［中］	inside	G2/K6
ながい	［長い］	long	G6
なっとう	［納豆］	fermented beans	G7
なな	［七］	seven	G1/K2
ななつ	［七つ］	seven things	K2
なに／なん	［何］	what	G1/K3
なのか	［7日／七日］	7th (day of the month)	G3
なまえ	［名前］	name	G1
なまごみ	［生ごみ］	kitchen garbage	G9
ならいます	［習います］	to learn	G6
なんじ	［何時］	what time	K3
なんにち	［何日］	what day of the month	K3
なんようび	［何曜日］	what day of the week	K3

[に]

に	［2／二］	two	G1/K2
にがつ	［2月／二月］	February	G3
にぎやか［な］		lively	G5
にく	［肉］	meat	G7/K7
にくや	［肉屋］	meat shop	K7
～にち	［～日］	day	G3
にちようび	［日曜日］	Sunday	G3/K3

にちようひん	[日用品]	daily necessities	G6
にほん／にっぽん	[日本]	Japan	G1/K3,K5
にほんご	[日本語]	Japanese language	G1/K5
にほんしゅ	[日本酒]	sake	K7
にほんじん	[日本人]	Japanese (people)	G1/K1,K5
にほんちゃ	[日本茶]	Japanese green tea	K7
にもつ	[荷物]	laguage	G9
にゅういんします	[入院します]	to be hospitalized	K10
にゅうがくします	[入学します]	to enter a school	K9
にんきがあります	[人気があります]	to be popular with	K10
にんじん		carrot	G7

[ぬ]

ぬぎます	[脱ぎます]	to take off (one's clothes)	G10

[ね]

ねこ		cat	G9
ねつがあります	[熱があります]	to have a fever	G10
ねつをはかります	[熱を測ります]	to take one's temperature	G10
ねます	[寝ます]	to sleep	G4
～ねん	[～年]	year	G3
～ねんかん	[～年間]	year (duration)	G4
～ねんせい	[～年生]	～year student	G1

[の]

ノート		notebook	G5/K5
のど		throat	G10
のどがかわきます		to be thirsty	G8
のぼります	[登ります]	to climb	G8
のみます	[飲みます]	to drink	G5/K7
のみもの	[飲み物]	beverage	G6/K6
のりば	[乗り場]	bus stop/platform	G4
のります	[乗ります]	to get on/to ride	G8
のりもの	[乗り物]	transportation	G4

[は]

は	[歯]	tooth	G10
パーティー		party	G3
バイク		motorbike	G4/K4
はいしゃ	[歯医者]	dentist	G10/K10
はいります	[入ります]	to join/enter	K9
はきけがします	[吐き気がします]	to feel like vomiting	G10
[ズボンを]はきます		to put on(trousers)	G10
はこびます		to carry	G8
はさみ		scissors	G6
はし		chopsticks	G7
ばしょ	[場所]	place	G4/K8,K9
はしります	[走ります]	to run	G8
バス		bus	G4/K4
バスケットボール		basketball	G1
パスタ		pasta	G7
バスてい	[バス停]	bus stop	G4
パソコン		personal computer	G6
はち	[８／八]	eight	G1/K2
はちがつ	[８月／八月]	August	G3
はつか	[20日]	20th (day of the month)	G3
バッグ		bag	G6
はっぴょうします	[発表します]	to give a presentation	G8
バドミントン		badminton	G1
はな	[花]	flower	G6/K6
はな	[鼻]	nose	G10
はなし	[話]	talk/conversation	K8
はなします	[話します]	to talk/to speak	G5/K8
はなび	[花火]	fireworks	K6
はなや	[花屋]	flower shop	G2
はやい	[速い／早い]	fast/early	G10
はやし	[林]	grove/japanese surname	K1
はらいます	[払います]	to pay	G5
バレンタインデー		St.Valentine's Day	G6
はん	[半]	half past	G3
ばん	[晩]	night	K4
パン		bread	G5
ばんごはん	[晩ご飯]	dinner/supper	G5/K4,K7
ハンサム［な］		handsome	G6
～ばんせん	[～番線]	platform	G4
ハンバーガー		hamburger	G7

はんぶん	［半分］	half	K3

【ひ】

ひ	［日］	sun/day	K3
ひ	［火］	fire	K3
ピアノ		piano	G1
ピーマン		green pepper	G7
ひきます	［弾きます］	to play	G8
ひこうき	［飛行機］	airplane	G4
ひざ		knee	G10
ピザ		pizza	G7
ビジネス		business	G1
びじゅつかん		musium of art	G8
ひだり／ひだりがわ	［左／左側］	left/left side	G2/K6
ひだりて	［左手］	left hand	K10
ビデオ		video	G8/K8
ひと	［人］	person/ human being	G6/K1
ひとつ	［一つ］	one thing	K2
ひとり	［一人］	one person	K2
ひま［な］		have spare time	G5
ひゃく	［百］	one hundred	K2
ひゃくえん	［百円］	100yen	K4
100 えんショップ	［100 円ショップ］	100 yen shop	G2
びょういん	［病院］	hospital	G2/K10
びょうき	［病気］	illness	G10/K10
ひる	［昼］	the daytime	K4
ひるごはん	［昼ご飯］	lunch	G5/ K4,K7
ひろい	［広い］	spacious/wide	G5/K5
びん		glass bottle	G9

【ふ】

ふあん［な］	［不安［な］］	auxious	K9
プール		pool	G8
フェリー		ferry	G4/K4
ふく	［服］	cloth	G6
ふくろ	［袋］	bag/sack	G9
ふじさん	［富士山］	Mt.fuji	K1
ふしんせつな	［不親切な］	unkind	K9
ふたつ	［二つ］	two things	K2
ぶたにく	［豚肉］	pork	G7
ふたり	［二人］	two people	K2
ふつか	［２日／二日］	2nd (day of the month)	G3
ふとります	［太ります］	to gain weight	G10
ふとん		futon	G9
ふとんかんそうき		futon dryer	G9
ふべん［な］	［不便［な］］	inconvenient	G5/K9
プラスチック		plastic	G9
プラットホーム		platform	G4
ふるい	［古い］	old	G5/K9
ふるほん	［古本］	secondhand book	K9
プレゼント		present	G6
フロアガイド		floor map	G6
ぶん	［文］	sentence	K5
～ふん／ぷん	［～分］	minute(s)	G3
ぶんか	［文化］	culture	K5
ぶんぐ	［文具］	stationery	G6
ふんすい		fountain	G2
ぶんぽう	［文法］	grammar	K5
ぶんぼうぐ	［文房具］	stationery	G6

【へ】

へいじつ	［平日］	weekday	G3
ベジタリアン		vegetarian	G7
へた［な］	［下手［な］］	unskillful	K6,K10
ベッド		bed	G6
ペットボトル		PET (plastic) bottle	G9
へや	［部屋］	room	G2/K8
へやばんごう	［部屋番号］	room number	G9
ペン		pen/marker	G2/K5
べんきょうします	［勉強します］	to study	G4
べんり［な］	［便利［な］］	convenient	G5/K9

【ほ】

ほうげん	［方言］	dialect	K7
ほうこう	［方向］	direction	K7
ぼうし	［帽子］	hat/cap	G10

ほうほう	[方法]	how to/method	K7
ほうめん	[方面]	direction	G4
ホームシック		homesick	G10
ホームページ		homepage	G8
ボールペン		ballpoint pen	G6/K6
ほか		other	G9
ぼく	[僕]	I (used by men)	G1
ほそい	[細い]	slender/thin	K6
ホチキス		stapler	G6/K6
ホテル		hotel	G2
ほねをおります	[骨を折ります]	to break bones	G10
ほん	[本]	book	G1/K5
〜ほん／ぼん／ぽん	[〜本]	counter for long things	G7
ほんだな	[本だな]	bookshelf	G6
ほんや	[本屋]	bookstore	G2

[ま]

〜まい		counter for papers	G2
まいあさ	[毎朝]	every morning	G4
まいしゅう	[毎週]	every week	G3/K4
まいつき	[毎月]	every month	G3/K4
まいとし	[毎年]	every year	G3/K4
まいにち	[毎日]	everyday	G3/K4
まいばん	[毎晩]	every evening/night	G4
まえ	[前]	front	G2/K6
まくらカバー		pillow case	G9
まじめ [な]		serious	G10
まずい		not delicious/tasteless	G5
マスクをします		to put on a mask	G10
まち		town	G2
まちます	[待ちます]	to wait	G8
まど	[窓]	window	G9
まんが	[漫画]	comics	G7

[み]

(はを)みがきます	[磨きます]	to brush teeth	G9
みぎ／みぎがわ	[右／右側]	right/right side	G2/K6
みぎて	[右手]	right hand	K10
みじかい	[短い]	short	G6
みず	[水]	water	K3
みせ	[店]	shop/store	G6
みせます	[見せます]	to show	G8
みそ		bean paste	G7
みそしる	[みそ汁]	miso soup	G7
みっか	[３日／三日]	3rd (day of the month)	G3
みっつ	[三つ]	three things	K2
みなと		harbor	G4
みます	[見ます]	to see/to watch/to look at	G5/K5
みみ	[耳]	ear	G10/K10
みりん		sweet sake	G7

[む]

むいか	[６日／六日]	6th (day of the month)	G3
むかえます	[迎えます]	to go and meet	G8
むしばがあります		to have a cavity	G10
むずかしい	[難しい]	difficult	G5
むっつ	[六つ]	six things	K2
むね	[胸]	chest	G10
むりょう	[無料]	free of charge	K9

[め]

め	[目]	eye	G10/K10
〜めい	[〜名]	counter for people	G7
めいしゃ	[目医者]	eye doctor	G10
めうえのひと	[目上の人]	one's superiors	K10
メール		email	G8
めがね		glasses	G10
めぐすり	[目薬]	eye lotion	K10
めしたのひと	[目下の人]	one's inferiors	K10

[も]

もういちど	[もう一度]	one more time	G10
もうすこし		some more/a few more/a little more	G6
もくようび	[木曜日]	Thursday	G3
もじ	[文字]	character	K5
もちます	[持ちます]	to hold/to have	G10
もどします	[戻します]	to return	G9

もの	[物]	thing	G7/K6
もらいます		to receive	G6
もり	[森]	forest/japanese surname	K1
もん	[門]	gate	K1

[や]

やさい	[野菜]	vegetable	G7
やさしい	[易しい／優しい]	easy/gentle	G5
やすい	[安い]	cheap	G5
やすみ	[休み]	rest/off/holiday	G3/K3
やすみます	[休みます]	to take a break	K3
やせます		to lose weight	G10
やっきょく	[薬局]	pharmacy	K10
やっつ	[八つ]	eight things	K2
やま	[山]	mountain	K1
やまだ	[山田]	Yamada (japanese surname)	K1
やまもと	[山本]	Yamamoto (japanese surname)	K1,K5

[ゆ]

ゆうがた	[夕方]	evening	K4
ゆうしょく	[夕食]	supper	K7
ゆうびんきょく	[郵便局]	post office	G2/K9
ゆうべ	[夕べ]	last night	G4/K4
ゆうめい[な]	[有名]	famous	G5
ゆっくり		slowly	G10

[よ]

ようか	[８日／八日]	8th (day of the month)	G3
～ようび	[曜日]	day of the week	K4
ヨガ		yoga	G8
よくしつ	[浴室]	bathroom	G9
よっか	[４日／四日]	4th(day of the month)	G3
よっつ	[四つ]	four things	K2
よにん	[四人]	four people	K2
よみます	[読みます]	to read	G5/K5
よる	[夜]	night	K4
よん	[４／四]	four	G1/K2

[ら]

ラーメン		Chinese noodle	G7
らいげつ	[来月]	next month	G3/K8
らいしゅう	[来週]	next week	G3/K4,K8
らいねん	[来年]	next year	G3/K4,K8
ランドリー		laundry	G9/K9

[り]

りゅうがくせい	[留学生]	international student	G1
りょう	[寮]	dormitory	G2
りょうきん	[料金]	fare/charge	K9
りようします	[利用します]	to make use of something	G8/K9
りょうり	[料理]	cooking	G1
りょうりします	[料理します]	to cook	G7/K9
りょこう	[旅行]	travel	K8
りょこうします	[旅行します]	to travel	G7
りんご		apple	G7

[れ]

れい		zero	G1
れいぞうこ	[冷蔵庫]	refrigerator	G9
レジ		register/casher	G6
レストラン		restaurant	G2/K2
レポート		report	G5
れんしゅうします	[練習します]	to practice	G9
れんらくします	[連絡します]	to contact	G9

[ろ]

ろく	[６／六]	six	G1/K2
ろくがつ	[６月／六月]	June	G3
ロシアご	[ロシア語]	Russian language	G8
ロッカー		locker	G9

[わ]

ワークショップ		workshop	G3/K3
わかい	[若い]	young	G6/K6
わかもの	[若者]	young person	K6,K10
わかります	[分かります]	to understand	G3/K3
わすれます	[忘れます]	to forget	G8
わたし	[私]	I	G1/K1
わるい	[悪い]	bad/wrong	G6
ワンピース		one-piece dress	G6

にほんちず（日本地図）

1 ほっかいどう(北海道)	13 とうきょうと(東京都)	25 わかやまけん(和歌山県)	37 とくしまけん(徳島県)
2 あおもりけん(青森県)	14 かながわけん(神奈川県)	26 しがけん(滋賀県)	38 えひめけん(愛媛県)
3 いわてけん(岩手県)	15 にいがたけん(新潟県)	27 きょうとふ(京都府)	39 こうちけん(高知県)
4 あきたけん(秋田県)	16 とやまけん(富山県)	28 おおさかふ(大阪府)	40 ふくおかけん(福岡県)
5 みやぎけん(宮城県)	17 いしかわけん(石川県)	29 ならけん(奈良県)	41 さがけん(佐賀県)
6 やまがたけん(山形県)	18 ふくいけん(福井県)	30 ひょうごけん(兵庫県)	42 ながさきけん(長崎県)
7 ふくしまけん(福島県)	19 やまなしけん(山梨県)	31 とっとりけん(鳥取県)	43 くまもとけん(熊本県)
8 いばらきけん(茨城県)	20 ながのけん(長野県)	32 おかやまけん(岡山県)	44 おおいたけん(大分県)
9 とちぎけん(栃木県)	21 ぎふけん(岐阜県)	33 しまねけん(島根県)	45 みやざきけん(宮崎県)
10 ぐんまけん(群馬県)	22 しずおかけん(静岡県)	34 ひろしまけん(広島県)	46 かごしまけん(鹿児島県)
11 ちばけん(千葉県)	23 あいちけん(愛知県)	35 やまぐちけん(山口県)	47 おきなわけん(沖縄県)
12 さいたまけん(埼玉県)	24 みえけん(三重県)	36 かがわけん(香川県)	

Inflection of Verbs

	ます form	じしょform	ない form	て form	た form	Volitional form	Imperative form	ば form	Potential verb	Passive verb	Causative verb	Causative passive verb
I	あそびます	あそぶ	あそばない	あそんで	あそんだ	あそぼう	あそべ	あそべば	あそべる	あそばれる	あそばせる	あそばせられる
	いきます	いく	いかない	＊いって	＊いった	いこう	いけ	いけば	いける	いかれる	いかせる	いかせられる
	およぎます	およぐ	およがない	およいで	およいだ	およごう	およげ	およげば	およげる	およがれる	およがせる	およがせられる
	かいます	かう	かわない	かって	かった	かおう	かえ	かえば	かえる	かわれる	かわせる	かわせられる
	かえります	かえる	かえらない	かえって	かえった	かえろう	かえれ	かえれば	かえれる	かえられる	かえらせる	かえらせられる
	ききます	きく	きかない	きいて	きいた	きこう	きけ	きけば	きける	きかれる	きかせる	きかせられる
	しにます	しぬ	しなない	しんで	しんだ	しのう	しね	しねば	しねる	しなれる	しなせる	しなせられる
	のみます	のむ	のまない	のんで	のんだ	のもう	のめ	のめば	のめる	のまれる	のませる	のませられる
	はなします	はなす	はなさない	はなして	はなした	はなそう	はなせ	はなせば	はなせる	はなされる	はなさせる	はなさせられる
	まちます	まつ	またない	まって	まった	まとう	まて	まてば	まてる	またれる	またせる	またせられる
II	かります	かりる	かりない	かりて	かりた	かりよう	かりろ	かりれば	かりられる	かりられる	かりさせる	かりさせられる
	たべます	たべる	たべない	たべて	たべた	たべよう	たべろ	たべれば	たべられる	たべられる	たべさせる	たべさせられる
III	します	する	しない	して	した	しよう	しろ	すれば	できる	される	させる	させられる
	きます	くる	こない	きて	きた	こよう	こい	くれば	こられる	こられる	こさせる	こさせられる
	－ませんか	－ことができる	－ないでください	－てください	－ほうがいい	－とおもう						
	－ましょう	－まえに、～	－ないほうがいい	－て、～	－(た)り、－(た)りする							
	－たい	－ために、～	－なくて	－てもいい	－(た)ら、～							
	－かた	－とき、～	－ないで	－てはいけない	－とき、～							
	－にいく	－ところ	－なければならない	－てみる	－ところ							
	－すぎる	－と、～	－なくてもいい	－ている	－(た)らいい							
	－そう	－な (Prohibition)	－ないつもりだ	－てから	－ことがある							
	－ながら、～	－つもりだ	－ないようにしている	－(reason)て、～	－あとで、～							
	－やすい／にくい	－ことになる		－ているところ	－まま							
		－ようにしている		－ていく／－てくる								
	けいご	－ようになる		－てしまう	－てあげる／くれる／もらう							
	お－になる	－ことにする		－てある	－ておく							
	お－する			－ても、～	－てほしい							

	Polite	
	Affirmative	Negative
Non-past	－ます	－ません
Past	－ました	－ませんでした

	Plain	
	Affirmative	Negative
Non-past	じしょform	ない form
Past	た form	－なかった
Plain Form +	－んです	－かどうか
	－し、－し、	－はず
	－なら	－らしい
	Noun modification	－のに、～
	－でしょう	－とおもう
	－そうだ	－ようだ
	－かもしれない	－ので

Combining numbers with counters

-まい [paper, shirt]	-年 [year]	-時 [hour]	-円 [¥]
いち まい	いち ねん	いち じ	いち えん
に　まい	に　ねん	に　じ	に　えん
さん まい	さん ねん	さん じ	さん えん
よん まい	よ　ねん	よ　じ	よ　えん
ご　まい	ご　ねん	ご　じ	ご　えん
ろく まい	ろく ねん	ろく じ	ろく えん
なな／しち まい	しち ねん	なな／しち じ	なな えん
はち まい	はち ねん	はち じ	はち えん
きゅう まい	きゅう／く ねん	く　じ	きゅう えん
じゅう まい	じゅう ねん	じゅう じ	じゅう えん
なん まい	なん ねん	なん じ	なん えん
-度★1 [occurrence, temperature] -だい [car, computer]	-年(間) [year-long duration] -じげんめ [class period]	-時間 [hour-long duration] -月★2 [month]	-年生 [grade]

★1 9度：温度(おんど) [temperature] と熱(ねつ)→○きゅう ど／○く ど

★2 4月：○し がつ ×よ がつ　7月：○しち がつ ×なな がつ

-か月 [month-long duration]	-さい [age]	-本 [long, slender object]		-分 [minute]
いっ かげつ	いっ さい	いっ ぽん	P★4	P
に　かげつ	に　さい	に　ほん	H★4	H
さん かげつ	さん さい	さん ぼん	B★4	P
よん かげつ	よん さい	よん ほん	H	P
ご　かげつ	ご　さい	ご　ほん	H	H
ろっ かげつ	ろく さい	ろっ ぽん	P	P
なな かげつ	なな さい	なな ほん	H	H
はっ／はち かげつ	はっ さい	はっ ぽん	P	P
きゅう かげつ	きゅう さい	きゅう ほん	H	H
じっ／じゅっ かげつ	じっ／じゅっ さい	じっ／ じゅっ ぽん	P	P
なん かげつ	なん さい	なんぼん	B	P
-こ [small object] -ページ [page] -かい★3 [floor] -回★3 [occurrence]	-さつ [book] -週間 [week-long duration] -てん [point]	-ひき [animal, fish] -はい [contents of a cup]		-分間 [minute-long duration]

★3 三がい：さんがい　三回：さんかい　何がい：なんがい　何回：なんかい

★4 いっぽん (Po)　にほん (Ho)　さんぼん (Bo)

Authors

Grammar	Chisako Umeda・Teruhiko Okamoto・Taeko Berwick・Toshinari Ito・Haruo Kanai
Reading	Chisako Umeda
Writing	Susumu Ideguchi・Tamiko Itabashi
Speaking	Chisako Umeda
Vocabulary exercises	Hiromichi Terajima・Kiyoko Kobayashi
Kanji and Vocabulary	Hiromichi Terajima・Kiyoko Kobayashi

Acknowledgement

We thank for the following people for completion of this textbook.

Akiko Shimizu・Akiko Honda・Tamaki Sumida・Michisuke Miyama・Hiroko Mansho・Yoshie Sasaki・Wakana Watanabe・Yoshie Itai・Chiho Suga・Miho Takahashi

The textbook for the beginning Japanese Part 1 was written by Chisako Umeda, Momoko Tsuchiya, Miyuki Tada and Sumiko Hachiwaka. It was used as a course pack for many years and was one of the important resources to help the authors write this textbook.

日本語５つのとびら
－初級編　１－

2009年10月20日　初版第１刷発行
2015年４月20日　第２版第１刷発行
2017年３月20日　第３版第１刷発行
2024年７月30日　第３版第３刷発行
［検印廃止］
編　著　立命館アジア太平洋大学
「日本語５つのとびら」編集委員会
編集委員会委員長　薬師寺公夫
初級編　編集主幹　梅田千砂子
執筆者　梅田千砂子　（立命館アジア太平洋大学）
岡本輝彦
バーウィック・妙子
伊藤俊也　（立命館アジア太平洋大学）
金居明生
寺嶋弘道　（立命館アジア太平洋大学）
小林潔子
板橋民子　（立命館アジア太平洋大学）
出口　将
発行所　株式会社凡人社
〒102-0093 東京都千代田区平河町 1-3-13
TEL：03-3263-3959／FAX：03-3263-3116

ISBN-978-4-89358-923-1